Lake George

Boats
and
Steamboats

William Preston Gates

© W. P. Gates Publishing Company

> *Dedicated to--*
>
> *I would like to dedicate this book to the men who influenced me the most in my youth,-the very same men who taught me to appreciate boats and boating: My father, William B. Gates, my two uncles, Robert A. Gates and Walter F. "Smokey" Gates, and my grandfather, E.F. Robert Preston.*

Published by:
W.P. GATES Publishing Company
William P. Gates
1 Glenwood Avenue
Queensbury, NY 12804
(518) 798-3609
  • or •
Box 405
Bolton Landing, NY 12814
(518) 644-9410

Copyright © 2003 by W.P. Gates Publishing Company
First Edition - First Printing
All rights reserved under International and Pan-American Copyright Conventions.
No part of this book may be reproduced or transmitted in any form without permission
in writing from the publisher and copyright holder.

Library of Congress Control Number: 2003092151
ISBN   #0-9672397-4-5 (Softcover)
ISBN   #0-9672397-5-3 (Hardcover) LIMITED EDITION

Cover Design: William P. Gates
Cover Painting by Ernie Haas.   Painted for William P. Dow, Lake George Steamboat Company
Title Page Lithograph: Harper's Weekly, July 25, 1891. Courtesy: Ed and Beth Becker
Technical Assistant: Donnaleen E. Gates

Other books by this author

W.P. GATES PUBLISHING CO.
William P. Gates

1 Glenwood Avenue
Queensbury, NY 12804
(518) 798-3609

Box 405
Bolton Landing, NY 12814
(518) 644-9410

Acknowledgements

In no particular order, I wish to thank the following individuals and organizations who helped to make this book possible.

Ron Alcan, Tom Apperson, Hague Historian Ethel Andrus, Frank Antos, Ted Arnstein, Sandi Aldrich, Scott Anderson, Mark Ackerle, Shirley Armstrong, Joe Zarzynski & Bob Benway of Bateaux Below, Inc., Dr. Russ Bellico, Dr. John Brothers, Director Pat Babe & the Bolton Historical Museum, John Beals, Dan Behan, Bolton Town Librarian Megan Baker, Betty Buckell, Ann Buckell, John Babe, Bob & Roz Brady, Steve Boyce & the Ticonderoga Heritage Museum, Jim Bissett, Jack Bryan, Mildred Busman, Scott Bauberger, Adam Bombard, Joan Baldwin, Lionel Barthold, Reg Ballantine, Bob Blais, Bob Bayle, Halley Bond of the Adirondack Museum, Pete Bombard, Tom & Carla Burlhoe, Keith Brown, Ed & Beth Becker, Jack Binley, John & Betty Barth, Fred Brown, Howard Bombard, Julia C. Beatty, Seddon Beatty, Jeff Beaton, John Bowers, Dick & Claire Bartlett, Tim Widner & Rebecca Pelchar & Maureen Dye & the Chapman Historical Museum, Francis Caldwell, Henry Caldwell & Black Bass Antiques, Ted & Jane Caldwell, Tom Conerty, Don Cornell, Nick & Carolyn Cutro, Mark Curri, Bruce Cole & Albert Fowler & Todd DeGarmo & Crandall Library, Leon Chase, Theta Curri, Pat Collins, Ray Ciccarelli, Craig Clesceri, Dr. G. Peter Cook, Jerry & Jane Crammond of the Silver Bay Association, Brian Cassidy, Dave Crook, Don Ceppi, Rick Connors, Richard Dean, Bill Dow and the Lake George Steamboat Company, Tony DePace, Frank Dagles, Mike DeLarm of Lake View Antiques, Charles Boylen & David Diehl of the Darrin Fresh Water Institute, Al Dunlop, Charlotte Drake, Jim & Kayce Dimond of Ephemerist Antiques, Al Dunlop, Don Dietterick, Charlotte Drake, Steve Draper, Lake George Village Historian Peggy Edwards, Wayde Earl, Don Eberle, Jerry Eichin, Paul Eckhoff, Dick Eger, Bob Ervien, Don Fangboner, Mark Frost & the Chronicle Newspaper, Darrell Finlayson, Peter Foster, John Fair, Dick & Yona Freidin, Bill Finnen & the Lake George Club, Mary Chester Flagg, Sherwood & Betty Finley, Sue Ferdinand, Larry Fueling, Kathy Flacke-Muncil & Rich Parker & Fort William Henry Corporation, R.Frulla, Jane Gabriels, Zandy Gabriels, Walter Grishkot, Brian Granger, Barbara Gates, Bud & Toni Gates, Mike & Allison Gates, Ryan & Lindsey Gates, Paul Goodness, Gordon Garlick, George Goodwin, Dr. Richard Garrett Jr., Bobby Gates, John & Debbi Gaddy, Ginger & Dottie Henry, Denise Huestis, Doug Houghton & Paul Jordan of Adirondack Boat Works, Sam & Pat Hoopes, Kam Hoopes, Hibbard Nash of Hall's Boat Corp., Tom Hirchburg, Bill Huus, Marie Ellsworth & Nikki Huus of Lake George Library, Wesley Huck Jr., Craig Hannon, Jack Howe, Russell & Isabelle Harris, Evelyn Hersh, John Hilton, Tony Hall of the Lake George Mirror, Allen Hall, Ernie Haas, Winter Horton, Teri Hoffman of the Antique Boat Society, Roger Howard, Roy & Jeanette Hunt, Philip Harris, Tony Hinman, Dave Hersh, Eric Huntington, Charles Houghton of Elco Boats, Karol Hines, Ed Hines Jr., Leah McGarr Hadley, Keigh Harrison, Jean Hadden, Dave Hoffey, Chuck Hawley, Fran & Dave Irons, Tom James, Dick & Mary Kowell, Jim Kneeshaw, Andy Keefe, William Ketchum, Marianna Klein & the Northern Lake George Yacht Club, Rich Kober, Ed Kluck, Steve Lapham, Buzz Lamb, Bruce Lundgren, Frank Leonbruno, Jeff Lawrence, Barbara Gates Lawrence, George LaPointe, Harvey Lambeth, Bill Lockhart, Craig Lonergan, Judy Larter, Tom Lynch, John Lustyik, John Lefner, Bob Lenz, Jim LaVere, Byron & Joan Lapham, Bea Lewis, Adam Lesser, Janet Marvel, Jack Mannix, Maggie McClure & the Lake George Historical Association, Bill Morgan, John Meyer, John Mason, Tom Muscatello, Gary Miller, John & Lisa Miller, David & Meredith McComb, Chris Mattoon, Dick & Mary Merrill, John Mathews, Peter Mason, Carol McCarthy, JoAnn Irish Mahoney, George McGowan, Jean Meyer, Dawn & Bus Macey, David & Jerry McAvinney, Mike Mason, David & Jeannette Maslanka, Dean Merrill, Joyce Miller & Adirondack Community College Library, Joe Morabito, Garth Monroe, Tom & Judy Moynihan, Ray Mound, Kathy Muncil & Rich Parker & Fort William Henry, Albert Nemathy, Peggy Nobles, John L. Jack Newkirk, Hank Overbeek, John & Anita Orlando, Dave Ostrow, Jayne O'Sullivan, Nancy O'Brien & the Adirondack Journal Newspaper, Ted Ornstein, Jane O'Connell of Hillview Library, Charles Peer, Ernie Whelden, Dave Pelchar, George Pencil, Francis Poutre, Ken Peters, George Painter & Camp Chingachgook, Tom Passaro, Mark Peckham, Bob Powell, George Pencil, Tom Pfeiffelmann, Dick Paris, Jim Quirk & Shoreline Cruise, Malanie Quigan, Rolf Ronning, Bud Raab, Deanne Rehm, MacLaren Richards of Riverside Gallery, Bob Rostetter, Tom Roach, Bill Richards, Leroy Ryder of the DEC, Tom Rhodes, Bud Rawson, Nancy Rooney, Dusty & Nancy Rhodes, Gavin Rooney, Mae Goodnow Rozell, Charlie & Anita Richards, Harold Ragotzkie, Rick Salerno, Chris Shaw, Ed Stanilka, Pete Smith, Marilyn Smith, Stuart Smith, Jim Smith, Greg Smith, Ralph Stiles, Larry Staats, Kim Staats, Bolton Town Historian Pat Steele, Kay Stevens, Roger Summerhayes, Tom Starr, Bill & Barb Streever, Dick & Pat Swire, Henry Heller Smith, Bill Smith, R. Paul McCarty & Sandra Spaulding & Pat Turner of the Fort Edward Historical Museum, Dan & Judy Starr, Peter Simon, John Skinner, John Sperry, Richard Sage, Fenton Sabo, Jim Shaughnessy, Don Snyder, Joe Scully, George Singer, Historian Marjorie Swan, John Smart, Mason "Doc" Saunders, Joe Snyder, Bill Sherman, Croswell Tuttle, Lee & Dottie Taber, Larry Turcott, Tom Turcott, Mike & Debbie Tasick, Jill Trombley, Robin Trudeau & the Hancock House Museum, Helen Thatcher Thomson, Esko Virta, Peter & Carol Van Dyck, Kate Van Dyck, Cornelia Wells & Trees, Historian Marilyn Van Dyke, Alex Virag, Historian Pam Vogel, Drew Van Der Volgen, Don & Dottie Vilmar, Don Volkman, Norman & Marian Wolgin, Ike Wolgin & the Lake George Kayak Co., Bill White, Hugh Allen Wilson, Tom Welch, Mike Wells, Warren Witherill, Dick & Joyce Willmen, Ernie Whelden, Dave Waters of Waters Edge, Mike White, Dee Wilson, Bob & Donna Wotton, Bob White, Wauneata Waller, Chapin Wallour, Linda Winslow, Raymond & Barbara Wright, Rich Watkins – and Donnie Gates. (Donnie and her technical skills deserve a special THANK YOU for helping to make this book possible.)

Foreword

Many wonderful thoughts filled my mind as I began to organize my years of research toward assembling this book. This topic is a familiar one to me, because "Lake George Boats and Steamboats" have been a part of my life since I was born. One of my first conscious memories is of riding with my family around Bolton Bay in my Uncle Bob's 1931 Chris-Craft 20 ft. Cadet Runabout named *Rags*. I sat in the rear seat enjoying the soothing hum from the engine as I watched the spray of water flying past me onto the wake we left behind.

My family's first home was located in downtown Bolton Landing on Main Street, so it was easy for me to walk to the steamboat landing in Roger's Park to watch the boats, – to watch the *Mohican* and the *Ticonderoga* as they passed by or came in to the pier for a landing. I remember being filled with wonder and excitement at these large vessels. Where did they come from? Where were they going? Who were these people that were so fortunate to ride on them?

As I grew a little older, boating with my friends in small rowboats and canoes out on the lake was as common an experience for us as riding our bicycles around town. Gradually, we challenged ourselves to expand our horizons and explore the lake further and further as we gained the skills and confidence to do so. Later, thanks to an old outboard motor, every new bay and every new mile taught us something new and interesting. Finally, during my early teens, we explored to Lake George's northern extremity, to the small dam at Ticonderoga. By "conquering" all of Lake George's 32 miles, we felt as if we had succeeded in climbing our own Mount Everest.

We now needed a new frontier to investigate—and it seemed that the next step for us was to snorkel and study the vast mysterious world beneath the lake's surface. It was very enlightening and enjoyable to search and discover this new frontier with its many challenges and surprises. Fish, rocks, shoals, old boats, dock cribs, anchors, fishing lures, old bottles—What great treasures would we discover tomorrow?

One of the many reasons I entered the teaching profession in 1968 was so I might have more time during the summer to enjoy boating and exploring Lake George, and I was very pleased when my children, Michael and Allison, enjoyed riding around the lake in our old 1938 Chris-Craft named *Alli* as much as I did.

In 1986, my summers changed forever when I began a new seasonal occupation which would place me out on the lake in the most enjoyable ways. I was asked to be a captain on the Sagamore Hotel's *Morgan* during its first 1986 summer, and as a captain for the Lake George Steamboat Company since 1987 on the *Mohican*, and now also on the new *Lac du Saint Sacrement*, I find myself back again to where I started out in my youth. I'm out on my favorite lake – with my family and friends – enjoying "Lake George Boats and Steamboats."

William Preston "Bill" Gates, 2003.

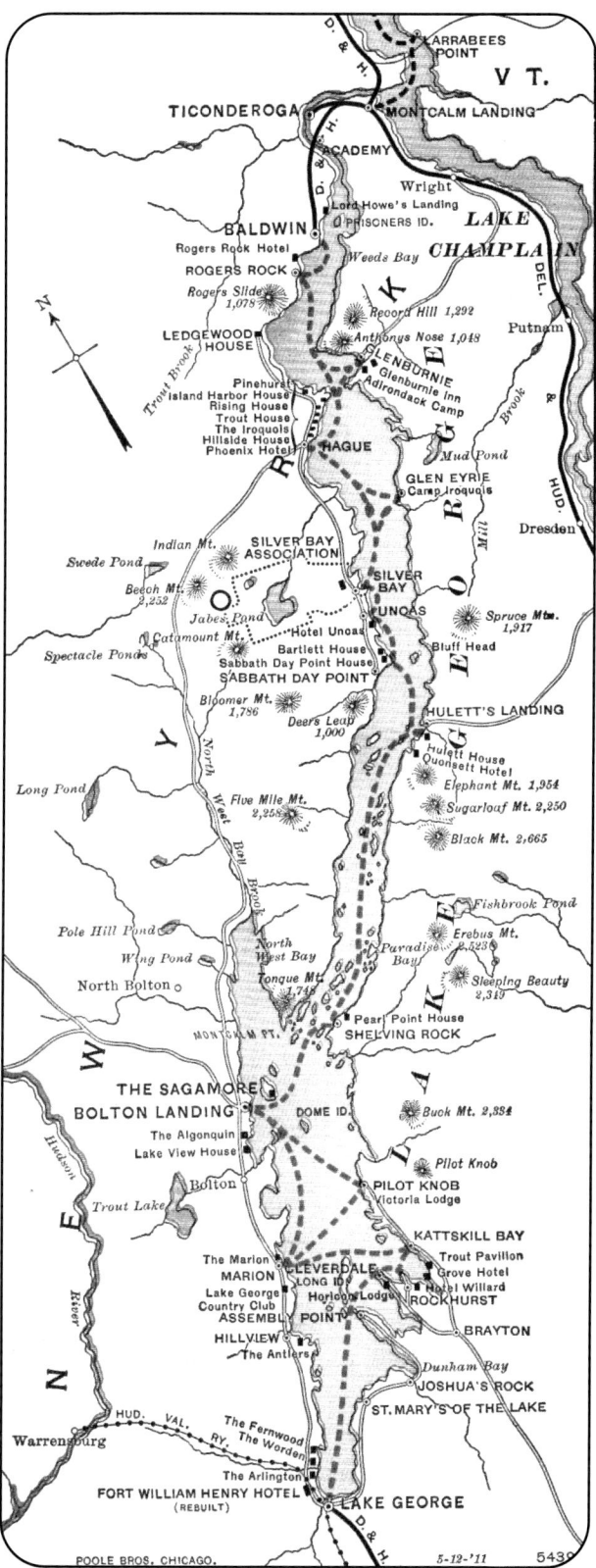

Map of Lake George showing the Steamboat courses to the early hotels and landings, 1911. Author's collection.

Introduction

When I was eight years old, I began collecting old and new Lake George post cards. In time, I added to my collection by including old Lake George books, maps, photographs, stereoptic cards and historical artifacts, which include boating and steamboating memorabilia. It then became apparent to me at some point that I should also begin photographing historic events, and photographing those artifacts that I was unable to obtain. Thus, my collection began growing in new ways.

I'm also very fortunate that my ancestors shared this same collecting hobby throughout their lives, and that many of these wonderful old Lake George treasures, from 1790 to the present, have now been passed down to me, so that I may share them with you. The more I explore around my family's 1830 Homestead, the more I uncover. In 1999, I discovered and published some of my Great Grandfather's "Turn-of-the-Century Scrapbook" focusing on the years 1899 to 1917, and I've also recently uncovered many more old photographs, books and articles which document rare information regarding Lake George's regional and boating history.

In 1999, I began writing articles for the Chronicle and Lake George Mirror newspapers, and I continued writing articles for the Chronicle in the form of a "Boat of the Week" series from 2000 to the present. My "Boat of the Week" series has been a tremendous boost toward bringing my boating collection up-to-date, thanks to all of the wonderful people around the Lake George region who have invited me into their boathouses and homes to share their boats and collections with me. I'm very much indebted to them, and as a result of their generosity, my research and collection increased to a point where I wanted to turn some of my treasures into this book, for your pleasure, and to ensure its preservation. I sincerely hope you enjoy "Lake George Boats and Steamboats" as much as I have enjoyed collecting it, writing it, working on it, and living it.

Bill Gates, 2003.
The "Huddle" at Bolton on Lake George, NY

List to the rippling waters,
   The tender flow of the tide;
It is sweeter than sweetest music
   As slowly we onward glide.
Out on the lake we linger
   In the hush of the summer night,
Two in a boat together,
   And life is a glad delight.

Here let us pause in the shadows,
   Hid by the fertile shore,
A moment to woo the silence
   And rest on the dripping oar.
You with your eyes so tender,
   Brimming with heaven's blue;
I with a heart o'erflowing
   And longing to speak to you.

See how the day's caresses
   Linger adown the west,
Where the beautiful golden portals
   Lead to a land of rest.
List how the strains of music
   Steal from the dreamy shore.
Oh, that we two together
   Were drifting for ever more!

Close to the shore we tarry
   Where the whispering willows bend,
For I have a tale to tell you
   That is sweet from beginning to end.
So the stars of the night may scatter,
   And the bird may fly to its nest;
I will murmur it low, "I love you,"
   And together we'll dream the rest.

Oh, beautiful hope of heaven
   That lives in a maiden's eyes!
I see in their depths the answer
   Ere the faltering lip replies.
     * * * * *
Out on the lake we linger
   In the hush of the summer night,
Two in a boat together,
   And life is a glad delight.
     —Arthur Lewis Tubbs.

Two in a Boat

Poem, from Lake George Mirror, July 15, 1893.
Courtesy: Bolton Historical Museum.

Photo, Two in a Boat.
Courtesy: Lake George Historical Association.

Elm Bark Canoe

Historians know very little about our first inhabitants in the greater Lake George region – and we know even less about the origin of the early Indians we discovered here upon our arrival. When the white man first arrived on this continent, only loose bands of aboriginal Algonquin Indians were found on the Eastern seaboard from the Mississippi to the Hudson Valley. Captain John Smith was captured by Algonquins, the early Dutch in New York, our Pilgrims and our Puritans were all in Algonquin territory, and the Algonquins were the first Indians Samuel D. Champlain encountered when he first arrived on this continent.

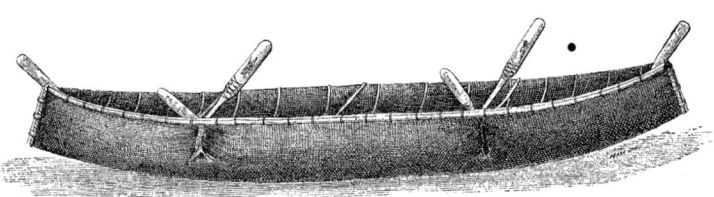

Elm Bark Canoe, early lithograph. Author's collection.

Another aboriginal group, the Iroquois, migrated from the northwest into the Mississippi Valley. From there they began separating—many migrated into the southwest and southeast while others settled in New York's Niagara region. When the Niagara Iroquois began to break apart, many drifted into Canada and along the St. Lawrence River Valley. The main stock were the Hurons which remained in Canada. The Onondagas, Cayugas, Senecas and Oneidas migrated into central New York and along the Finger Lakes while the Mohawk group remained in Montreal which became their capital. The Mohawks were now at the height of their power as they controlled all the territory from the St. Lawrence to the Mohawk River headwaters. The Adirondacks and Vermont were their hunting grounds.

The Mohawks became involved in a disastrous war with their fellow Hurons in 1550 which weakened them significantly. Around this time, they became united with their four Indian neighbors for protection—the Onondagas, Cayugas, Senecas and Oneidas. The Five Nation Iroquois Confederacy, or League of the HO-DE'-NO-SAU-NEE, was now formed at the suggestion of the Onondagas. The Tuscaroras of the Binghamton region later joined this alliance in 1722. This powerful nation became the most warlike and dangerous ever known in this region, and they terrified their enemies for good reason. During the second half of the 1600s and the early 1700s, they killed many thousands of any tribe that was within their reach with the firearms they had received from the Dutch, Swedes, English and French. They waged constant warfare.

The Mohawks controlled the entire eastern half of present day New York State, including the Lake George region. Their primary settlements were along the southern bank of the Mohawk River east of Utica, but they would spend the warm summer months hunting and fishing on our lake which they called, AN-Di-A-Ta-Roc-Te (Lake That Shuts Itself In). Longhouses once occupied strategic locations on the lake at Assembly Point, Tongue Mountain and Sabbath Day Point, to name a few. It is not uncommon even today to uncover arrowheads or stone tools at these, and many other sites, around the lake and along nearby streams.

Because the Iroquois traveled mostly on foot along ancient Indian trails, boats were essential for occasional and temporary use. In the few places where a boat was regularly required, dugouts were utilized, however, dugout canoes were too heavy to transport to distant locations. The Iroquois solved their need for a temporary craft by adopting the "bark canoe", "GA-SNA" or "GA-O-WO".

The Hurons, in contrast, were experienced canoeists. They acquired their canoeing knowledge from their neighbors, the Algonquins, who traded with them for maize. Huron canoes were made from the paper birch which was most plentiful in their northern habitat.

The Iroquois canoes on Lake George, however, were not made of birch bark as many would imagine—they were made instead of elm bark, or occasionally the bitternut-hickory. These canoes were clumsy, dangerous for crossing rough lakes, impossible for rapids and rivers, and most unsuitable for long voyages. Because elm bark warped easily, they were disposable craft, providing service for no longer than one year to their hunters and war parties. After use, they were hauled out of the water to dry. If canoes were still usable at the end of the season, the Iroquois would often bury them in the sand to preserve them through the winter.

Hulls were fashioned from one single piece of elm bark at the location where they were needed. They preferred the white elm. Felling of trees was avoided for fear of harming the delicate bark. The outer side of the bark was turned inward; both ends of the canoe ended plainly and sharply with a vertical prow where they were sewn with strips of inner bark from the basswood. The inside of the canoe was kept to form by bent wooden ribs made of young ash saplings placed 6 to 10 inches apart. The bottoms were wide and flat athwartships providing stability for carrying heavy burdens, yet these canoes were exceptionally light in weight. Thwarts were made of very small saplings, tapered at the ends, so they were pliable enough to be bent around the gunwales. To seal leaks, the Iroquois used a wad of the pounded inner bark of a dead red elm which they would crush into a sticky paste that swelled when damp. They also used moss, grass, tallow, gum or clay. Large tears were repaired by sewing an elm bark patch over the holes. The floor was protected with pieces of bark or light branches laid over the ribs. Frequently, the sides were decorated with a stripe of red paint.

The smallest canoes were 12 feet long, however, Iroquois warriors built very large models, up to 40 feet long, capable of carrying 30 men, two-by-two, standing or seated. Popular for fur trading, they could carry up to 1,200 pounds of fur. By 1750, the Iroquois were using square blanket-sails to propel their elm bark canoes on larger lakes like Lake George. Unfortunately, not one of these elm bark canoes survives today.

Bateaux

The French and Indian War was waged between France and Britain from 1755 to 1763, and many battles were fought over control of the strategic Lake George water highway. In March of 1757, the 1500 French, under the command of Rigaud de Vandreuil, unsuccessfully attacked Fort William Henry, using Diamond Island as a command post, but they did succeed in destroying several hundred bateaux which had been pulled up onto the shore. In 1903, the remains of an early sloop was discovered in 15 feet of water off shore; it was soon raised onto the beach in front of the fort. The sloop was 44 feet long, 14 feet wide, 7 feet deep and was constructed of black oak. A Spanish coin was found aboard dated 1743. Soon afterward, the boat was cut up and made into souvenirs which were sold to the tourists.

In the struggles during the fall of 1758, it became essential for both sides to have a fleet of boats that were stable, dependable and easy to construct;–the bateaux were the perfect boats for transport and battle. The French had first used them in New York in 1666 to explore our northern border. The British first utilized them later during Queen Anne's War, between 1702 and 1713, along the Mohawk River.

The Lake George bateaux averaged 25 to 36 feet long, 4 to 5 feet wide and had flat bottoms for maximum stability. They were strongly constructed of pine planking mounted on oak frames and were capable of carrying up to 22 soldiers. With both bow and stern ending at a point, they were easy to build and to maneuver. Bateaux were propelled by oars or poles and often would be steered by a stern sweep acting as a rudder.

Because it was too easy to be surprise attacked while hiking along Lake George's rocky tree-lined shores, the troops preferred the safety of distance allowed by paddling down the open lake. In July of 1758, more than 900 British bateaux were used in the unsuccessful attack against Fort Ticonderoga (then called Fort Carillon) by the Abercromby Expedition. This July 5th expedition was so large–it has been written that, "when the flotilla was three miles on its way, the surface of the lake was completely hidden from sight."[8]

In the fall of that same year, the British intentionally sank over 260 bateaux near what is today called Wiawaka so they could be protected from another possible French attack by wintering them under the ice of Lake George. In the spring of 1759, most of these bateaux were retrieved for reuse, however, 7 were left submerged because they had drifted into deeper water and were not easily recoverable. Time has taken its toll on these hulls leaving only the flat bottom planks, some cleats and many lower rib pieces intact.

In April, 1776, under orders from the Continental Congress, Benjamin Franklin, Samuel Chase and Charles Carroll traveled down Lake George in a 36 foot bateau on their way to Canada. Three months later, each of these men signed the Declaration of Independence in Philadelphia.

Bateau replica constructed by Ted Caldwell and students from Bolton Landing, Newcomb and Minerva Schools. Photo by Author.

In 1992, this sunken fleet was placed on the National Register of Historic Places thanks to the efforts of Joseph Zarzynski, Bob Benway and the membership of Bateaux Below, Inc. The dive site is rated as "Intermediate" and is accessed on a "first come, first served basis".

An 8th bateaux, which was constructed by local teachers and students, was recently sunk beside the others to help us learn more about the British's early sinking techniques and about deterioration rates in fresh water. Undoubtedly, there are remains of other historic bateaux waiting to be discovered and preserved on the bottom of Lake George.

1757 Sloop discovered in 1903 in 15 feet of water off Fort William Henry.
Courtesy: Pat Babe, Bolton Historical Museum.

Land Tortoise (Radeau)

England and France were engaged in many battles here on Lake George during the French and Indian War period, and each was equally determined to take control of this important region. After the French General Marquis de Montcalm captured Fort William Henry in 1757, the British and her allies planned an offensive to retake control of Lake George.

Captain Samuel Cobb supervised the construction of a flat-bottomed warship called a "radeau" which in French means raft. She was crudely pointed in the bow and had seven openings or ports in her sides for cannon. Launched on October 20, 1758, she was 52 feet long, 18 feet wide and was rowed with 26 sweeps (oars) with sails as an option. The crew inside were partially protected by high sloping sides which projected inward.

To protect this craft from being destroyed by the French during the winter, the radeau, named *Land Tortoise*, was carefully sunk beneath the southern ice of Lake George during the night of October 22, 1758 in such a way that it could be easily recovered in the spring, however it slipped into deeper water and was not recoverable. The British were forced to build another one in 1759 which they named the *Invincible*.

Land Tortoise sketch by Donnie Gates.
© W.P. Gates Publishing.

In 1990, Joe Zarzynski, Bob Benway and other divers of Bateaux Below, Inc. made the remarkable discovery using side-scan sonar. They found the *Land Tortoise*, located slightly over one mile north of the Lake George Steamboat Company's Steel Pier, in 100 feet of water. For the next four years, it was secretly studied by volunteer divers under the supervision of professional researchers. To dive this site, you must first register at the N.Y.S. Dept. of Environmental Conservation booth at Lake George's Million Dollar Beach.

Boating has significantly progressed here on Lake George since 1758, of course, however it is vitally important that we all know, understand and appreciate our boating origins and history. Although the *Land Tortoise* is not within easy viewing range for most of our citizens, it is important for everyone to be aware of its presence and historical significance. Centuries ago, this lake which we all enjoy so much today, was a major battlefield. Nations won and lost, lives were spared and lost–and the fate of this region became defined.

In 1995, this valuable "Gun Battery" was placed on the National Register of Historic Places. I find it interesting to note that most of today's pleasure boaters pass by the two buoys marking this site totally unaware that below them lies "the oldest intact warship in North America".

1759 "A Perspective View of Lake George". Sketch by Henry Skinner. Radeau *Invincible* and sloop *Halifax*.
Courtesy: Marjorie Swan, Warren County Historian.

Petti-auga

During 1768, a New York real estate investor, Samuel Deall, purchased a large tract of land at Ticonderoga and launched Lake George's first "Petti-auga". It was described as follows: "This odd word, of no discernable ancestry, was applied to an equally unusual craft—a flat bottomed contraption with leeboards in lieu of a keel, two masts and two sails, all managed by one man who was also helmsman and very frequently drunk." [31] In short, it was little more than a small commercial sailing barge. Deall also operated a petti-auga franchise from Ticonderoga on Lake Champlain.

After Fort Ticonderoga was captured and the Revolution began in earnest in the Lake George region, commercial endeavors halted abruptly on the lake, however later, during the very early 1800's, boat building became an even larger industry for Ticonderoga than lumbering.

Petti-auga: Model by Denise Huestis.
Photo, Courtesy: Steve Boyce,
Ticonderoga Heritage Museum.

James Caldwell

Robert Fulton's *Clermont* was the first steamboat, right? Not true. As far back as the 1780's, John Fitch and James Rumsey were in heated competition to achieve steamboat success. Both made major progress and both built and piloted functional steamboats. Of the two, John Fitch's successful boat, *The Steamboat*, propelled by duckfoot paddles, was the most durable by logging over 1000 miles in 1790. During that same year, Robert Fulton was still in London embarking upon an unsuccessful career as an artist. Fulton began showing interest as a nautical engineer much later in 1793 after becoming friends with Rumsey. By 1796, Robert Fulton began devoting all of his time and resources towards improving and developing the new invention to make it commercially successful. It took him eleven more years to achieve his goal when his steamboat sailed from New York City to Albany in 32 hours on August 19th, 1807. The history books are incorrect again by calling his ship the *Clermont*. It was first named *The North River Steamboat* – and later *The North River*. After a complete rebuild during the winter of 1807-1808, he reregistered and renamed it *The North River of Clermont*.

Following Fulton's example, the Winans brothers built the steamboat *Vermont* at Burlington, on Lake Champlain, which was a widely publicized operation in 1808. Because the towns around Lake George were small and because the new steamboat was often believed by many to be a creation of the Devil, steamboating did not begin here on Lake George until 1817. On April 15th, 1817, the Lake George Steamboat Company was incorporated. With John Winans on the new board, it can be assumed that he was the inspiration for this new com-

The Steamboat - America's first workable steamer - 1790 - built by John Fitch. Length, 60 ft. Print, Author's collection.

North River Steamboat, (later named *Clermont*) - 1807 - built by Robert Fulton. Length, 133 ft. 78 tons. Print, Author's collection.

James Caldwell - 1817 - first Lake George steamboat. Sketch by Donnie Gates.
© W.P. Gates Publishing.

pany, and with James Caldwell's financing, it might also easily be assumed that their first steamboat would be named for him, the *James Caldwell*. (The original name for today's Lake George Village was Caldwell, named for his family.)

The *James Caldwell* was built at a cost of $12,000 in Caldwell, probably on Pine Point. She was similar in shape to the canal boats of the period with two long boilers and a tall brick smokestack. She was 80 feet long, 20 feet wide across the beam, drafted 8 feet and displaced 120 tons. Her boilers burned wood and developed 20 horsepower propelling it along at just 4 mph with John Winans as her first captain.

She undoubtedly suffered frequent breakdowns because her engine was "third-hand" having previously been aboard Lake Champlain's *Champlain* and *Vermont* (which sank in 1815). The trip down the lake took an entire day, and was equal to the speed of a rowboat. On one voyage, she was struck by lightning, but was mostly undamaged and continued her season.
After only four struggling seasons, she burned mysteriously at her dock in Caldwell in1821, with many joking that she had caught fire from "over insurance". The reality was that her owners did not recover much of their investment, so two years passed before a new vessel, the *Mountaineer* (*I*), was built to replace her.

Mountaineer (I)

Mountaineer (I) - 1824 - Sketch by Donnie Gates.
© W.P. Gates Publishing.

No original drawings or paintings of the *Mountaineer* survive today. To create this sketch, I compared the evolution from the *James Caldwell* to the *William Caldwell* and determined what the *Mountaineer* might have looked like.
(The author).

There isn't any record of a commercial steamboat on Lake George during 1822 and 1823. With Hague and Bolton as the only viable towns along the lake at that time, business was probably very slight.

The *Mountaineer* (I) was built in 1824 on Pine Point in Caldwell (Lake George Village) at a cost of $12,000 by James Baird of the Lake House Hotel with the assistance of Captain and boatbuilder Jahaziel Sherman. She was 100 feet long, 16 feet wide at her beam, drafted 8 feet and displaced 125 tons. Her 20 horsepower steam engine propelled her along at 6 mph under the command of Captain Lucius C. Larabee.

Her wooden hull was of a unique design with no rib frames. Three layers of oak planking were laid in alternating horizontal and vertical directions giving the hull the extreme flexibility to, "bend and twist like an eel".[8] Making two trips to Ticonderoga each week, with the other days being used for sightseeing excursions, her first short season was a success. Fare was $2.00.

With no piers constructed along the lake, and to guarantee the fastest possible voyage, Captain Larabee would tow a small yawl (rowboat) behind the *Mountaineer* and passengers would have to be rowed out and then climb aboard the yawl to be winched alongside to board. He had different standards for the ladies: he would try to stop for them, but every male had to be "yawled in".

The *Mountaineer* (I) was retired after 13 years of service in 1836 and allowed to sink and rot away in Ticonderoga Creek. As late as the 1890's, her remains could still be seen.

William Caldwell

Steam packet *William Caldwell* - May 1, 1844 - from Lake George Steamboat Company poster.
Courtesy: William Dow, Lake George Steamboat Company.

The *William Caldwell* was then built near the northern outlet of Lake George at Ticonderoga, about a half-mile north of today's Baldwin Pier, by Captain Jahaziel Sherman of Lake Champlain. With prominent double stacks spewing black smoke, it began operating in the spring of 1838 by making daily 8:00 AM round trips from the Lake House dock in Caldwell to Ticonderoga and back. While at Ticonderoga, it would remain at her dock for 3 1/2 hours daily so her passengers could visit the ruins of Fort Ticonderoga. At 3:00 PM she would leave for the return trip to Caldwell. She appeared in an 1838 W.H. Bartlett lithograph near Black Mountain.

A woman named Atherton operated the first horse and carriage service for passengers who needed overland transportation from Ticonderoga to Lake Champlain to catch the steamboats waiting there. Later, Captain William Baldwin took over this service and operated it for many years. For this reason, this shoreline is still named Baldwin today.

This third Lake George steamboat, the *William Caldwell*, was named for the son of James Caldwell who was the first patent holder of today's Lake George Village. The boat was approximately 110 to 140 feet long (accounts vary), 17 feet wide at her beam and had a draft of 8 feet. Built at a cost of $20,000, her wooden hull could displace 150 tons in weight. She was powered by an "old-fashioned Fulton type of steeple engine" which operated a "horizontal cross beam up and down" providing 40 horsepower which propelled this vessel up to 12 mph. Her captain throughout her years of service was Lucius C. Larabee. This famous early Lake George Steamboat Captain, and an ancestor of mine, Elias S. Harris, began his illustrious steamboating career on the *William Caldwell*. At the age of 15 he was a fireman and soon he was called upon to land a yawl at the Bolton and Hague docks. The Pilot, William Potter, was his first instructor in navigating this large vessel around the lake.

By 1848 the *William Caldwell* was showing signs of deterioration. In that same year she was retired and abandoned in the bay north of today's Shepard Park in Lake George Village where she eventually sank and disintegrated.

There wasn't any steamboat service of any kind during the 1849 season, however this would be the very last year where no commercial lake transportation would be available. With the launching of John Harris's *John Jay* in 1850, passenger boats have been faithfully plying the waters of Lake George every summer since.

William Caldwell model. Unknown builder.
Courtesy: Ethel Andrus, Hague Town Historian. Photo by author.

John Jay

John Jay at Cook's Landing.
Courtesy: Ed and Beth Becker

When the steamboat *William Caldwell* was retired and dismantled in 1848, no new ship was ready to replace her. 1849, therefore, was a discouraging season for the travelers that sought passage down Lake George. During that quiet summer here at the lake, John Jay Harris of Harrisena, Queensbury was observing the completion of his new steamer built by H.R. Dunham & Company at Ticonderoga Creek which he launched in the spring of 1850. Built at a cost of $26,000, the *John Jay* was much more powerful and stylish than any of her three predecessors.

She was 145 feet long, drafted 8 feet and was 20 feet wide across her beam. With her wooden hull made totally of oak, she displaced 250 tons as her 75 horsepower wood-fired steam engine moved her at 13 miles per hour. Although only two old lithographs of the *John Jay* exist to show us what she looked like, Captain Oscar Finkle of Bolton Landing described her as being "painted white with a lower and upper deck, the latter being approximately fifteen feet above the guards". A canopy roof made of wood was later added. With Captain Lucius C. Larabee aboard, she made daily 7:00 AM trips from Caldwell to Cook's Landing at Ticonderoga where she met the stage coaches which brought passengers to and from the landing on Lake Champlain. In a rare document loaned to me by Philip Harris, a descendent of John J. Harris, John was only able to insure his new boat in 1850 for $4,000 to cover, "her engine, boilers, machinery, tackle, apparel and furniture."

In the spring of 1854, the Lake George Steamboat Company received its new charter by an Act from the New York Legislature. The company, which was soon to build the new Fort William Henry Hotel, was now authorized to charter or purchase Lake George vessels "propelled solely or partially by the power or aid of steam or other expansive fluid or motive of power". The *John Jay* was then purchased for $18,000 and the company placed Captain Josea B. Farr in command. Captain Farr soon became the first president of the company. In time, he was replaced by Captain James Gale, who became the company treasurer and later became manager of the new hotel. . John Jay Harris's brother Elias S. Harris was his pilot, his engineer was Daniel Scott and John's cousin Leander Harris was one of his deckhands.

Tuesday July 29th, 1856, had been a typical, very warm, Lake George summer day. The *John Jay* left Cook's Landing, Ticonderoga at 6PM, much later than usual. After traveling about six miles south past Waltonian Island, a fire was discovered which caused great alarm aboard. In Pilot Harris' own descriptive words—"Before we reached Friend's Point, a severe shower came up. The wind struck the steamer as we passed the point, coming over the mountain with terrible force. The gale struck the top of the smoke stack and stopped the draught. The pressure was so heavy that it burst open both doors of the furnace. Wood was used for fuel. The fireman had just placed a pile of wood near the furnace doors—. When the doors flew open, the hold was suddenly filled with red-hot embers—. The alarm went through the boat from deck to deck."

The pilot house was not immediately aware of the extent of the fire because communication was relayed by voice during this early era. Unfortunately, the *John Jay* had just missed an easy opportunity to safely beach close-by among the islands. Suddenly, the ship lost all steering as the tiller ropes below-deck were burned away by the rapidly spreading fire. In a gallant display of heroism, Pilot E.S. Harris ran through the smoke and flames to the after-part of the promenade deck where he steered the boat by hand using the emergency tiller. The smoke was so thick that he was blinded and could only guess when to turn in towards Hague. The *John Jay* missed the intended sandy shore and struck a large exposed rock which caused it to careen further outward into the lake a significant distance. This last series of events, combined with the spreading flames, caused the passengers to panic. As their options ran out, people ran to every corner of the ship seeking safety. With the paddlewheels still in motion, passengers began jumping overboard, only to be pushed further from shore by the wheels' current. Many were saved by clinging to life-preservers, tables, chairs or steamer trunks that had been thrown overboard to them, however, the lives of 6 passengers were lost, five women and one man, in the only deadly accident in Steamboat Company history.

The *John Jay's* officers and crew acted heroically throughout this tragedy to save lives and administer comfort to the distressed passengers. The ship's carpenter William George leaped onto the rocks to safety while carrying a female passenger who was in terrible distress. In doing so, he dislocated both of his ankles. Passenger William Brunet, an assistant at Garfield's Hotel, dove into the depths and retrieved three bodies, the first one being saved by resuscitation. Even "Old Dick the Rattlesnake Man", (Richard Shear), saved the life of a young girl by throwing overboard his wooden box filled with snakes so she could climb upon it.

The wreck of the *John Jay* still lies on the bottom of Lake George in the shallow waters south of Cook's Islands at Temple Knoll, a haunting reminder of that tragic night back in 1856 when the lives of six passengers were lost. Although her rotting wooden remains will someday dissolve finally into dust, the name Calamity Rock, the rock she struck while trying to seek safety, will forever stand guard as a monument and will forever keep her memory alive.

**(Author's Note) Throughout the 18 years I have been a boat captain on Lake George, I have always been most fascinated with the story of the *John Jay*. Although I'm proud that John Jay, Leander and Elias Harris were some of my steamboating ancestors, my strongest interest lies in the study of the misfortunate timing and series of unavoidable events which had to coincide to cause the loss of six lives and the destruction of the ship.

Calamity Rock. Photo by author.
Courtesy: John and Betty Barth.

Minne-Ha-Ha (I)

Minne-Ha-Ha at Fort William Henry Hotel dock, Caldwell.
Courtesy: Maggie McClure, Lake George Historical Association.

Following the loss of the *John Jay*, plans were immediately set in motion to replace her. Salvaging the boilers from the *John Jay*, the *Minne-Ha-Ha* (meaning "Laughing Waters" from Longfellow's Hiawatha) was launched and christened on May 12, 1857 near Caldwell (Lake George Village). She was the first ship on Lake George to offer the appearance of a modern steamboat. Built to carry up to 400 passengers, the *Minne-Ha-Ha* left Caldwell at 7:30 a.m., traveled the full length of the lake to Ticonderoga and returned to Caldwell at 6 p.m. With James Gale as her first captain and Elias S. Harris (John J. Harris' brother) as her pilot, she was a magnificent ship in skilled hands. Soon thereafter Harris became captain. He later described her by saying, "This boat was one of the fastest and finest steamers of her day, and admired by steamboat men as well as all others." The *Minne-Ha-Ha* was the last of the wood burning large steamers on Lake George and used six cords of wood per round trip: the ones to follow burned coal.

She cost $20,000 to build, was 144 feet long, 22 feet wide at her beam, and drafted 8 feet. Displacing 260 tons, her 75 horsepower engine propelled her along at 13 mph. In 1869, she was replanked and renovated. One of her distinguished passengers that year was said to be Civil War Potomac Army Commander Major-General George B. McClellan. In 1871 twelve year old future President Theodore Roosevelt rode the Minne-Ha-Ha with his family while vacationing at Caldwell.

After 20 years of successful service, the *Minne* was retired in 1878. Her steam engine was sold for $16,000 to a boat-builder in Vancouver, British Columbia, but the boat's usefulness didn't end there. Cyrus Butler, owner of the Horicon Pavilion Hotel at Black Mountain Point, purchased the hull and utilized it for additional rooms for 50 guests and a dining hall for his hotel. The iron mooring rings are still visible along the shore today.

Eventually, the hull went into disrepair and sank in the shallow bay in 14 feet of water. It was later dismantled and the remainder was dynamited. Her keel is still totally visible to this day on the bottom. I've snorkeled over it on dozens of occasions during my lifetime.

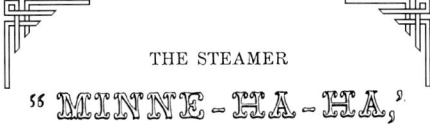

1868 Advertisement.
Courtesy: Henry Caldwell, Black Bass Antiques.

Minne-Ha-Ha Assembly Room

Minne-Ha-Ha (I).
Photos by Seneca Ray Stoddard.

Top left and right photos: At Black Mountain Point. Courtesy: Lake George Historical Association.

Center and bottom left photos: Private collection.

Bottom right photo: Courtesy: Ike Wolgin.

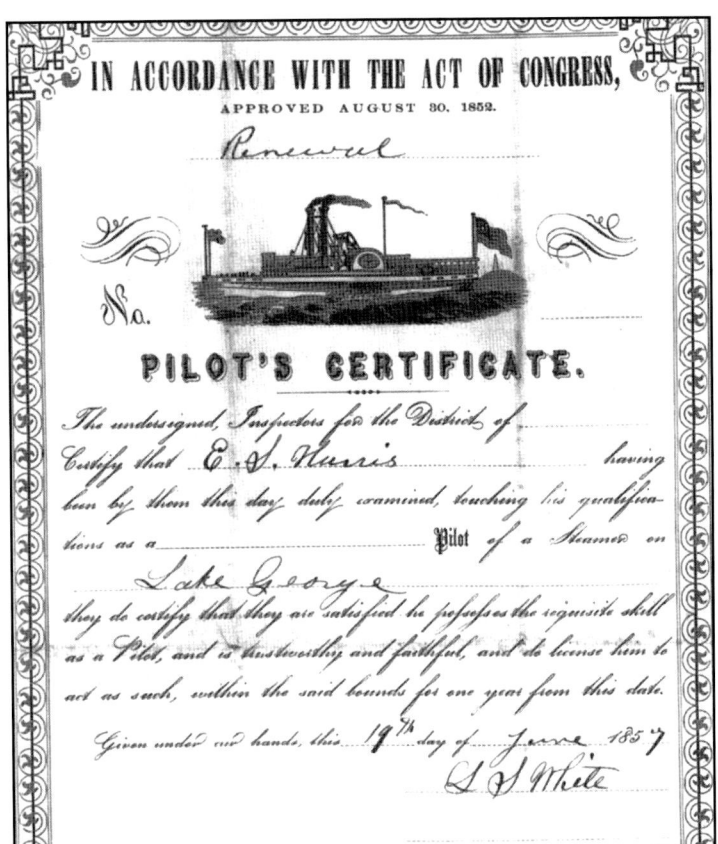

Captain Elias S. Harris

Left: 1857 Pilot's Certificate.
Courtesy: Jane O'Connell, Hillview Free Library.

Above Photo: Courtesy: Ed Stanilka

Ganouskie

By 1869, it became clear that the *Minne-Ha-ha* (I) was unable to provide adequate daily service to all the new passengers arriving by trains at both ends of Lake George. In the late spring of that same year, the wooden-hulled *Ganouskie* was constructed at Caldwell (Lake George Village) at a cost of $20,000. She was christened with the early Indian name given to our present day Northwest Bay.

The *Ganouskie* weighed 67 tons and was 72 feet long, exactly the same length as the Sagamore Hotel's *Morgan* of today. Her beam was 20 feet, draft was 7 feet and she was the first propeller-driven steamboat on Lake George—propelled by a single screw at 11 mph. Her steam engine was shipped by water from Philadelphia to Fort Edward where it was then carted to Caldwell in pieces and installed.

At a speed of 11 miles per hour, her job was to carry up to 50 passengers southward while the *Minne-Ha-Ha* (I) carried them north. This was the first time two steamboats provided simultaneous service on the lake.

The *Ganouskie* sported an unusual round pilot-house and an observation cabin on her upper deck. Originally, she burned wood for fuel, but in 1877 she was converted to coal with the installation of new coal grates, and her upper deck was modified to carry more passengers.

Ganouskie.
Courtesy: Lake George Historical Association.

Her first captain was Arnold Hulett who founded Hulett's Landing on Lake George's northeast shore. From 1870 onward, the *Ganouskie* carried mail. That same year her open deck was decked over. In 1880, she grounded on the rocks off Sabbath Day Point and was pulled safely off by Cyrus Butler's *Meteor*.

Ganouskie was laid up in the Baldwin Shipyard in 1884, and in 1885 her engine was dismantled. During 1886 she was sold to Captain G.W. Howard who moored her along the southwest shore of Big Burnt Island in the Narrows where she became a floating saloon. Her machinery was sent to Shelburne Harbor on Lake Champlain. For the amusement of the patrons, a rattlesnake was displayed in a cage on the bar.

Above: *Ganouskie*, Wilson House, Bolton, showing new upper deck. Courtesy: Lake George Historical Association.
Right: *Ganouskie* Certificate of Inspection, 1878. Courtesy: Don Cornell.

Owl

Owl at Caldwell. SR Stoddard photo. Courtesy: Bolton Historical Museum.

In 1871, the *Owl* was brought up the Hudson River and launched on lake George, reportedly by General Banks, builder of the cog railway up Prospect Mountain. By 1873 she was being utilized for picnic and fishing charters only under the ownership of Captain Lee Harris. The propeller driven *Owl* was 30 feet long, 7 feet wide and drafted a light 3 feet 6 inches, allowing the boat to lay up close to the shoreline for easy wilderness access. With a top speed of 8 mph, up to 25 guests were initially charged fares of $3.00/hour, $15.00/day. Later in her career they were raised to $5.00/hour, $25.00/day.

She ran most of her charters from the Fort William Henry Hotel in Caldwell. Famed local photographer Seneca Ray Stoddard once chartered her for improving his new Lake George Maps. During the 1870's, the *Owl* was one of only three or four power driven boats on Lake George. In 1881 the *Owl* was sold to Hiram Hyde who operated charters from the Trout Pavilion Hotel in Katskill Bay.

Lillie M. Price

Lillie M. Price. Photo by S.R. Stoddard.
Courtesy: Peggy Edwards, Lake George Village Historian.

The story of the *Lillie M. Price* is also the story of the unusual man who built her and owned her—Colonel Walter M. Price. Colonel Price was born to a poor family in England in the early 1800s. His first marriage failed rather quickly and soon after he took on a manual job in the export trade. In addition, there were rumors that he was also involved with another young woman who began chasing him in desperation. To escape his troubles, Walter Price sailed off to America for a new beginning. In New York City he worked at a succession of jobs which included a coal company and a brewery. At the brewery he discovered a $3000 error in the bookkeeping. He was rewarded by increased responsibility and salary—and in a short period of time, Walter owned the company. He next formed the Empire Brewery which became a successful monopoly over most of his competitors.

His new found riches brought him into contact with the high society he craved to be associated with. In only a few years, he was married to a succession of wives. He soon was charged with bigamy, although he claimed that his first marriage in England was invalid. Newspapers across America published the scandal.

It became fashionable at the time for the wealthy to build their summer mansions throughout the Adirondacks. So many of the large estates were established between Bolton Landing and Caldwell (Lake George Village) that this ten miles of Lake George shoreline became known as Millionaires' Row. Colonel Price built his on the west side of Route 9 where today's Twin Birches Motel is located. Although it was torn down many decades ago, we refer to it today as the "Upper Price Manor" because his son William built his own "Lower Price Manor" just north of Lake George Village across from today's Northway Exit, a mansion that still stands today. (Actually, Walter Price was not a true colonel. He received that honorary status after he single-handedly outfitted an entire Union Army regiment in the Civil War.)

Colonel Price next became financially involved in the construction of the new Fort William Henry Hotel at the head of the lake; it was said that he was the only financial backer for the project. His latest marriage was to an upstairs maid at Price Manor, Constance Fallon. They had two daughters which were both deaf-mutes. When it was decided that the new hotel needed its own small steamboat for transporting guests, the new steamer built in 1871 was named for his favorite daughter—Lillie Minne-ha-ha Price. Colonel Price commissioned a figurehead to be sculpted of the beautiful Lillie which was mounted on the bow.

The *Lillie M. Price* was 61 feet long, had a 14 foot beam and drafted 6 feet burning slab wood for fuel. Her master was Captain Edwin White; her pilot was Burr Phelps of Pilot Knob whose family's name is today attached to Phelps Island. The boat would make daily trips to the Sherman House Hotel in the Narrows, into Paradise Bay and back for a fare of $1.50. In August of 1874, she struck a small fishing boat with three aboard and sank it; fortunately there were no fatalities.

In 1880 her pilot-house was removed and her propeller was repaired. During this renovation, guests from the Crosbyside Hotel in Caldwell were forced to attend church by rowing across the bay in small boats or traveling around by carriages.

After incorporating in 1885, the five corporation directors continued to keep the *Lillie M. Price* at the Fort William Henry Dock for a yearly fee of $25. Captain Moses

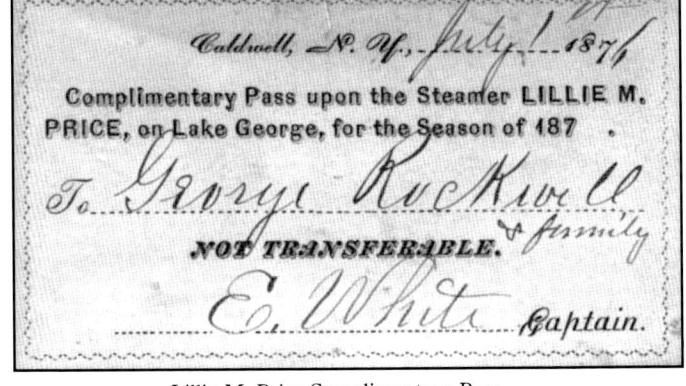

Lillie M. Price Complimentary Pass.
Courtesy: Lake George Historical Association.

Finkle became her new captain. By 1888, she began to show serious deterioration. She was scrapped at the end of the 1888 season. The figurehead of Lillie was then removed and given to the family.

It is interesting to note that Colonel Price had become a serious alcoholic towards the end of his life. When he died in 1876, many legal battles occurred for control of his estate between most of his heirs and former wives. Price Manor was then sold to settle the finances.

There was a happy ending for Lillie Minne-ha-ha Price. She became an artist, and in 1892, at the age of 21, she met and married Adolph Pfeifer who was one of the founders of the Union League for the Deaf. The life story of Lillie M. Price would probably be long forgotten here at Lake George if the steamboat built in her honor had been christened by any other name.

Julia

The *Julia* was brought to Lake George from New York City in 1873 by Captain Frank Van Wormer who sailed her from the Trout Pavilion. She was the very first privately owned steam yacht on Lake George. The only other steamboats at that time were the sidewheeler *Minne-Ha-Ha* (I) and the propeller driven *Ganouskie*. Passing through a series of owners, she was still transporting passengers on Lake George in the mid 1880's.

Julia, first private commercial steam yacht on Lake George. Author's collection.

Mystic

Mystic at the Lake-View House.   Courtesy: Private collection.

When the Lake-View House opened in 1875 in Huddle Bay, Bolton, a little south of the Algonquin, it could accommodate 25 guests. Later it was enlarged to hold 100. Most of their patrons arrived in Bolton Landing on the steamers *Minne-Ha-Ha* or *Ganouskie*. The Lake-View would then dispatch a small steamboat to ferry passengers to the hotel. The unusual looking *Mystic* was one of these small craft. Notice that the *Mystic* was propelled by two paddle wheels.

Meteor

Meteor at Black Mountain Bay, 1880. Floating hotel *Minne-Ha-Ha* (I) at left.
Courtesy: Lake George Historical Association.

The *Meteor* was built on the Hudson River and exhibited in Machinery Hall at the United States Centennial Exhibition in Philadelphia. Launched at the William Kapella Shipyard the spring of 1876, she was 51 feet long, 10 feet wide at her beam and drafted 4 feet 4 inches. Sporting a 4 foot wheel, her 2 cylinder engine with steel shaft propelled her along at 11 mph.

In 1877 the *Meteor* was brought to Lake George by Cyrus Butler. When she was not being used for personal pleasure, she was frequently chartered for use by the Rogers Rock Hotel. Captain S.W. Clark of Ticonderoga carried up to 40 guests and charged $25/day or $5/hour.

Increasingly, the *Meteor* was hired as a workboat. Her most publicized work project was to tow the retired *Minne-Ha-Ha* (I) to Black Mountain Point in 1877 to become part of the Horicon Pavilion Hotel.

In 1880, Captain Clark towed a barge of building materials from the Fort William Henry dock to Bluff Head and other points. That same year the *Ganouskie* became stranded on a rocky shoal near Sabbath day Point. The *Meteor* successfully puller her off.

In June of 1892, the town of Hague voted to remove two large boulders that had been partially blocking the road for years. Steam drills did the drilling with the steam being carried in pipes from the steam powered *Meteor* anchored off shore below.

The *Mohican* (I)s engine wouldn't fire up in the spring of 1995 so again the *Meteor* was called upon; she towed it to the Baldwin shipyard near Ticonderoga for repairs. She also was used frequently to tow barges of wood to the paper and lumber mills. While towing a barge of pulp to the Ticonderoga paper mill during August of 1995, the *Meteor's* fire box apparently spewed some stray sparks onto a pile of firewood being used along with coal for fuel. The *Meteor* was totally destroyed.

H. Colvin

Little has been recorded about the *H. Colvin*. She was built during the fall and winter of 1875 and launched in June of 1876. A commercial side-wheeler steamboat of simple design and construction, she was about 50 feet long and sported a 10 foot beam.

H. Colvin.
Courtesy: Rebecca Pelchar & Maureen Dye, Chapman Historical Museum.

Pampero

Pampero ready to race, 1880's. Photo, Author's Collection.

Boat racing on Lake George is as old as boating itself. Most Lake George boating enthusiasts have read many accounts of *Ankle Deep's* Gold Cup Race in 1914 and *El Lagarto's* three successful years in the mid 1930's. Ironically, an early eyewitness who attended each of these historic competitions said that none of *Ankle Deep's* or *El Lagarto's* performances were able to compare to an early race he witnessed between the *Pampero* and the *Dandy*. Orson Culver Richards(1873-1958) was so impressed with this historic event that he described it in detail in his journals in 1948. His great nephew Bill Richards of Pilot Knob recently shared this important history with me.

Before you read the story of the race, I'd like to tell you a little about the *Pampero's* history. Pampero is a South American term meaning, "a strong west wind across the pampas", according to Webster. The new $30,000 teak and mahogany *Pampero* was built at the Continental Iron Works in Brooklyn to be exhibited in Philadelphia at the 1876 U.S. Centennial Exhibition. She was purchased at the Exhibition by the Commodore of the New York City Yacht Club, Harrison B. Moore. *Pampero* was unique because her ribs were made of galvanized steel. She was fast, with a length of 54 feet, an 8 foot beam and a draft of 2 feet 6 inches.

In 1877, Mr. Moore brought the *Pampero* to his summer home on Heart Bay at the northern end of Lake George. She was still very fast 11 years later in 1888—so fast, that a wager was made between Moore and Captain Boyer of the steam yacht Dandy. The race was to be held the following year, 1889. In Orson Culver Richards' own words (and with my own additions)—

"I want to tell you about what I think was the greatest sporting event ever held on Lake George. It was the race between the *Pampero* and the *Dandy*. The (*Pampero's*) boiler was a Roberts 4 [[ft. by 6 ft. and her engine was a triple expansion with cylinders 5 [[in., 9in. and 14 in. diameter—stroke was 9 in. The *Dandy* came up from Long Island Sound. (She was) about five feet shorter than the *Pampero*. –This race was to settle an argument (and) was from Fourteen Mile Island to the Fort William Henry (Hotel). The stakes were a thousand dollar bet and a dinner for their friends at the hotel. (In addition, the loser was to pay all the expenses for the *Dandy* to Lake George and back, plus the cost of all wine consumed by both crews.)

The race had a lot of publicity and the *Horicon* (I) took aboard (the judges and) a lot of enthusiasts-. Amasa Howland, Eber Richards and I –went directly to the starting line (on the *Horicon*)-. Captain Harris of the *Horicon* told his passengers to spread out and keep the boat trim, that he could do only 19 mph and would try to keep up with the racers.

The *Pampero* was black, her boiler was black, her stack was black and the smoke from it was black. (The day before the race *Pampero* was lifted from the water and her bottom was rubbed with black stove polish to reduce drag.) She was burning the finest grade of soft coal, saturated with kerosene and packed in little paper bags. Her boiler was so large that the condenser couldn't handle the steam so they took out the condenser, therefore losing the benefit of the vacuum, but making up for it in the extra amount of steam going through the engine. A short exhaust pipe was installed on the low pressure outlet. Her machinery was heavy and she sat low in the water. She gave the impression of brute strength.

In contrast was the *Dandy*. She was of light mahogany and all of her finish was shining brass, polished like a mirror, her boiler, engine jacket and stack, all brass, and she appeared graceful as the most finished dancer. No smoke from her stack, no cloud of white steam from her exhaust pipe—her condenser was taking care of that. She was light in the water and slid through with no sound on a wave that rose gradually from her bow to a point amidships and then fell away gradually to the stern. I have seen photographs to illustrate shapes and wave lines of prominent boats and only once have I seen a photograph of a boat throwing a similar wave line.

The two boats went across the starting line together, the *Horicon* just back of them and a little to the east.–The boats set

Pampero and *Horicon* (I). Photo by Fred C. Thatcher. Courtesy: Jim Shaughnessy.

tled down to business. The *Pampero* was throwing the spray and literally plowing up the lake. The *Dandy* was gliding along as though she was greased. The *Pampero* was throwing fire and black smoke in the air and mingled with it was that cloud of white steam from the exhaust pipe. The *Dandy* sailed along, no fuss, everything quiet, everything serene—but she began to fall behind, not much, but definitely she was slipping, and in about two miles the *Pampero* was out in front three or four boat lengths.

The next thing we knew, the *Pampero* was slowing up—something was wrong—the *Dandy* went by her and the *Horicon* caught up with her. *Pampero* was in trouble. They were squirting water on something. Someone said the fireman had fainted, but –they were (actually) cooling down a hot box. In a very short time the *Pampero* began to pick up speed and soon was really doing business. She was right close off the *Horicon's* bow and the *Dandy* was out in front an eighth of a mile. We could see the crew working on the *Pampero* and there wasn't any sick fireman; he was a busy fireman. The flame and smoke against the darkening sky as we went towards the finish was a picture. The *Pampero* began to gain, the gap between the two racers was getting smaller and as we approached Tea Island, a mile from the finish, the gap was only a hundred feet. Could she make it? The *Pampero* would catch her in the next mile! No! The Dandy must have something up her sleeve, something in reserve, so the conversation went on the *Horicon*. I pounded my Dad on the shoulder until it was black and blue. THEN! Off Tea Island came a puff of steam from the *Dandy*. She stopped, and as we went by they were shoveling her fire overboard. She had blown a tube in her boiler and was out of the race. She was carrying 240 pounds of steam at the time. She still had the reserve to call on and the *Pampero* would never have caught her IF the tube hadn't blown. I heard the engineer on the *Pampero* say he was carrying 350 pounds and we know she was using every ounce. (The *Pampero* had won!)

(Later that day,) the sun had dipped behind the mountains, the boats and the crews were cooling off at the Fort William Henry dock, the men were talking it over and I was right there listening. I have seen the Gold Cup races, have seen *El Lagarto* do 70 MPH, have seen the *Hawkeye* blow a cylinder head off at full speed—I was there when *Ankle Deep* broke her shaft and the Count (Mankowski) went overboard, and I have seen the *Ellide* travel in the thirties. For beauty, drama, excitement and sustained interest, nothing ever happened on Lake George to equal that race between the *Pampero* and the *Dandy*."

In 1891, Moore was upset briefly when he lost the $300.00 propeller in the Narrows which had propelled his prized boat to victory, however, the following year he waged a new race between his *Pampero* and *Horicon* (I) herself. The July 1892 race was on the regular course followed by the *Horicon* between the Rogers Rock Hotel Pier and Hague, a distance of approximately 6 miles. The *Pampero* won by a quarter of a mile during a "gale west wind" according to *Horicon*'s Pilot W. Warren Rockwell.

In 1910, the Lake George Steamboat Company purchased the *Pampero* for $1200 from Harrison Moore to run opposite the *Mercury* from the Fort William Henry Hotel for picking up passengers at several of the smaller private docks around the southern end of the lake. Captain Herbert Barber, Engineer Clayton Newell and purser Kenneth Noyes traveled up the west shore to the Hotel Marion, crossed to Assembly Point and returned along the east shore. After two successful seasons, she was replaced by the new *Mountaineer* (II). In 1916, *Pampero* was sold James McCabe of Ticonderoga for towing booms of logs to a sawmill on Lambshanty Bay. Her rotting remains can still be seen today on the shore of the bay.

LOCAL MOTOR BOAT SERVICE ON LAKE GEORGE

Beginning July 1st the Power yacht "Pampero" will leave Lake George (railway dock) daily, Sundays inclusive, at 9.00 A.M. and 3.00, 5.00 and 7.00 P.M. for Marion House and return, following closely the west shore of lake to the Country Club and Hotel Marion, crossing the lake to Assembly Point and Dunham's Bay, returning to Lake George via the east shore. Fare fifty cents for the round trip, occupying about one and one-half hours. Twenty-five cents between any two landings. Tickets on sale only on board. This service will continue in effect until about September 10th.

Pampero advertisement, 1911. Courtesy: Dick and Mary Kowell.

Horicon (I)

Horicon (I). Courtesy: Lake George Historical Association.

By the mid 1870's, the 25 year old *Minne-Ha-Ha* was in need of replacement, thus the new *Horicon* (I) was built, totally of wood–eighty freightcar loads were required. Her second-hand boiler and engines came from the steamboat *Champlain*, on Lake Champlain, which had been wrecked north of Westport the previous year. Her bell had sailed on Lake Champlain's *United States* which sailed from 1847 to 1873. A magnificent sidewheeler, no expense was spared to make her the very best. She boasted grand saloons and imposing cabins; her main saloon on her promenade deck being 108 feet long and 27 feet in width. It was finished in all native woods. Originally the dining saloon was in the hold, as was the trend of the day, but later it was moved to the main deck aft. A carved American Bald Eagle with gold leaf was mounted on the top of her masthead throughout her years.

The graceful new *Horicon* (I) was launched at Cook's Landing in 1877, her name derived from the fictitious Indian name for Lake George referred to in James Fenimore Cooper's novel "Last of the Mohicans". Built at a cost of $75,000 dollars, she was 195 feet long, 30 feet wide at the beam, drafted 9 feet and could carry 1000 passengers.. Displacing 643 tons, her 270 horsepower engines propelled her along at a speedy 20 mph. She was once clocked with Captain Elias S. Harris aboard from the Fort William Henry to Cooks Landing at 1 hour, 45 minutes. This new steamer was a steady craft which, "made quite a dent in our crystal clear waters and a pilot had to be constantly on his toes," according to Pilot Walter Harris.

First Captain Charles P. Russell ran daily trips north opposite the *Ganouskie*. In 1892, The Lake George Mirror reported, "Captain Reeves, of the steamer *Horicon*, gave his passengers a musical treat recently. The Marion House orchestra played several pieces on the down trip and as far back as Pearl Point, where a social hop was given". During that same summer the Mirror, "–noticed two well-known faces aboard the *Horicon* July Fourth, Mr. Carl Schurz and Dr. Jacobie, who were on their way to the Sagamore, near where the two gentlemen built handsome cottages this spring", (in Bolton Landing). On August 20, 1892, the Mirror gave this interesting account,–"The other evening, as the steamer *Horicon* was landing at the Sagamore dock, an Indian basket peddler attempted to go ashore. He made a misstep and fell into the lake. He could not swim, and were it

---

On a Lake George Steamer

She is sitting on the deck with her sister,
(I've been furtively watching afar.)
No masculine eyes could have missed her -
The steamers particular star.

The girl in the blue flannel jacket
Over there by the railing -- don't look!
Her breastpin's the little gold racquet,
A rose in the end of her book.

With a big parasol, polka-dotted,
She keeps off the sun (and men)
But from under that 'brella' (polka-spotted)
She gives me a glance now and then.

Too bad that the age has departed
For slave with umbrella and fan;
How I'd spread that 'umbrell' (polka-dotted)
And gyrate her Japanese fan!

Poem by W.S. Rossiter, Lake George Mirror, August 26, 1893. Courtesy: Darrell Finlayson.

not for the presence of mind and timely action of Chas. G. Prindle, the steward of the boat, he would have drowned. Mr. Prindle seized a pike pole and pulled the victim out of the water in the nick of time. This is the third life he has saved this season."

In 1898, the successful steamboat *Horicon* made 119 trips down the lake and grossed a record $38,935. During the winter of 1901-1902, she was completely renovated at a cost of $25, 057. Her hull was completely replaced, with the exception of her keel.

Sailing for 34 consecutive seasons, the *Horicon* was commanded by a succession of seven captains. Still in good condition at the end of her career, she was retired and dismantled in 1911 to make way for the new steel-hulled *Horicon* (II) which replaced her.

Above: Cup, Champlain Transportation Company.
Courtesy: Diver, Craig Hannon.

Right: *Horicon* (I) passengers, Long Island ahead.
Courtesy: Private collection.

Below: Lithograph. *Horicon* (I) at Caldwell.
Courtesy: Henry Caldwell.

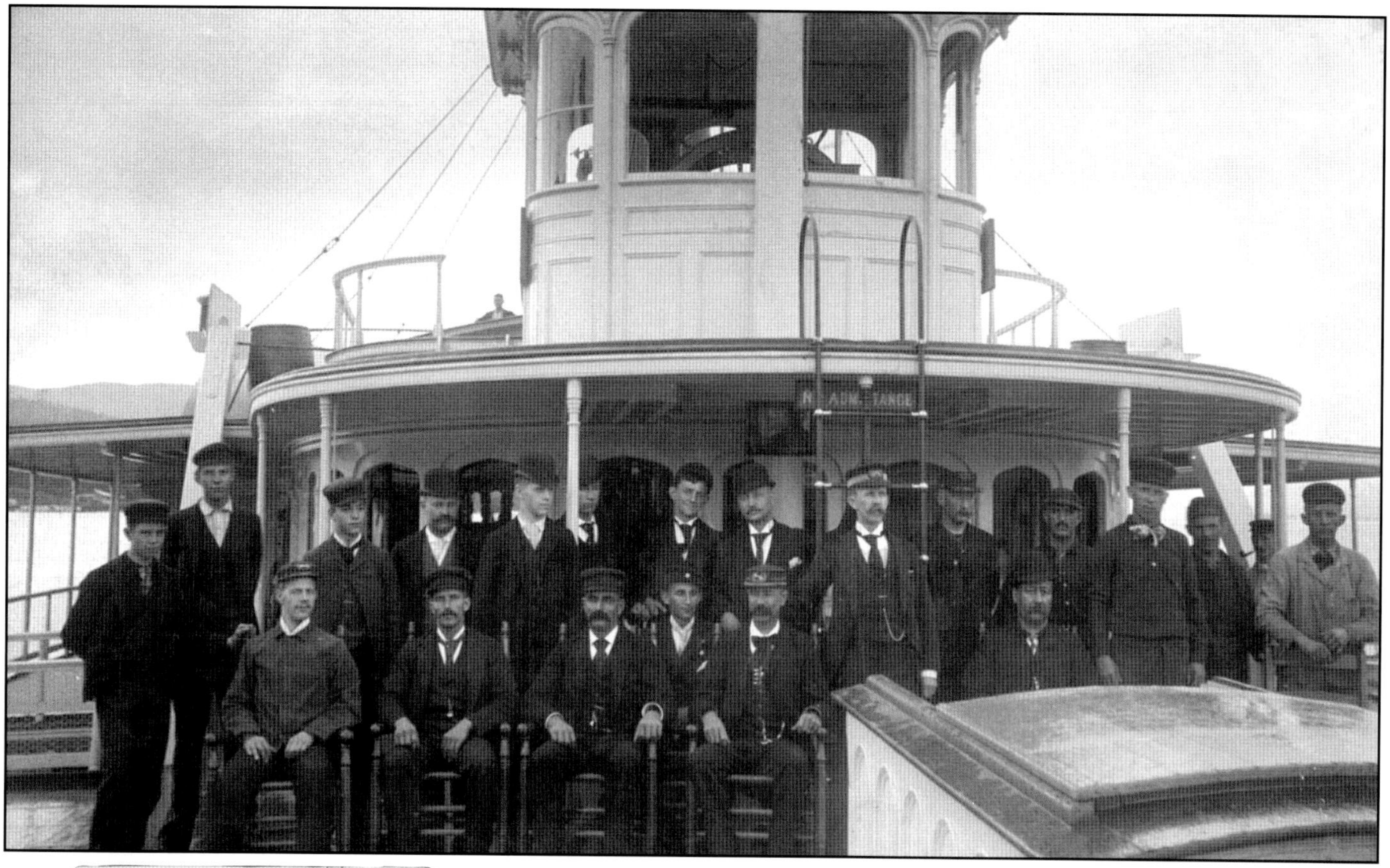

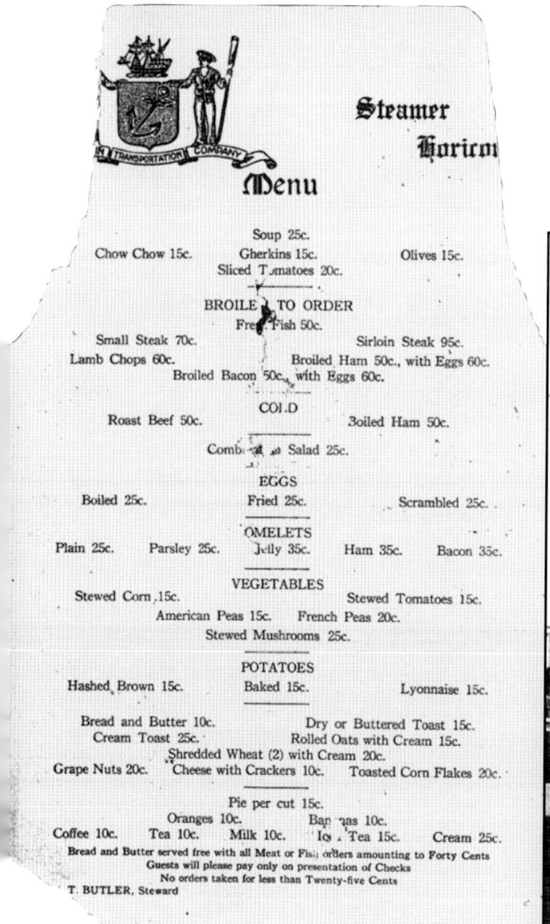

Steamer Horicon

Menu

Soup 25c.
Chow Chow 15c. Gherkins 15c. Olives 15c.
Sliced Tomatoes 20c.

BROILED TO ORDER
Fresh Fish 50c.
Small Steak 70c. Sirloin Steak 95c.
Lamb Chops 60c. Broiled Ham 50c., with Eggs 60c.
Broiled Bacon 50c., with Eggs 60c.

COLD
Roast Beef 50c. Boiled Ham 50c.
Combination Salad 25c.

EGGS
Boiled 25c. Fried 25c. Scrambled 25c.

OMELETS
Plain 25c. Parsley 25c. Jelly 35c. Ham 35c. Bacon 35c.

VEGETABLES
Stewed Corn 15c. Stewed Tomatoes 15c.
American Peas 15c. French Peas 20c.
Stewed Mushrooms 25c.

POTATOES
Hashed Brown 15c. Baked 15c. Lyonnaise 15c.

Bread and Butter 10c. Dry or Buttered Toast 15c.
Cream Toast 25c. Rolled Oats with Cream 15c.
Shredded Wheat (2) with Cream 20c.
Grape Nuts 20c. Cheese with Crackers 10c. Toasted Corn Flakes 20c.

Pie per cut 15c.
Oranges 10c. Bananas 10c.
Coffee 10c. Tea 10c. Milk 10c. Iced Tea 15c. Cream 25c.

Bread and Butter served free with all Meat or Fish orders amounting to Forty Cents
Guests will please pay only on presentation of Checks
No orders taken for less than Twenty-five Cents
T. BUTLER, Steward

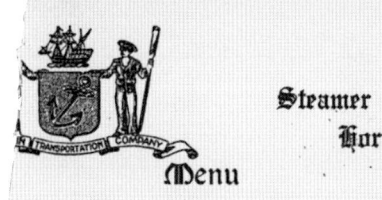

Above: *Horicon* (I) Officers and Crew. Courtesy: Lake George Historical Association.

Left: *Horicon* (I) Menu. Courtesy: William Dow, Lake George Steamboat Company.

Below: *Horicon* (I) at Pearl Point, S.R. Stoddard photo. Courtesy: Hugh A. Wilson.

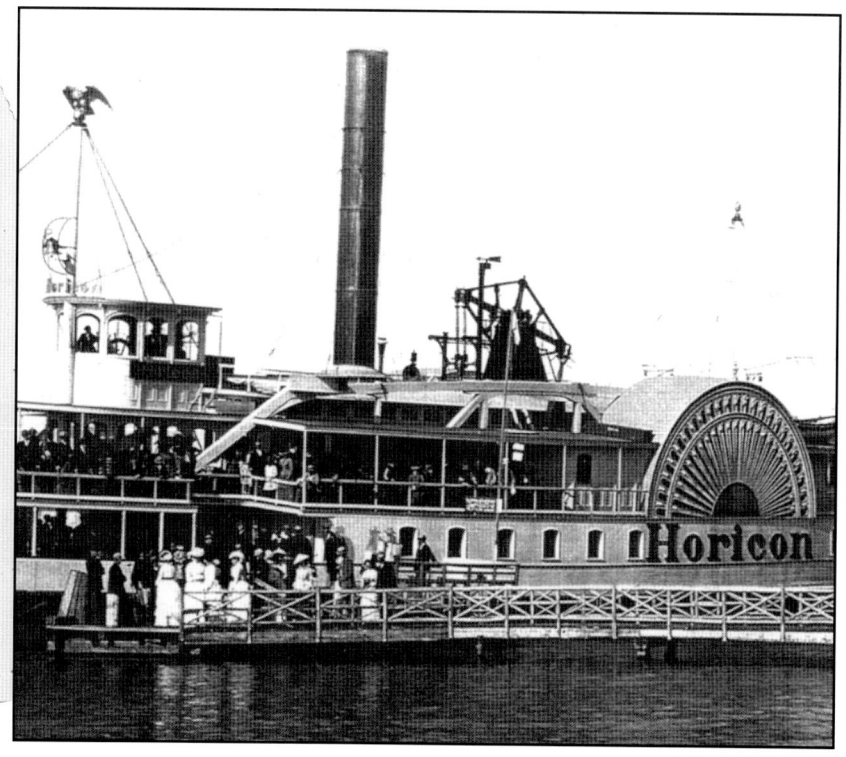

Banshee

Jay Taylor and his wife Amelia are shown here in the *Banshee,* meaning "Irish Ghost". Taylor was the first Ranger to reside on Glen Island beginning in 1921. When he died in 1936, his wife was appointed to replace him, a job she held until she retired in 1954. Interestingly, there were two later State Boats, both with the name *Banshee.*

Courtesy: Leah McGarr Hadley.

J. Henry Rushton

Above: Rushton rowboat at Bolton Landing. Circa 1900.
Courtesy: Lake George Village Historian.
Right: Rushton "Iowa" rowboat owned by the author.

J. Henry Rushton was born in 1843. Being small in build and in poor health, he moved to Canton, New York while he was in his late twenties and secured a job as a clerk in a shoe store. At the age of 32, he built a small boat for himself which was very light in weight making it easy for him to carry. A man saw his beautiful boat and pressed Henry to sell it to him. He did—-and that is how the Rushton Canoe business began.

In the beginning, Henry began building boats for the locals around Canton. Soon, people from around the world began seeking his boats because of their light weight and strength. He built skiffs, rowboats, guide-boats and canoes, and published his first catalogue in 1877 which was mailed as far as Australia, England and France. J. Henry Rushton was a master at publicizing his business, and by 1880 he was enjoying success and fame. Many magazine articles featured the Rushton Canoes with Rushton occasionally contributing an article himself on "Hints on Canoe Building" for Forest and Stream Magazine.

Although the motor boat was beginning to gain favor here on Lake George at that time, there were many who favored the convenience, silence, tradition and portability of the canoe. Undoubtedly, many of the locals on Lake George were attracted to the Rushton Canoes because several fine original examples can still be found around the lake in boathouses, sheds and barns. In that regard, I am the proud owner of an "IOWA" Rushton that has been passed down through my Bolton Landing family to me.

J. Henry Rushton died in 1906, but a century later, his beautifully crafted boats still live on in the Adirondacks and on Lake George.

American Canoeing Association

American Canoe Association Regatta, 1882. Photo by S.R. Stoddard. Courtesy: Private collection.

In the spring of 1880, John Henry Rushton received an invitation in the mail to attend "The National Canoe Congress" on Lake George, (later named "The First Call"), for the purpose of organizing a national canoeing organization. Rushton was asked to bring five of his canoes for the exhibit, and he brought a sixth to be given away as a prize for the paddling race. Camping grounds for the event were provided by the Fort George and Crosbyside hotels at the southern end of the lake. Nearly 40 canoeists from around the nation were in attendance that first year, and all canoe types were represented; sail, wooden, canvas, clinker-built, open and decked. Canoes were arranged by the Association into four classes,–the big sailing canoes with centerboards and several hundred pounds of ballast, the light paddling canoe, sailing paddling canoe, and paddleable sailing canoe. Contests were offered for sailing, paddling, racing and dumping, an event where a canoeist must overturn his canoe, right it again, climb aboard and continue paddling.

On August 3, 1880, the first day of the three day event, most of the day was spent ironing out details and electing officers. The original plan was to call themselves "The National Canoe Association", however, many present were from Canada so the name became "The American Canoe Association". The races on the 4th and 5th were so successful that the decision was unanimous to hold the 1881 convention on Lake George once again, and of all the canoes on display, a Rushton was chosen as the best, winning "First Premium". The New York Times wrote of the event that, "A Rushton was unanimously recognized as the most beautiful and serviceable boat of the kind to be found in this country or in England. The builder has certainly succeeded in building the strongest, lightest, most graceful, and most useful paddling canoe that has yet been devised."

Three of the founding members fell in love with the lake so deeply that they immediately purchased the Three Sisters Islands five miles up the lake where the meetings were held, and offered them for camping during the 1881 and 1882 conventions. They renamed the island group–"The Canoe Islands", a name they still proudly hold today.

A.C.A. Members at Crosbyside, 1882. Photo by S.R. Stoddard. Courtesy: Private collection.

By 1882, the American Canoe Association conference on Lake George had grown to 260 members. The August 26, 1882 Harper's Weekly magazine described this third annual event as follows;–"The canoeists camp at Lake George is on Lorna Island, one of a group of three known as the Canoe Islands. In its irregularity, its quaint appointments, and its variety of composition, the camp of the canoeists stands pre-eminent for picturesqueness. Its central object is a snug log cabin, which forms the permanent head-quarters of the Association. The canoeists are a jolly lot, and after supper, and after the stern duty of washing dishes has been performed to the satisfaction of the autocratic cook, the gatherings around the camp fires are enlivened by an infinite fund of jest, anecdote and song; nor are practical jokes beneath the dignity of the canoeist when in camp."

Harper's goes on to say, "The second day of camping was ladies' reception day, and extensive preparations were made to render the appearance of the camp as attractive as possible. Tent flags were drawn aside, and the brightest-colored blankets placed on top of the neatly made beds. Festoons of gay flags were strung among the trees, and long lines of canoes were drawn up on shore, and arranged with all sails set, so as to show to the greatest advantage.

The convention closed on Friday night by a business meeting and banquet at the Crosby House. At the banquet were distributed the prizes of the Regatta, which were merely silken flags, it being the policy of the Association not to offer any prizes of sufficient value to attract other than the most honorable competition."

As the membership broke up camp and sailed off in a variety of directions the following morning, they sounded their good-bye's with boatswain's whistles, bugles, conchs, steam-whistles, fish-horns and any other device suitable for making noise. Each horn sounded with three long blasts and one short, the official saluting signal for the American Canoeing Association.

In 1888, the Warrensburg News wrote,–"This year's meet of the American Canoeing Association has come to an end and has passed into canoe history. It doubtless compares favorably with any of its predecessors. Many strong friendships were formed, and it is rumored that at least one canoeist found him a partner from the ladies' wing of the Association. It will be a handy arrangement for next year's meet, as one boat will do for both. The steamer Ticonderoga (I) made a special trip to the dock on Long Island to carry away the enormous amount of material incident to a camp of 300 canoeists."

Left: Postcard. Courtesy: Henry Caldwell.

Below: August 26, 1882, HARPER'S WEEKLY Lithograph "The Canoe Regatta on Lake George" Sketch by F. H. Taylor. Courtesy: MacLaren Richards, Riverside Gallery.

Smith-Granger Rowboats

During the 1880's, rowboats were very popular at all of the hotels along the Lake George shoreline. Guests used them for pleasure, fishing and transportation. Cottage owners also used them for after dinner enjoyment. Rowers frequently sang songs and played musical instruments while rowing these boats, which were decorated with flowers and lanterns.

In 1885, Fred R. Smith of Bolton Landing began designing and building rowboats at his lakeside boat shop named, The Smith Company, later to be named, F.R. Smith and Sons. Between 1885 and 1926, he built nearly 600 boats, many with the help of his longtime employee George C. Granger. The Sagamore Hotel reportedly purchased over 200 Smith-Grangers over the years.

The first boats were of lap strake construction with three-inch wide planking. On many boats, natural crooked White Oak was utilized for knees, stems, ribs and seat braces. Select White Cedar was the primary choice for planking. Everything was fastened together by copper clout nails.

Above Circle: Oar with Smith "S" insignia. Courtesy: Joan Baldwin, F.R. Smith & Sons.
Below: *Bipkins'* wine-glass stern. Courtesy: David & Meredith McComb.

The design of these craft is distinctive, especially its "wine glass" shaped transom. Quickly the Smith-Granger rowboats overtook any new competition;– they became known as the "Lake George Rowboat". Although there is some variation in length because of special orders, most tend to average 15 feet, 8 1/4 inch in length.

John Boulton Simpson of Green Island in Bolton Landing special-ordered four of these rowboats. The most well known, the *Helen*, named for one of J.B. Simpson's daughters, is on display at the Adirondack Museum in Blue Mountain Lake. Another Smith-Granger rowboat, the *Pollywog*, owned by Helen later in life, was accidentally run over in the late 1930's by the famous Gold Cup racer *El Lagarto* piloted by George Reis. Luckily, its occupant was able to jump clear before the collision. To preserve that near-tragic moment, George had a wall display made for Helen which displays his damaged propeller and her *Pollywog* seatback. It is still on the wall of her former boathouse today.

During the past seventy-five years, these unique rowboats disappeared from view. Most rotted away and were scrapped decades ago, however, a few have managed to survive, thanks mostly to the efforts of old Lake George families who stored them away safely many decades ago.

In August of 2001, a group of Bolton residents organized the first annual Smith-Granger Rowboat Regatta which was held in Bolton Landing. Over a dozen rowboats were on hand. Each boat carried a descendent of Fred R. Smith. In 2002, the event was opened up to other vintage rowboats, and over fifteen of these beautiful craft simulated a race across Bolton Bay– a beautiful sight to see.

Above: *Pollywog,* Courtesy: Paul Eckhoff.
Helen, Courtesy: Halley Bond, Adirondack Museum.
Right: 2002 Rowboat Regatta at Bolton Landing.
Photo by Author.

Josie C

The *Josie C* was built for the Trout Pavilion hotel in Katskill Bay by Captain Hiram Hyde in 1883. She was used for excursions to the Narrows and to pick up guests from the train at Caldwell. Capable of carrying up to 60 passengers, she was 56 feet long with a beam of 12 feet, 6 inches.

Josie C. Big Burnt Island in background with old *Ganouskie* as a floating saloon. The Hudson Falls Waite Hose Company aboard, 1885.
Courtesy: Sandra Spaulding, Fort Edward Historical Museum's Cronkhite Collection.

Ticonderoga (I)

Ticonderoga (I). Named for Fort Ticonderoga. Notice painting of the ruins of the fort on the paddle wheel shroud.
Courtesy: Fort Edward Historical Museum.

Horicon (I) and *Ticonderoga* (I), 1900. Courtesy: Lake George Historical Association.

When the railroad line from Glens Falls to Caldwell (Lake George Village) was completed in 1882, the small steamboat *Ganouskie* was unable to handle the increasing crowds who wanted to travel to Lake George. The side-wheeler *Ticonderoga* (I) was constructed and launched in 1883 to accommodate these new passengers. She was the last large steamboat to be constructed entirely out of wood and the last also to be launched at Cook's Landing at the Lake's northern end. With a construction cost of $77,000, she was 172 feet long, carried a 28 foot beam and drafted 9 feet.

Under the experienced hands of her first captain, James H. Manville, this 500 ton ship was capable of attaining a speed of 20 miles per hour. From 1884 to 1901, she sailed simultaneously with her sister ship, the *Horicon* (I).

During the season of 1886, the *Ticonderoga* suffered mechanical difficulties when her walking beam failed. She had to be towed from the Kattskill Bay area to her pier at Caldwell. On another occasion that same year, a young Hague woman fell overboard and drowned before she could be recovered.

It is unfortunate that a listing of passenger names was not kept on ledger books as was done at the early hotels. I'm certain there would be many surprises. Civil War veteran General William Sherman rode aboard the *Ticonderoga* in 1885. In that same year, Ulysses S. Grant rode aboard the *Horicon* (I).

After an evening charter cruise, the *Ticonderoga* left the Kenesaw House Hotel at Fourteen Mile Island and returned to

Ticonderoga (I) burning. August 29. 1901. Courtesy: Pete Smith.

the Baldwin (Ticonderoga) pier. Her fires were stoked at 2 AM and the crew sought some well needed rest. The following morning, August 29, 1901, the boat left Baldwin at 7:27 AM and headed south. Soon thereafter, a fire broke out below deck as she approached Roger's Slide. The vessel quickly landed at the nearby Roger's Rock Hotel pier, however, her wooden construction caused her to burn very rapidly. The Lake George Mirror reported, the smoke, " soon became so dense that the stokers were compelled to leave their posts and scramble up the iron ladders–holes were cut through the deck in two or three places and streams of water poured on the flames, which up to this moment had been confined between decks."

Captain Frank G. White remained with his ship until the lines burned which held her to the pier. She then drifted northward across the bay to Hawkeye Point. Although the *Horicon* came quickly to her aid, it was too late. She sank in the shallows, leaving only her ironwork for the salvagers.

Above: *Ticonderoga* (I). Courtesy: Ethel Andrus, Hague Town Historian.
Below left: *Ticonderoga* (I) Bell now hangs on a Lake George cottage wall. Courtesy: Mary Chester Flagg.
Below right: *Ticonderoga* (I) postcard. Courtesy: Dick and Mary Kowell.

D.W. Sherman

D.W. Sherman. Courtesy: Lake George Village Historian.

The *D.W. Sherman* was named for its owner, Darwin W. Sherman, owner the Marion House Hotel on the southern end of Boon Bay on Lake George's west side. She was later operated by the Fort William Henry hotel in 1883 while under command of Captain Harvey Crandall. In 1898, H. Gordon Burleigh of Whitehall and Ticonderoga purchased her from Crandall. In this photo, the *D.W. Sherman* has stopped in the Narrows to watch a forest fire.

Pocahontas

Pocahontas at Silver Bay with Governor Charles Evans Hughes aboard. Courtesy: Hague Town Historian.

Most old Lake George boats passed through the hands of several owners during their lifetime, however none had a more interesting lifetime than the yacht *Pocahontas*. She was built in 1885 for manager Henry E. Nichols of the Lake House which once stood on the site of today's Shepard Park in Lake George Village. Seneca Ray Stoddard described her that same year in his guidebook as a "new and graceful craft". Named for the Indian maiden Pocahontas of Captain John Smith fame, this new bright white steam powered launch was 55 ft. long with a 10 ft. beam and could carry up to 75 passengers. She was used by the hotel for six summers to shuttle hotel guests around the lake.

In 1891 the *Pocahontas* was purchased by George H. and LeGrand C. Cramer of Trinity Rock and Cramer Point who immediately changed her hull color to a bright yellow. With a new boiler and engine installed, Captain Almon Burton and engineer Willis Call were able to increase its speed to 13 mph.

In August of 1892, the Lake George Mirror wrote, "*Pocahontas* with Secretary of the Navy on board went through a terrific storm of wind, thunder and lightning, hailstones and immense rain recently near Dome Island which tested her seaworthiness and strength as hardly ever before. She took the squall right in the teeth and rode it out with an ease and jollity greatly to the comfort and delight of all on board, and as a climax to a very stirring experience, such a double rainbow appeared as is never seen anywhere else than on the most coquettish of lakes."

In 1895 *Pocahontas* was unsuccessfully advertised for sale by George Cramer. With a now elderly Captain Lee Harris aboard, she was leased to Captain Charles Wood who used her for excursion runs to the Narrows and to other landings during the summer of 1900. In 1901 she was purchased by millionaire Royal C. Peabody of Wikiosko, a Lake George mansion that still survives today. Three years later in 1904, he sold it to his brother George Foster Peabody of the mansion Abenia who used it frequently to entertain the rich and famous in America who came to visit him. His original boathouse remains today as the Boathouse Restaurant.

George Foster Peabody was a close friend and business partner with Spencer and Katrina Trask of the Three Brother Islands in Bolton. Spencer Trask frequently stayed on Clay Island during the summer of 1906 to escape the pressures of entertaining at his Saratoga summer estate, Yaddo. He had no intention of building another large estate. He was only interested in finding a private hideaway to construct a small cottage. Katrina had other ideas. It was her vision that the three small rocky Three Brother Islands be developed into a Venetian style estate by connecting the islands with two covered bridges. During the winter that followed, the Trasks purchased as many old stone walls as possible from the local farmers who gladly delivered their "winter cash crop" by horse teams pulling sleds of rocks across the ice. These rocks were used to "beef up" the islands to make them suitable for building a new artist colony for writers, musicians, and artists selected by a committee. Artists' living quarters were located in rooms on the second floors of the covered bridges. The Trask's final personal touch was to rename the islands Triuna which means "Three in One".

Pocahontas. 1906. Three Brother Islands in background before development by the Trasks. Courtesy: Dick and Pat Swire.

Spencer Trask was suddenly and tragically killed in a railroad accident on December 31, 1909 at Croton on the Hudson. Soon after, George Foster Peabody declared his longtime affection for Katrina. In Katrina's personal memoirs entitled, STORY OF LAKE GEORGE, she described being met at the Lake George Train Station by George Foster and the *Pocahontas* – "When I arrived at the Station, Foster stood there smiling welcome, and led me to his boat, the *Pocahontas*. It was filled with flowers—roses, roses, roses everywhere, tall and bowing, fragrant and silent, but speaking more eloquently than words. To the stern of the *Pocahontas* he led me, placed me amidst the luxurious cushions, the great red roses stood on either side. Then to my surprise and delight we began to glide down the lake. We moved as though we were in Venice, that magic land of dreams—that city of the senses—".

The northern island at Triuna was where the servants cooked and lived. This was also the island that housed their boats. At four o'clock in the morning during August of 1913, a fire started on the *Pocahontas* which was docked at the northern island. Having been recently converted to burning the dangerous naptha fuel, the fire spread rapidly due to the fuel's explosive com-

Pocahontas at Three Brother Islands. Courtesy: Dick and Pat Swire.

bustion and the strong winds. Most of the structures on the northern island were lost and considerable damage was done to buildings on the other two islands. Fortunately, Katrina's home was spared. The fire aboard the *Pocahontas* soon burned her mooring lines and she drifted out into the bay where she burned to the waterline and sank. Her keel and a few ribs still lie on the bottom today near the old dock site. Also lost were 'three motorboats, five rowboats, the docks, boat houses, a storage gasoline tank, coal bunkers, the servant's quarters and the large laundry building", according to the Glens Falls Times.

Katrina supervised the rebuilding of the islands from Yaddo in Saratoga. Although she lived for another ten years, she never again left Yaddo's boundaries and therefore never returned to the Triuna Islands during her lifetime. It is interesting to note that George Foster Peabody continued to express his love for Katrina Trask until she finally agreed to marry him in 1921. Unfortunately, Katrina died only 11 months afterward.

I'm certain that shallow water explorers have accidentally stumbled upon the remains of the *Pocahontas* repeatedly over the past seventy years—totally unaware that they are viewing the final remains of one of the most interesting and colorful vessels ever to have plied the waters of our beloved Lake George.

Above: Spencer and Katrina Trask entertaining on Triuna. Dome Island in background. Courtesy: Dick and Pat Swire.
Above left: Naptha cover discovered recently by Pat Swire while snorkeling around the Three Brother Islands.

Arcadie

George O. Knapp at Shelving Rock owned a small fleet of boats to accommodate guests at both the Pearl Point Hotel and the Hundred Island House. Shown here is his electric launch named the *Arcadie* which is Greek meaning: "A scene of simple pleasure and quiet."

Arcadie at Pearl Point. Author's collection.

Bluebird

When she died, Katrina Trask left the Triuna Islands in the care of George Foster Peabody. Peabody's pleasure craft *Bluebird* was used daily by his caretaker, Harold Rozell Sr., for transportation and errands to the mainland. More than once, the Rozell's spent the winter on the islands. Harold also used it occasionally for his own family outings on his days off, as shown in this photograph. When Peabody died in 1938, Triuna became a part of Yaddo and was used as an artists colony until it was sold in 1940.

Bluebird in early 1930's with Triuna caretaker Harold Rozell Sr., wife Ruth, daughter Ruth and son Harold Jr. Courtesy: Mae Goodnow Rozell, wife of Harold Jr.

Katrina

In 1900, the *Katrina* was owned by F.R. Smith of Bolton. She was later owned by Bolton's Wilson Brothers. *Katrina* was 35 feet long, had a 10 foot beam and could carry up to 35 passengers. Occasionally, she was leased out for towing and hauling purposes. On November 23, 1914, the *Katrina* was docked at John Boulton Simpson's boathouse on Green Island. A fire broke out and burned the boathouse, Clarence Wilson's *Katrina*, Simpson's *Calypso* and John Travers' gasoline launch.

Katrina with C.E. Wilson at stern & unknown woman.
Courtesy: Hugh Allen Wilson.
Katrina hauling wood to build an ice house, Sept. 30, 1913.
Courtesy: Rich Watkins.

Cozy

Cozy at Pilot Knob. Author's collection.

Cozy was built on the Hudson River near New York city in the late 1890's. In 1889, she was brought through the Champlain Canal by Eber Richards of Pilot Knob and lifted onto a flatbed train car at Fort Edward. While being lifted out of the water, the forward cable broke and the bow dropped with a splash into the canal. Fortunately, she was not damaged. From 1889 to 1892 Cozy was used for the transportation of mail and vegetables from Butternut Creek (Katskill Bay) to Victoria Lodge (Pilot Knob). In 1890, Cozy was changed over from naptha power to steam for safety reasons. The July 22, 1893 Lake George Mirror stated that, "Arrangements have been made with the steamer Cozy and Commander Wands to take entire charge of the Katskill Bay delivery of Sunday papers."

Cecilia

The Sextons of Hague built many boats for Lake George customers at the turn of the Twentieth Century. Wildman Sexton began the family business in the 1890's by building "carvel" style rowboats from 14 to 16 feet long, featuring a high back seat for passenger comfort. Later, his son Jesse expanded the business by building motor launches, canoes and naptha launches.

Jesse's Cecilia was approximately 50 feet long. She was owned by Captain James C. Leach of Ticonderoga who used her for excursions around the northern end of the lake. Cecilia could be rented by the hour or by the day.

Cecilia. Oval, Courtesy: Henry Caldwell. Above, Courtesy: JoAnn Irish Mahoney.

Uncas

Jesse Sexton built the Uncas for Smith Sexton, his cousin who ran a small cottage rental business next to the Uncas Inn near Hague. To launch her in 1910, Jesse used skids and rollers pulled by five teams of horses to access the lake hundreds of feet in distance from his shop. The Uncas was nearly 50 feet long, could carry up to 30 passengers and had her own covered pier. Later in her life she made trips along the full length of the lake, stopping at many of the small hotels along her route.

Uncas launched in Hague, 1910. Courtesy: Hague Town Historian, Ethel Andrus.

Uncas at the Uncas Dock. Courtesy: Hague Town Historian.

LAKE GEORGE
1906, by D. Watson

My holidays hath come, and I
To fair Lake George again will hie,
" And leave the mad'ning crowd behind,"
A thousand pleasures there to find,
Forgetting city din and strife,
I will renew the springs of life,
Woo nature at her very best,
And for a time have perfect rest.

From when French Point the steamer bounds,
Until the lake's extreme she rounds,
What visions of delight we see,
Our hearts are filled with ecstacy.
See yonder crystal riv'lets glow,
As down the mountain side they flow,
Thus as we wind by hill and gorge
We are entranc'd with fair Lake George.

And when we've sailed thy waters o'er,
We love to wander by thy shore.
Or climb the hills some crag to view,
And in thy woodland game pursue,
Or nestle by a shady nook,
Lull'd by the music of some brook,
Thus shall we take our diverse way,
And peaceful spend each happy day.

Around thy islands we will row,
Or to some cove a fishing go,
Enhale the fragrant laden breeze,
Shed by the wild flow'rs and the trees,
And when the sun dips in the west,
We too will seek our peaceful rest,
And thus when holidays are done
We'll wish they only had begun.

Snapshot

The *Snapshot* was built and owned by Fred C. Thatcher, famed early photographer in Bolton Landing and Lake George Village. He was the son of Julius "Jule" Thatcher, Ticonderoga photographer. Fred built *Snapshot* in 1910 and used her to access all areas of Lake George, whereas his father Jule used a small yellow rowboat and his wagon, pulled by his horse Jen, for transportation. Eventually, Fred gave *Snapshot* to Captain Marty Fisher. All that remains of *Snapshot* today is her anchor which is owned by the Thatcher family.

Snapshot. Fred C. Thatcher Collection.

Ella

The *Ella* was Jesse Sexton's personal gasoline powered motor launch. Named for Jesse's wife, *Ella* was 34 feet long and was capable of carrying 15 passengers. Jesse rented it out for $1.00/hour or $8.00/day. He built his boats during the winter months so he would be available to operate his rental business in summer.

Ella. Author's collection.

Gypsy

The nearly 50 feet long *Gypsy* was also built and owned by Jesse Sexton and used for rental excursions. The *Gypsy* was frequently rented for fishing trips as well and was the most popular and successful of his two boats due to its larger size. On Sundays, the *Gypsy* carried passengers to the Catholic church across the lake at Huletts.

Gypsy. Author's collection.

Idler

Idler, built by Jesse Sexton, cruising in Bolton Bay. Courtesy: Bolton Historical Museum.

Saunterer

The *Saunterer*, built by Jesse Sexton, was a private naptha launch owned by Colonel William D'Alton Mann of Hague and New York City. Col. Mann, who received his title during the Civil War, owned a New York newspaper named "Town Topics" which focused on celebrity gossip. It was told to me that he padded his profits by receiving large payments to keep certain names out of print.

At Hague on lake George, he was at first a squatter who built a large home named "Saunterer's Rest" on one of Hague's nearby Waltonian islands. The flamboyant Mann later cut his home into two parts to move it across the bay to the mainland after New York State claimed all of the islands.

Saunterer among the Waltonian Islands. Courtesy: Hague Town Historian.

Mohawk

Mohawk at Uncas. Twelve passenger launch built by Jesse Sexton for his cousin Smith Sexton.
Courtesy: Hague Town Historian.

Passaic

Passaic. Author's collection.

P*assaic*, built by Jesse Sexton, was mentioned in a turn-of-the-century Lake George Mirror as follows: "Mr. Wm. T. Pratt the G.P.A. of the Minneapolis, St. Paul & Sault Sainte Marie R. R., who has recently erected a neat comfortable cottage on his island, "Leontine," in the bay opposite the Algonquin took a party of guests for a sail on his launch, "*Passaic*" through the Narrows and Paradise Bay piloting the boat himself like a veteran. Mr. Pratt is known to railway officials from coast to coast as "Uncle Bill the Prince of Goodfellows." Mr. and Mrs. Pratt and family are entertaining Miss Helen Gildersleeve of Pittsburg, who by the way is a charming young lady with a beautiful voice."

Locust

Locust. Courtesy: Pete Smith

The *Locust* was a masterpiece of style and function. She was 67 feet long, sported a 10 foot beam and drafted 5 feet. Built for a large estate down the Hudson, Will and Harvey Crandall purchased her and brought her to Lake George in 1891 and modified the interior to carry up to 50 passengers charging a daily rental fee of $25.00. She ran out of the lake's southern basin alternating from the Lake House Hotel, Pine Point and the Fort William Henry. After a successful passenger career, the Locust was purchased by the American Graphite Company in Hague which supplied graphite to the Dixon and Ticonderoga pencil companies. With James McCabe from Ticonderoga as her captain, she was used to haul coal barges until the end of her days, around 1915.

Locust hauling coal barge at Hague for American Graphite Company. Courtesy: Hague Town Historian.

Rachael

To give an accurate overall account of Lake George's boating history, it is essential to point out that there were occasional tragedies, as you would expect, on a lake so large and well traveled. On August 3, 1893, the Hundred Island House below Shelving Rock Mountain was holding a social event with additional guests invited from other nearby cottages and hotels. The Kenesaw House on Fourteen Mile Island rented the small steamer *Rachael* from manager Philips of the Pearl Point Hotel to transport passengers across the narrow channel. (The 55 feet long, 9 inch beam *Rachael*, built by Chris Bates at Caldwell, was launched in 1982 and was owned by D.W. Sherman of the Hotel Marion.)

It was a rough, dark and stormy night when the small *Rachael* made the crossing. To further set the scene for tragedy, the *Rachael's* captain, Cromwell Barber, was not available that evening and was replaced by his inexperienced pilot, Claude Granger. The engineer was John W. Brisbin.

Rachael steamed to her doom on August 3, 1893.
Sketch by Donnie Gates.
© W.P. Gates Publishing.

With twenty three passengers aboard, the *Rachael* struck the remains of an old dock crib near the mainland and careened lakeward into the darkness. She first tipped over sideways and within only a few seconds was on the bottom taking nine lives along with her. Eight were women who had been trapped in the *Rachael's* cabin where they sought shelter from the wind and rain. Coroner Streeter had the grim task of dealing with the bodies which were laid out the next day in the Hundred Island House billiard room.

The *Rachael* was raised with the help of two large scows and taken to the Marion House where ten large holes were repaired. This tragedy was the final blow to the Hundred Island House. It closed permanently at the end of the 1893 season. The following year, the hotel was purchased by George O. Knapp, first president and co-founder of Union Carbide Corporation, who renovated it into his personal summer home.

Fanita

Fanita launched, 1890. J.B. Simpson and daughter Fanny on bow for christening ceremony. Notice champagne bottle on bow stem.
Courtesy: Bolton Historical Museum.

Commodore John Boulton Simpson was a wealthy Millionaire's Row "cottage" owner on Green Island in Bolton Landing. His title refers to his status of Vice-Commodore at the Lake George Yacht Club. His Lake George mansion, named Villa Nirvana, still stands proudly today next to the Sagamore Hotel, behind the cruise-boat Morgan's summer pier.

John Boulton Simpson loved boats. In 1890, he launched the 80 foot hull of his Fanita, a boat which is still talked about proudly today around Bolton. Over 40 family and friends were on hand for the launching as Bolton photographer Jules Thatcher recorded the moment. She had an 11 foot beam and required a crew of four. Her steam engine produced 125 hp and propelled her along at 16 mph.

The Fanita was named for one of Mr. Simpson's daughters, Fanny. This $16,000 private yacht was the most elegant on the lake and one of the fastest for several years until the 40 mph Ellide came along. Because the Sagamore Hotel did not have its own boat, the Fanita was used frequently for hotel excursions.

The Simpson family spent their winters in New York City. Every June, their private railroad car would arrive at the Caldwell Railroad Station (Lake George Village), where the waiting Fanita would transport the group to Green Island in the capable hands of Captain Clarence Wilson and Engineer Henry Truax, both of Bolton Landing.

J.B. Simpson proudly entered Fanita in every annual regatta on the lake, many of them planned under his leadership. He also entertained guests aboard and annually transported his longtime male friends to a carefully planned Chouder Party on one of the islands. Each guest was handed his own personal bottle of champaign upon arrival at the island for the feast.

Fanita spent her winters in a large storage barn on the west side of the island which still stands today. Only recently, the name "Fanita", in delicately carved woodwork, was removed from its peak. In 1896, Fanita was lengthened 15 feet as part of a major improvement project.

During 1914, the Fanita was nearly lost. A fire burned the Simpson boathouse to the water's surface, taking two other yachts with it. Fortunately, Fanita was saved.

Before the Simpsons eventually sold the boat to George McCabe of Ticonderoga, much of her finery was removed. McCabe carried up to 30 passengers aboard, however, soon his business declined. The Fanita's life ended in the narrow creek at the north end of Lake George where she was pulled onto shore and burned.

Today, her wheel, clock, chair and trophies are part of a permanent display at the Bolton Historical Museum, along with numerous photographs.

Fanita extended 15 feet in 1896. Photo by Jule Thatcher.
Top photo, courtesy: Lake George Historical Association. Bottom photo, courtesy: Hugh Allen Wilson.

Fanita's interior was decorated with tufted red velvet and fitted out with elegant furnishings and china.
Jule Thatcher photos and *Fanita's* Clock. Courtesy: Bolton Historical Museum.

Fanita decorated for regatta at Villa Nirvana.
Courtesy: Bolton Historical Museum.

Fanita's lifeboat is now owned by the William Dow family and hangs today in the Lake George Steamboat Company's old D&H Train Station.

Fanita's wheel is now on display at the Bolton Historical Museum.

Fanita's regatta signal cannon is owned by the Bixby family of Bolton Landing and is still used for special events. Photos by Author.

Fanita Jr.

After the turn-of-the-century, John Boulton Simpson owned this Fay and Bowen named *Fanita Jr.* Standing is Captain Henry Truax of Bolton Landing. Seated far right is Simpson's daughter Helen. In back seat is Clara Krumbholz, wife of the Sagamore Hotel's General Manager T.E. Krumbholz.

Photo right. Courtesy: Bolton Historical Museum.

Photo below. Courtesy: Ike Wolgin.

Folly

Folly was also owned by John Boulton Simpson, seated left with rifle. Thatcher photo. Courtesy: Bolton Historical Museum.

Vassar

Vassar. Electric boat owned by John Boulton Simpson's daughter Helen, seen here. Boat named for Vassar College, attended by Helen's older sister Fanny.

Above photo courtesy: Bolton Historical Museum.

Right photo courtesy: Ike Wolgin.

Cadet

J.B. Simpson of Bolton Landing once owned the *Cadet*. Before he owned her, she was named *Olive*. *Olive* was built in 1893 by N.E. Porter in Alexandria, near Mossy Point. She was 45 feet long, had a 10 foot beam and was powered by a triple expansion steam engine. Raphael Porter bought her in 1894 and she was transported to Lake George for use at the Rising House Hotel. In 1898, J.B. Simpson bought her, lengthened her to 48 feet and changed her name to *Cadet*. Around 1900, F.R. Smith of Bolton Landing bought her and used her for a steam powered excursion boat at his marina; later she carried cargo. By 1910 she was outdated; power boats were replacing steam. She was taken out into 50 feet of water, scuttled and forgotten. With the help of "side-scan sonar", she was rediscovered on November 8, 1997 by Joe Zarzynski and Bob Benway of Bateaux Below Inc., a non profit group dedicated to preserving underwater shipwrecks. In May of 2002, *Cadet* was placed on the National Register of Historic Places.

Above, *Cadet* (former *Olive*). Drawing by Mark Peckham, State Coordinator, National Register of Historic Places.
Courtesy: Mark Peckham and Bateaux Below, Inc.

Below, *Cadet* today, drawing from 1998-1999 fieldwork.
Courtesy: Joseph W. Zarzynski & Bob Benway, Bateaux Below, Inc.

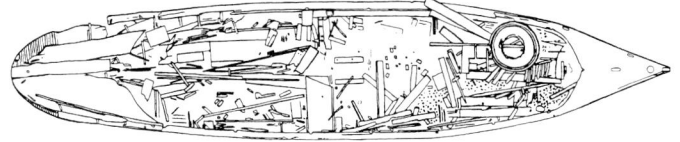

Gypsy
(owned by J.B. Simpson)

Gypsy. Above photo taken in front of J.B. Simpson's "Villa Nirvana" on Green Island. Notice *Fanita*'s old signal cannon on bow.

Photo left, aboard *Gypsy* in 1915. Helen Simpson at far right and J.B. Simpson seated next to captain.

Courtesy: Bolton Historical Museum.

Blythe

Blythe. Nearly identical to J.B. Simpson's *Gypsy.* Courtesy: Pete Smith.

River Queen

The Steam yacht *River Queen* was transported to Lake George from down the Hudson River in 1890. It was owned by T.E. Roessle who operated the Fort William Henry Hotel. The hotel and boat were sold the following year to William Noble of the Hotel Grenoble, New York City. Noble installed a new steam engine in her during extensive renovations and kept Captain Leander Harris in command for charters from $15 to $25 per day.

In 1891, one of the most magnificently beautiful boating pageants ever held was carried out on Lake George. Nearly every private yacht on the entire lake participated and nearly every part of the lake's shoreline was illuminated. An August 1891 Lake George Mirror headlined: "The Grandest Venetian Feast of Lanterns on Record–Handsomely Decorated Steam Yachts, Blossoming with Beautiful Girls–Who Won the Prizes." It went on to say, "Fifty miles of shore line blazing with colored fires, illuminated with Chinese and Japanese lanterns, the glare of the whizzing rockets, brilliant scintillations of roman candles, booming of cannon, illuminated steam yachts and beautiful girls. Such was the scene witnessed on the shores of Lake George Tuesday night. That the Lake George Carnival was a great success no one can gainsay. Lake George hotel men, cottagers, and steam yacht owners entered into the carnival enthusiastically, and there could be but one result–the grandest aquatic carnival, Venetian festival or Chinese feast of lanterns ever given in the United States."

River Queen in the Narrows. Courtesy: Private collection.

The *River Queen* was one of the first prize winners–"A beautiful transformation was brought about for the occasion in the River Queen–the lines of the steamer were completely hidden under a mass of white and gold. A bower of beauty", which was decorated to represent Cleopatra's Barge.

By the end of the cenrury, the *River Queen* was sold to Jay Smith who used her to haul coal and lumber barges at the northern end of the lake. While on the job in early winter, she struck ice and sank into 8 feet of water in Ticonderoga Creek near Cooks Landing. She was later raised and was reportedly used for serving food to other boaters who entered Paradise Bay.

River Queen hit ice and sank in 8 feet of water in Ticonderoga Creek. Courtesy: Hague Town Historian.

Island Queen

Island Queen (former *L.G.A.*). Courtesy: Bolton Historical Museum.

Assembly Point received its name in 1887, named for The Lake George Assembly who began holding camp meetings there. Previously, this 40 acre penninsula was known as West Point. Dr. Drurie Sanford. who owned Long Island and South Island (later named Speaker Heck), suggested the project and oversaw planning and construction. An auditorium was required and a large dock needed to be constructed at the end of the point. Two of the large steamers would stop daily to drop off mail and passengers.

In 1890, a new boat was constructed at the head of Van Warmer Bay by Captain Everett Harrison of Glens falls for the purpose of carrying passengers to Assembly Point. For a fee of only $1, she also carried passengers to Paradise Bay twice daily from Caldwell. She was also operated by Captain's George Harris and Hiram Hyde. Moses Finkle was Pilot. She was 90 feet long, had an 18 foot beam, had a 4 ft. 6 inch draft and could carry 250 passengers at 12 mph. Originally she was named the *L.G.A.* (Lake George Assembly), however, the following year her name was changed to *Island Queen*. Signs were placed at the various landings around the lake announcing that the *Island Queen* would pick up passengers and carry them to the services and lectures. The June 14, 1890 Lake George Mirror stated, "The handsome new excursion steamer, the *L.G.A.*, is almost ready for launching. Recently an additional force of workmen were put on, so that the craft may possibly be running on schedule on or about July 10. It may be said that the *L.G.A.* will be worthy of our beautiful lake. The steamer was built entirely by day's work and out of the best material. It should be entitled to receive the confidence and endorsement of the public."

The *Island Queen* also participated in the famous Lake George Pageant of 1891. The Mirror wrote, "The parade was headed by the *Island Queen*, under Captain Harrison, which was hansomely decorated with flags, bunting and chinese lanterns. On the upper deck of the craft were seated the members of the Warrensburg band, who discoursed as the different landings were passed."

On November 12, 1892, at the end of only her third successful season, the *Island Queen* totally burned at her Cedar Landing pier in Katskill Bay.

Caprice

The Ripple news of August 18, 1883 stated, "– a party of young people under the kind chaperonage of Mrs. Larremore and Mrs. Livermore set out from the Sagamore (Hotel) in the steam yacht *Caprice* to attend a complimentary hop given by the proprietor of the hotel at Hulett's Landing. After a sail of an hour and a half, the party landed at Hulett's and were warmly welcomed by a committee of the young ladies of the house." The Ripple went on to say, "The sail homeward (at 11 pm) was enlivened by songs and choruses, to which the accompaniments of Mr. Tobey on the banjo added great effect." *Caprice* was also used for towing barges. An 1890 news account says one barge she was towing began to sink near Diamond Point and the towline between them had to be cut. In 1891, Commodore J.B. Simpson used the *Caprice* for preparing his annual chowder party–"The steamer *Caprice* left the landing at the Sagamore Friday morning with all the necessary supplies and made the run down the lake to the Indian Kettles in short order." On August 9, 1893, the Mirror reported that, "West Wildy, pilot of the steam yacht *Caprice*, and engineer Seth Truesdale, saw a deer swimming in the lake near Anthony's Nose Saturday. The animal swam along the rocks for some distance and then at the first favorable opportunity left the water and ascended the mountain slope." That same newspaper also said, "The Steam yacht *Caprice* made the last two trips on Sunday for the newspaper service. Captain Wood of the *Mamie* was taken suddenly ill and was unable to fill his contract for the season."

Caprice. Courtesy: Bolton Historical Museum.

Ellide

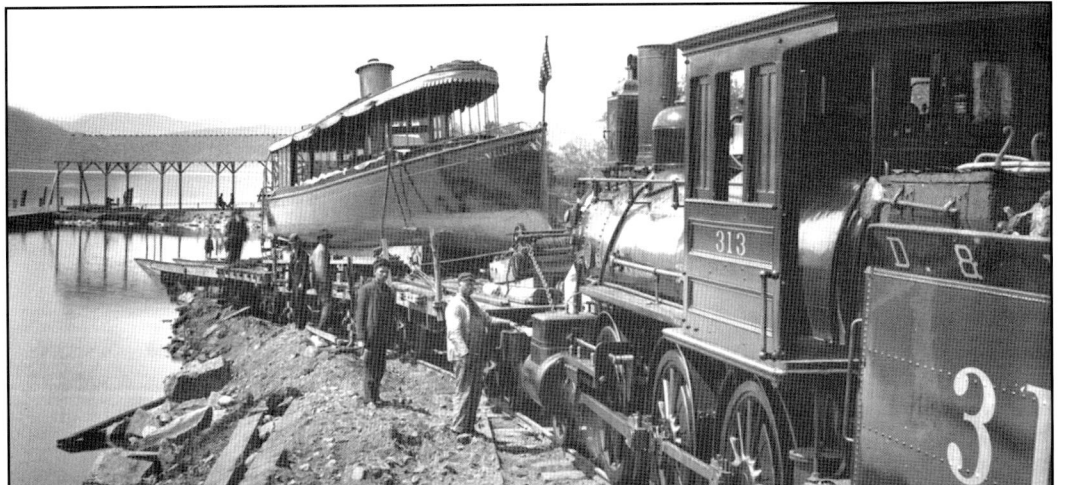

Ellide launching at Baldwin, 1897. Photos by Julius "Jule" Thatcher. Courtesy: Jim Shaughnessy.

Commodore Ebenezer Burgess Warren owned the Warren Roofing Company in Philadelphia. A successful millionaire, he often boasted that he, "retired in 1873 to be a fisherman". While vacationing at the Mohican House in Bolton Landing, he formed a partnership with three other vacationers who conspired to build the first Sagamore Hotel on Green Island during 1882 and 1883. Each of these developers built a summer "cottage" (mansion) on the island, adjacent to the hotel. Warren's cottage "Wapanak" still stands.

In 1897, he ordered the construction of the *Ellide* at a cost of $30,000 to replace his *Cyric*. He had been teased once too often by J.B. Simpson about his sluggish *Cyric*. *Ellide* was designed by Charles D. Mosher and built by Samuel Ayres & Sons in Nyack, New York. She steamed under her own power up the Hudson, traveled up the Champlain canal and was delivered to Baldwin by railcar.

Her captain was Captain Elias Harris' son, George B. Harris. Hoping it would be the fastest boat on Lake George, to his own surprise, the *Ellide* was the fastest boat in the world for two years. During 1897, speed trials were formally conducted with *Ellide* developing top speed of 40.2 mph while producing 910 hp. In 1901, the fastest boat on the lake, and world, became the 50 mph *Arrow*, designed by the same architect and owned by a New York City industrialist.

Mr. Warren stored the *Ellide* during the summer months at his elaborate "Fisherman's Cottage" which was located on the site of today's F.R. Smith & Sons boathouse in Bolton Landing. During the winter, it was stored in a long barn on the west side of Green Island, north of the Sagamore Bridge.

Ellide, 1897. Record speed 40.2 mph. Rare Postcard: Author's collection.

The *Ellide* was 80 feet long, with an 8 foot 4 inch beam, a 2 foot draft and a displacment of 13 tons. Her hull was divided by 5 steel bulkheads creating 6 water-tight compartments. She was double planked with mahogany and all was fastened with "Tobin Bronze" bolts.

Her steam engine was a brass 800 horsepower Mosher Patent Quadruple Expansion unit of "cylinders 9, 13, 18 & 34 inches in diameter by 10 inches stroke" capable of a clocked official speed of 40.2 mph. The boiler was a Mosher Water Tube, similar to 9 in use at that time by the United States Navy. In fact, the Navy considered purchasing the *Ellide* from Warren in 1898 for conversion use as a torpedo boat in the Spanish American War, however the war ended before any purchase was made.

When E.B. Warren died, *Ellide* was sold to W.W. Burton of Lake George who used her for charter and sightseeing excursions. She was stored in her Green Island boathouse where she was eventually scrapped.

Top photo, *Ellide* running a mile in 1 min. 3 1/2 sec. Courtesy: Ike Wolgin.
Above left, *Ellide* dressed for a regatta in Bolton Bay. Courtesy: Bolton Historical Museum.
Above right, *Ellide* racing in 1897. Courtesy: Lake George Historical Association.

Cyric

Cyric in Bolton Bay, owned by E. Burgess Warren. Courtesy: Hugh Allen Wilson.

The *Cyric* appeared on Lake George in June of 1891. It was built by Samuel Ayres of New York City for E. Burgess Warren, owner of Wapanak cottage on the east side of Green Island in Bolton Landing. The *Cyric* was housed in the boathouse of Warren's elaborate "Fisherman's Cottage" (today F.R. Smith's Marina). The mahogany planked *Cyric* was 52 feet long, 7 feet 9 inches across her beam and was powered by compound steam engines. Her new boathouse was built on Green Island's east side.

That same 1891 summer found the *Cyric* participating in the huge Lake George Floating Pageant. *Cyric* was the 14th steam yacht in line in the grand parade. The Mirror stated, "The *Cyric* was beautiful in yellow and white and shone like a diamond among a constellation of gems. Mr. Warren was seated forward engaged in telling guests some remarkable fish stories. The craft bore a load of handsome ladies and I began to pity the victims selected as judges, who were expected to decide as to the merits of the boat carrying the most beautiful load."

E. Burgess Warren was an avid and successful fisherman. He and his captain, Alex Taylor, fished for bass from the *Cyric* nearly every day and in all kinds of weather. During a severe summer storm in July of 1901, the Troy Times reported that *Cyric* capsized, "a half-mile east of Dome Island and opposite Camp Andrews, where the water is more than 100 feet deep. Mr. Warren was on a fishing trip when a heavy thunderstorm, accompanied by a strong wind, suddenly passed over the lake. The canvas curtains had been pulled down and fastened to keep out the rain. A teriffic gust of wind struck the yacht, and not finding a vent through the upper works forced the boat over, and it rapidly filled. The boat was kept afloat by a large air-tight compartment in the bow." Mr. Warren's life was saved by Captain Alexander Taylor, Engineer John Mead of Caldwell and Steward Robert Thompson as they all held on to the capsized boat until help arrived. They were rescued 40 minutes later by John Harris of the steamer Sagamore. The *Cyric* was later towed to shore after the storm passed. Soon thereafter, a young boy dived into the lake and recovered Warren's gold watch.

In 1897, Warren replaced the sluggish *Cyric* with a new and much faster boat, the *Ellide*. The *Cyric* spent the next series of years towing log booms to the sawmill in Bolton Landing where Lamb's NO-RO-WAL marina is located today.

Her final long-time owner was Art Louis who rebuilt her into a simple gasoline-powered cabin cruiser. By 1936 she was on the marine railway most of the time on the Harris Bay side of Cleverdale. She was never launched during W. W. II. She further deteriorated and had to be destroyed after the war.

Wapanak

Wapanak, also owned by E. B. Warren, was named for his home "Wapanak" on Green Island. She was 32 feet long, 6 feet wide. Warren sold her in 1892. Notice the first Sagamore Hotel in background which burned in 1893. Courtesy: Hugh Allen Willson.

Geneva

Geneva at BayView, 1893. (Gazebo is now on Treasure Point). Photo by Jule Thatcher. Courtesy: Jim Shaughnessy.

In 1891, *Geneva* was brought to Lake George by William Demuth of New York City, owner of William Demuth and Company, wealthy manufacturer of cigar store Indians. Demuth and his family summered at the Fort William Henry Hotel until he moved into his own luxurious "cottage", Bay View, at Bolton Landing in 1893. Demuth loved boating and fishing and spent most of his time here at Lake George in his *Geneva*.

He and the *Geneva* also participated in the magnificent Lake George Floating Pageant in 1891. Mrs. Demuth had the boat equipped with over 400 small red fairy lamps. The Lake George Mirror described *Geneva* as, "the most artistically decorated steam yacht in the parade. A wagon load of handsome evergreen wreaths were used to decorate the saloon windows, running vines twined and tristed their tendrils around the stanchions and on the after deck, forward, and in every place where it was

Geneva at 1891 Lake George Floating Pageant. Courtesy: Bolton Historical Museum.

possible for a pretty girl to pose, there she was, resplendent in Turkish, Spanish and golden and crimson silk costumes. On the upper deck at the prow stood the living figure of a sailor in naval costume, who maintained this picturesque position, as well as though part of the boat. On the forward deck was Christopher Columbus in regal attire and aft of the stack were a group of native Indians costumed in war paint, clubs, feathers, etc., who went through the act of killing and tomahawking each other in thorough Mohican style. One feature of the *Geneva's* load of fair freight was the artistic grouping. As the yacht moved by the piers, not a motion was made, each beautiful maiden a picture in herself, the whole a dream of fair women." The man on the bow was Harold St. John, an entertainer at the Fort William Henry Hotel.

Demuth's *Geneva* and his beautiful Bay View estate were both sold in 1915 to John B. Warden who later sold both again in 1922 to Madame Marcella Sembrich, retired soprano from the Metropolitan Opera in New York. Sembrich was not interested in boating; her focus was on teaching aspiring young singers. She quickly sold the *Geneva* to Frank Bates of Lake George, had the boat storage barn removed, and there, three years later, she built her new pink stucco studio which is now open to the public every summer as part of the Marcella Sembrich Museum. Very interestingly, when the museum had new hardwood floors installed in 2001, the *Geneva's* concrete launching ramp was discovered in its entirety beneath the studio floor.

Geneva & Fanita Officers and Crew. Standing: Capt. George Harris of the *Geneva*, Douglas Thompson, Wm. Plumb fireman of the *Fanita*, George Granger engineer of *Fanita*, John Seward, engineer of *Geneva*. Seated: Capt. Clare Wilson of the *Fanita*, Harry Finkle, sailor of *Geneva*, Henry Wilson, sailor of *Fanita*.
Courtesy: Bolton Historical Museum.

Camera

The *Camera* was built in 1890 for Glens Falls photographer George W. Conkey. By 1891, Conkey would act as captain and photographer simultaneously, taking his passengers around the lake for photographs.

The *Camera* came along just in time to participate in the 1891 Floating Pageant. The Mirror said, "The yacht *Camera* was chartered by the Russian Consul General, who by the way had five boats in the parade, and was a marvel of beauty. In the rear of the *Camera* was a boat converted into a swan, floating gracefully on the water. The snowy plumage was admirably counterfeited."

One of Conkey's distinguished guests was George O. Knapp of Chicago, President of Union Carbide. In the late 1890's, the *Camera* gave Knapp and his family a tour of the Narrows. Learning that the Hundred Island House was for sale along with the Pearl Point Hotel and a large parcel of lakeshore and mountainside property, Knapp immediately purchased and developed it into his expansive summer estate.

> THE CAMERA—The steam yacht "Camera" can be chartered by parties for pleasure, or wishing to have photographic views taken at different points on the lake. The steamer was built last year. New engines this year. Address, George W. Conkey, Central House, Caldwell, Lake George, N. Y.

Camera Ad: Lake George Mirror, June 20, 1891.
Author's collection.

Camera at 1891 Lake George Floating Pageant. Courtesy: Fort Edward Historical Museum.

Mamie

The 45 passenger sight-seeing boat *Mamie* was built and launched on Lake George in June of 1891 by Captain Minard "Min" G. Wood of Assembly Point and Harris Bay. She was 51 feet long and 10 feet 2 inches wide at her beam. Named for Wood's daughter, the *Mamie* was powered by the same 40 hp steam engine that had powered the *Pocahontas*.

In 1893, *Mamie* left the Fort William Henry Hotel twice daily making trips to Paradise Bay and back. Amazingly, Captain Wood made 16 brief scheduled stops each way, picking up and dropping off passengers. The fare was only $1.00.

To further boost Min's profits, he also delivered mail, newspapers and made freight deliveries to each hotel along his route.

Mamie. Photo by Fillmore of Ticonderoga. Courtesy: Ike Wolgin.

The Excursion Steamer Mamie

Will make regular daily trips, except Sunday, via the "One Hundred Islands," to Paradise Bay, making the intermediate landings on flag or notice to the captain, as per the following schedule:

Going North.			Going South.	
A. M.	P. M.		P. M.	P. M.
9 00	2 00	Lv....Fort Wm. Henry Hotel....Ar.	1 10	6 40
9 03	2 03	............Lake House............	1 07	6 37
9 10	2 30	............Crosbyside............	1 00	6 30
9 20	2 40	...........The Antlers............	12 50	6 20
9 28	2 50	....Assembly Point (L. G. A.)....	12 42	6 12
9 40	3 10	..........Horicon Lodge...........	12 30	6 00
9 43	3 13	..........Sheldon House...........	12 27	5 57
9 46	3 16	...........Grove Hotel............	12 24	5 54
9 50	3 20	.........Trout Pavilion...........	12 20	5 50
9 52	3 22	..............Albion..............	12 18	5 48
9 55	3 25	..........Katskill House..........	12 15	5 45
10 08	3 38	..........Marion House............	12 02	5 32
10 25	3 55	..............Bolton..............	11 45	5 15
10 35	4 05	............Sagamore..............	11 35	5 05
10 46	4 16	............Kenesaw...............	11 24	4 54
10 51	4 21	........Hundred Island House......	11 19	4 49
10 54	4 25	............Pearl Point...........	11 16	4 46
11 05	4 35	............Paradise Bay..........	11 05	4 35

Fare for round trip, $1. Proportionate rates for intermediate landings. M. G. WOOD, Captain.

SUNDAY NEWSPAPER STEAMER MAMIE.

Leave Caldwell at 11:20 A. M., arrive at Roger's Rock at 3:30 P. M. Will carry a limited number of passengers from the foot of the lake. Passengers wishing to catch the sleeper at Caldwell can flag the Mamie.

Mamie. Top photo, *Mamie* at 1891 Lake George Floating Pageant.
Courtesy: Fort Edward Historical Museum.
Left, Summer schedule, Lake George Mirror, July 22, 1893.
Courtesy: Bolton Historical Museum.
Above, Fall schedule, Lake George Mirror, September 9, 1893.
Courtesy: Bolton Historical Museum.

Helen (I)

Helen (I) in the Narrows, early 1890's. Courtesy: Fort Edward Historical Museum.

Helen (I) was owned by Frederick O. Burhans of Warrensburg and New York City who used her as his private yacht during the early 1890's. Occasionally, *Helen* was also hired for excursions.. In 1891, at the Lake George Floating Pageant, it was reported that the *Helen* was in sixteenth position in the Grand Parade. "There was a lively crowd aboard, and as the boat steamed slowly and majestically by the piers, three hearty cheers, Lake George hurrahs, were given by the merry party aboard. The *Helen* was resplendent in her decorations. Her decks and saloon and quarters were appropriately festooned with clouds of bunting, and as she went steaming on her way, the scene reminded one of fairyland. The Lake House was well represented on board."

Helen was sold shortly after 1894 when Frederick and his brother commissioned the construction of *Helen* (II).

Helen (II)

Helen (II) under construction at Caldwell, 1892.
Courtesy: Lake George Historical Association.

Helen (II) was built in 1892 by Chris Bates of Caldwell who had a boat construction shop across the road from the courthouse. *Helen* (II) was owned by brothers Frederick and Charles Burhans, both summer Warrensburg residents. This *Helen* was 65 feet long and 9 feet 6 inches wide at the beam. Powered by a 75 hp steam engine, she was quite fast for her day.

In July of 1897, while *Helen* was docked overnight at Crosbyside, vandals drilled four holes in her hull below the waterline and pushed *Helen* out onto the lake with the intent of sinking her. She listed heavily, sank and was very difficult to retrieve, however she was brought up and put back in commission. That same year, *Helen* finished her season by making the last fall runs for *Mohican* (I) after she had mechanical difficulties.

In 1898, Engineer C. Wood became Captain C. Wood.

Kismet

Kismet built at Caldwell. Courtesy: Lake George Village Historian.

Kismet was built at Chris Bates' boat shop in Caldwell where the bank now stands near the old courthouse, and was launched by Henry Nichols, proprietor of the Hundred Island House, for George O. Knapp. In 1894, *Kismet* was an important member of the fleet of boats available at the Hundred Island House in the Narrows along with *Vanadis* and a large fleet of rowboats made by Rushton and Smith. Her main task was to transport new guests from the train station at Caldwell to the hotel. Almon C. Burton was her captain in 1894.

Kismet usually wintered at Crosbyside, and thus was frequently the first steam-powered vessel to operate on the lake every spring. One spring, when the ice broke up, *Kismet* had already been launched. North winds carried so much ice into Caldwell Bay that Henry Nichols and the proprietor of Crosbyside were unable to use the boat and had to walk instead to Caldwell.

Pastime

Pastime at 1891 Floating Pageant. Courtesy: Fort Edward Historical Museum.

Pastime was owned by Commander A.G. Davis of Baltimore, Maryland, owner of the cottage Wambek. During the 1891 Floating Pageant, Wambek cottage "gave a brilliant illumination. His *Pastime* "was the ninth boat in line. The *Pastime* was beautiful with Japanese lanterns, bunting and flags. Commander Davis was an imposing figure on the after deck surrounded by handsome ladies. His boat was a bower of beauty."

Marion

Above three photos of *Marion* on Lake George. Courtesy: Fort Edward Historical Museum.
Below, *Marion* towing barge on Champlain Canal. Courtesy: Fort Edward Historical Museum.

Chris Bates built the Marion at Caldwell for D.W. Sherman of the Marion House during the winter of 1890-1891. With a 65 feet length and a beam of 10 feet, Bates had to build a new and longer shed to accommodate her for construction. Marion was named for Sherman's wife, as was his hotel, and was launched in August of 1891 in the command of Captain Ollie Smith.

The Marion was used mostly by the hotel for transporting guests, however she was also available for charter. The Marion annually attended the popular Hague Regatta. It was reported that, "At 12 o'clock, the handsome steam yacht Marion swept across the lake to Assembly pier, and with the flag of the Lake George Mirror to the fore, departed with a merry party on board, bound for the regatta in Hague."

In 1901, she was purchased by Fred Howland of Kattskill Bay and remodeled. The Howland family used Marion several years for their private summer use. She was sold during World War I, and in 1918 was transported from Baldwin to Lake Champlain by train. She lived the remainder of her life towing Champlain Canal barges. A few years later she sank and had to be destroyed.

Mohican (I)

The *Mohican* (I) was designed by Henry T. Marvin of Brooklyn and was built in Caldwell on Pine Point in 1894 for young Captain Everett Harrison of Glens Falls to operated his own Paradise Bay Line. She cost $15,760 to build. The ship was named for the Mohican Indians who once spent their sum mers in the region now known as Bolton Landing.

A few months after completion, she sank at the Fort William Henry dock, was raised and repaired and spent the remainder of the season carrying freight and passengers to the towns and hotels along the lake. She was purchased the following winter (on February 12, 1895), by the Champlain Transportation Company, (owners of the Lake George Steamboat Company) for $13,000. Extensive imptovements were made which included a new main deck, steam heat, carpeting, toilet facilities, etc. She displayed the traditional elk antlers which indicated that she was the fastest vessel in the fleet. With 20 years of experience as a Pilot behind him, Captain Wesley Finkle now was in command and he remained in command for the remainder of the Mohican (I)'s fourteen years.

The *Mohican* (I) closely resembles today's *Mohican* (II), however she was fourteen feet shorter and was constructed entirely of wood. Her pilot house and cabin were of varnished cherry. She was 93 feet long, 17 feet wide across her beam, drafted 6 1/2 feet and weighed 150 tons. Her 200 horsepower steam engine pushed a single propeller. The engine was later replaced by a Fletcher built steam engine numbered 199.

Sailing daily from Baldwin at 7:20 am, the "*Mo*" stopped at all of the landings when signaled and arrived at Caldwell in time to catch the 11:25 am southbound train. On her return trip, she left the pier at 2:45pm, touched all the landings again, arriving at Baldwin at 6:30pm. During the busy summer season, she made regular trips to Paradise Bay in the Narrows.

The *Mohican* (I) was retired in May of 1908 when today's steel-hulled *Mohican* (II) replaced her. She was dismantled at the Baldwin drydock that same year.

Above, *Mohican* (I), 1894, built on Pine Point. Courtesy: Lake George Village Historian.
Below, *Mohican* (I), 1894, owned by Everett Harrison. Private collection.
Right, *Mohican* (I), 1895 to 1908, L.G. Steamboat Company. Ballast has been added. Courtesy: Bob Benway.
Right, 1902 Schedule. Courtesy: Dick and Mary Kowell.

New York to Montreal
VIA LAKE GEORGE AND LAKE CHAMPLAIN
CONDENSED TIME TABLE—JUNE 23, 1902.

STATIONS.	ROUTE.	Daily ex. Sunday	Daily ex. Sunday
Lv. NEW YORK	N.Y.C. & H.R.R.	9.55 AM	12.10 AM
"	West Shore R.R.	7.10 "	9.30 PM
"	Night Boats.		6.00 "
"	Day Boats.		8.40 AM
" Albany	D. & H.R.R.	1.10 PM	7.00 "
" Troy	"	1.50 "	7.00 "
" Schenectady	"	1.45 "	7.00 "
" Saratoga	"	3.00 "	8.20 "
" Fort Edward	"	3.35 "	8.45 "
" Glens Falls	"	3.52 "	9.05 "
" CALDWELL	L. G. Steamers.	4.30 "	9.30 "
" Assembly Point	"	4.45 "	9.45 "
" Cleverdale	"	4.50 "	9.50 "
" Rockhurst	"	4.55 "	9.55 "
" Trout Pavilion	"	5.00 "	10.00 "
" Kattskill	"	5.05 "	10.05 "
" Marion	"	5.20 "	10.20 "
" Bolton	"	5.35 "	10.35 "
" Green Island	"	5.40 "	10.40 "
" Fourteen-Mile Island	"	5.50 "	10.50 "
" Hundred Islands	"	5.55 "	10.55 "
" Pearl Point	"	6.00 "	11.00 "
" Hulett's	"	6.40 "	11.35 "
" Sabbath Day Point	"	6.50 "	11.45 "
" Silver Bay	"	7.00 "	11.55 "
" Hague	"	7.25 "	12.10 PM
" Rogers' Rock	"	7.45 "	12.30 "
Ar. BALDWIN	"	7.50 PM	12.50 "
Lv. FT. TICONDEROGA	L. C. Steamers.		1.20 "
" Larrabee's	"		1.30 "
" Port Henry	"		2.35 "
" Westport	"	6.45 AM	3.20 "
" Essex	"	7.35 "	4.05 "
" Burlington	"	9.00 "	5.20 "
" Port Kent	"	9.40 "	6.00 "
" Bluff Point (Hotel Champlain)	"	10.10 "	6.35 "
" Cliff Haven (Landing for Catholic Summer School)	"	10.15 "	6.40 "
Ar. Plattsburgh	"	10.30 "	7.00 "
" Rouses Point	D. & H.R.R.	1.40 PM	8.10 "
" St. Johns	G. T. Railway.	2.35 "	8.42 "
Ar. MONTREAL	"	3.20 "	9.35 "

Breakfast, dinner and supper are served on Lake Champlain and Lake George steamers, on the American plan.

New York City Information Bureau, 21 Cortlandt St.

Montreal to New York
VIA LAKE CHAMPLAIN AND LAKE GEORGE.
CONDENSED TIME TABLE—JUNE 23, 1902.

STATIONS.	ROUTE.	Daily ex. Sunday	Daily ex. Sunday
Lv. MONTREAL	G. T. R'way.	10.15 AM	6.30 PM
" St. Johns	"	11.00 "	7.35 "
" Rouses Point	D. & H.R.R.	11.40 "	8.10 "
" Plattsburgh	L. C. Steamers	3.00 PM	7.00 "
" Cliff Haven (Catholic Summer School)	"	3.05 "	7.05 "
" Bluff Point (Hotel Champlain)	"	3.10 "	7.10 "
" Port Kent	"	3.50 "	7.40 "
" Burlington	"	5.20 "	8.40 "
Ar. Essex	"	6.00 "	9.25 "
" Westport	"	7.20 "	10.10 "
" Port Henry	"		10.50 "
" Larrabee's	"		12.10 PM
" FT. TICONDEROGA	"		12.25 "
" BALDWIN	L. G Steamers	7.20 AM	1.00 "
" Rogers' Rock	"	7.25 "	1.05 "
" Hague	"	7.40 "	1.35 "
" Silver Bay	"	7.55 "	1.45 "
" Sabbath Day Point	"	8.10 "	2.00 "
" Hulett's	"	8.20 "	2.10 "
" Pearl Point	"	8.50 "	2.40 "
" Hundred Islands	"	8.55 "	2.45 "
" Fourteen-Mile Island	"	9.00 "	2.50 "
" Green Island	"	9.10 "	3.00 "
" Bolton	"	9.15 "	3.05 "
" Marion	"	9.30 "	3.20 "
" Kattskill	"	9.45 "	3.45 "
" Trout Pavilion	"	9.50 "	3.50 "
" Rockhurst	"	9.55 "	3.55 "
" Cleverdale	"	10.00 "	4.00 "
" Assembly Point	"	10.10 "	4.10 "
Ar. Caldwell	"	10.35 "	4.30 "
" Glens Falls	D. & H.R.R.	11.44 "	5.25 "
" Fort Edward	"	12.00 M	5.40 "
" Saratoga	"	12.35 PM	6.12 "
" Schenectady	"	1.20 "	9.30 "
" Troy	"	1.45 "	7.30 "
" Albany	"	2.00 "	7.35 "
" New York	N.Y.C. & H.R.	5.30 "	12.02 "
"	West Shore.	7.45 PM	8.00 "
"	Night Boats.		6.00 "
"	Day Boats.		5.30 PM

The morning trains from Montreal have no boat connection through Lake Champlain. Take P. M. trains leaving Montreal at 6:30 or 8:10 P. M. and lodge at Hotel Champlain or on board steamer Vermont at Plattsburgh. Cool, comfortable and clean staterooms with meals on board and use of stateroom to end of Lake Champlain journey at Fort Ticonderoga the following day.

New York City Information Bureau, 21 Cortlandt St.

Mohican (I), 1908, on Baldwin Drydock to be dismantled. Courtesy: Bolton Historical Museum.

Mary Anderson

The *Mary Anderson* ran out of Huletts Landing during the very early 1890's, probably between 1890 and 1895. She was originally owned by and named for *Mary Anderson*, an attractive Shakesperian actress who lived from 1859 to 1940. She used the *Mary Anderson* for excursions on the Hudson River. In 1890, she married aristocrat Antonio deNavarro and moved to England; her boat then appeared at Huletts on Lake George with Albert Jakeway as pilot.

Mary Anderson. A painting in gouache and oils, early 1890's. Courtesy: John Smart.

Isolde

The *Isolde* was owned by Camp Andrews of Phelps Point and Andrews Bay, Pilot Knob. This property was first settled by John Andrews of Patten's Mills who purchased these lands in 1869. John loved camping and soon he was inviting his friends to camp here with him. One of his camping friends was Andrew Smith of Poughkeepsie, famous for his Smith Brothers Cough Drops. Smith purchased nearly 200 acres from John Andrews and developed it into a summer colony known as Camp Andrews.

During the 1890's, Camp Andrews owned the steam yacht *Isolde* which was mainly used for pleasure rides and picking up the mail at Katskill Bay. Although modified significantly, *Isolde* was still around at the onset of World War II. Her owner at the time, Mrs. Isabelle Fursman, donated the *Isolde* to the war effort in England where it served during the war.

Top, *Isolde*. Conkey Photo. Courtesy: Lake George Historical Association.
Above, *Isolde* blowing her steam whistle, 1890's, at Camp Andrews, Pilot Knob.
Courtesy: Roy and Jeanette Hunt.

Theta

Theta at Pilot Knob. Courtesy: Roy and Jeanette Hunt.

In 1884, Victoria Lodge was built at Pilot Knob by John and Victoria Harris. Among the frequent guests was Eber Richards of Sandy Hill (Hudson Falls). Eber was a successful lumberer. In 1888, he purchased 175 feet of shoreline and soon built his summer home here. In 1892, Eber had his own small steam yacht, the *Theta*, named for his Union College fraternity, the *Theta* chapter of Psyupsilon. Theta was 45 feet long and had a 6 1/2 foot beam. Eber bought her in New York City and steamed her up the Hudson, through the Barge Canal, up the Champlain Canal where she was loaded onto a freightcar at Sandy Hill and transported to the Caldwell Station and launched onto Lake George.

Theta had a small "yacht piano" aboard which was one of five ever made by the Columbia Piano Company. It was special-ordered for Eber's son Frederick and his bride Constance who were married aboard on June 12, 1895. This piano had only 65 keys instead of the usual 88.

Eber Richards died in 1912. *Theta's* piano was moved into Theta Cottage where it was used for another 60 years during Sunday Hymn Sings. Never once tuned, the piano was auctioned off during the early 1970's.

The *Theta* was sold in 1912 by Edward Peck Culver who handled Eber's estate. Many of *Theta's* removable memorabilia were removed at the time of the sale, and these historic items are still being preserved today around the Pilot Knob area by family and friends.

Theta Name Board. Courtesy: Roy and Jeanette Hunt.
Theta photo. Courtesy: JoAnn Irish Mahoney. Clock from *Theta*. Courtesy: Bill Richards.

Crusader

Crusader was owned by Mr. and Mrs. William T. Wells of Bolton Landing's Crown Island and Melbourne, Florida. Wells was President of the Rustless Iron Company in New York City. In 1897, he ordered construction of the *Crusader* by Chris Bates in Caldwell at a cost of $5,000. With a length of 60 feet, a beam of 10 feet and a powerful triple expansion steam engine, she was a fast boat. Several years later her boiler was replaced. Her original boiler was discarded into the lake and is still there, near her old pier at Crown Island. Eventually *Crusader* was sold to the Silver Bay Association to run alongside their *Oneita*.

It is interesting to note that Dr. Irving Langmuir also owned Crown Island several decades later. In the early 1930's, Dr. Langmuir won the Nobel Prize for his research on Surface Chemistry while working for the General Electric Company.

Crusader at Crown Island, Bolton Landing. Courtesy: Lake George Historical Museum.

Wanda

The steamboat *Wanda* was owned by W.H. Beardsley of New York City who had purchased all 12 acres of Fourteen Mile Island from the Delaware & Hudson Company. He built a new summer home here during 1905–1906. It still stands on the southern end of the island and is owned today by Sherwood and Betty Finley. Beardsley was a successful businessman who had achieved great wealth as Secretary of the Florida East Coast Railroad and as a Director of the Standard Oil Company. Beardsley loved the lake and he loved to fish from his *Wanda*.

In 1908, he sold the old Kenesaw Hotel adjacent to his home to Jules and Fred Thatcher who were important early photographers around the Lake George region. It is interesting to note that when the Thatchers tore down the hotel, over 50,000 square feet of the old hotel's lumber was shipped to both Ticonderoga and Caldwell and was reused.

The Finley's have wonderfully maintained Beardsley's home and have preserved its original splendor–and they have treasured and preserved the *Wanda's* old bar which once entertained the lake's elite 100 years ago.

Wanda. Top photo and bar cabinet, courtesy: Sherwood and Betty Finley. Lower photo, courtesy: Lake George Village Historian.

Oneita

During the summer of 1895, Horatio Sanford of Long Island and Assembly Point sold his small steam yacht, *Gladys*. She left Lake George and was shipped to Buzzards Bay, Massachusetts where President Grover Cleveland frequently used her for his fishing trips.

Sanford replaced *Gladys* with a new $5,000 naptha launch built by the Charles Seabury Company at Morris Heights, New Jersey. He shipped her to Lake George and christened her *Oneita*. She was 47 feet 6 inches long, 7 feet 5 inches at the beam, reached a speed of 9 mph and gracefully displayed a long "clipper" bow and a solid canopy. In 1897, Sanford sold *Oneita* to Silas H. Paine at Silver Bay. The Silver Bay Association used the 35 passenger *Oneita* for their outings up into the 1920's when she was sold.

Oneita at Silver Bay. J.S. Wooley Photo. Courtesy: Mike DeLarm, Lakeview Antiques.

Oneita at the Silver Bay Association. Courtesy: Jane Crammond, Silver Bay Association

Iroquois

Industrialist LeGrand C. Cramer of Troy, New York, and Cramer Point on the southwestern shores of Lake George, built a beautiful summer mansion named Trinity Rock which still stands today. In 1902, he ordered a new yacht to be constructed by the Gas Engine & Power Company and the Charles L. Seabury & Company Consolidated at Morris Heights, New Jersey. This completed craft was sailed up the Hudson River and Champlain Canal where it was lifted onto a D & H Railroad flatcar and carried overland two miles to the marine rail track at Baldwin near Ticonderoga. There it was launched and christened—the *Iroquois*.

The *Iroquois* was 75 feet long, had a 12 foot beam, drew 4 feet of water, weighed 35 tons and averaged at a speed of 13 mph. She was powered by a triple expansion steam engine and was schooner rigged (meaning she was also equipped with sails). The boat was easily recognizable due to her white painted hull, mahogany woodwork, and upswept bow with a 14 foot bowsprit. There was a 14 foot room aft containing lockers and a toilet and an awning across the entire deck. She was lighted by electricity which also powered her unique searchlight. In addition, there was a complete galley, sleeping berths, a coal bunker forward and life preservers for all passengers. Cramer's crew of three consisted of a pilot, engineer and one deckhand. "She made a very trim appearance", according to an August 1902 Lake George Mirror. In September of that same year, the Mirror wrote, "As the *Iroquois* was passing the Mother Bunch islands, a fine specimen of deer was discovered swimming in the lake. The *Iroquois* started in pursuit and after a half hour's struggle, the animal was lassoed. The deer weighed 245 pounds."

In 1909, Cramer sold the *Iroquois* and purchased his new *Winnish*. The *Iroquois* now went through a series of owners. Elmer Burton and Frank Cotton used the *Iroquois* to carry passengers and deliver mail, and in 1909, Cotton and Burton had a contract with the Glenburnie Inn at Anthony's Nose to provide one hour lunch cruises from the hotel. According to historian Betty Buckell, the boat had so many mechanical difficulties that they soon lost the contract because they were unable to maintain the agreed upon schedule. My research shows their new 1919 schedule included full-length lake trips: "NORTHBOUND-Leave Lake George Station Dock 9:45AM, Arrive Baldwin Dock 1:10PM. SOUTHBOUND-Leave Baldwin Dock 1:20PM, Arrive Lake George Dock 4:50PM".

The Silver Bay Association owned her the following year in 1920. Captain F. Banker carried 30 passengers aboard and also used her to tow coal barges out of Hague. When the Lake George Steamboat Company began using *Horicon* II as a "SHOW BOAT" in the early 1930s, they leased the *Iroquois* for transporting passengers from the Silver Bay Association's caretaker Walter McDonald. Captain Marty Fisher was her Master.

For many years, the *Iroquois* lay idle at Adolph Och's boathouse which is now the Boathouse Restaurant. By the mid 1930s, the *Iroquois* was in very poor condition. To prevent her from sinking, she was partly hauled ashore at the end of Warner Bay. Her boiler and steam engine had been removed, most if her had been stripped—only her 2 inch shaft and propeller remained below deck.

Croswell Tuttle of Lake George had always been fascinated by her. He purchased the *Iroquois* in 1937 for only $50.00 off her latest owner from Glens Falls who was willing to donate her original compass and wheel which he had stored away. Although dismayed at her poor condition, Croswell and his friends, Stanley Rymkewicz of Glens Falls and Helen Ketchum of Luzerne, made the *Iroquois* operational again by installing a gasoline powered Buick automobile engine. Croswell recently told me that the engine was "a straight eight—very large and very heavy— to shift it required use of feet as well as hands". Only able to go forward in first gear, it went just 5 mph. On her new maiden voyage, Tuttle ran his yacht from Warner Bay to his family's boathouse near Tea Island. Stanley remained in the pilothouse as engineer—Croswell steered and signaled Stanley, who actually controlled speeds with a series of signal bells and jingles. Helen came along for the ride.

Tuttle and his friends enjoyed the *Iroquois* for the next three years. When Croswell Tuttle returned from World War II in October of 1945, he saw that the *Iroquois* had been totally vandalized and stripped. Only her propeller and original large brass stern mounted deck-plate remained on the rotting hull which had completely deteriorated due to weathering. Croswell then went away for a week-long vacation. When he returned, his father had the remains of the boat destroyed.

Today, the original 42 inch propeller is still owned by Croswell, and the 1902 brass deck-plate is owned by Henry Caldwell of Bolton Landing.

Iroquois. (Clockwise) Propeller, courtesy: Croswell Tuttle. *Iroquois* at Silver Bay, courtesy: Hague Town Historian. Brass Deck Plate, courtesy: Henry Caldwell. Croswell Tuttle, Hannah Ericson and an Alaskan scout aboard *Iroquois*, 1937, courtesy: Croswell Tuttle. *Iroquois* at Halycon, courtesy: Croswell Tuttle. Men aboard *Iroquois* at Silver Bay, courtesy: Esko Virta.

Vanadis

Vanadis launching beside the old Caldwell Courthouse, 1897. Courtesy: Jack Mannix.

Union Carbide co-founder George O. Knapp purchased the Pearl Point Hotel and the Hundred Island House Hotel beneath Shelving Rock in the Narrows at the end of the nineteenth century. He closed both hotels, tore them down and built his summer mansion into the mountain hillside keeping all employees of both hotels as his personal staff. He then hired the Bates brothers at Caldwell to construct his new yacht *Vanadis* in 1897. The 70 passenger *Vanadis* was steam powered, 65 feet long, with her own set of china and silver. Captain Stephen Harrris and Engineer George Ferris were in command with Captain Almon Burton of the *Pocahontas* taking over in 1898 and Captain Edward Irish eventually following him. Knapp also owned the steam yacht *Kismet* at the same time.

On November 18, 1909, the *Vanadis* was secured for the night. Fires were carefully banked and the crew went to bed. Everyone was awakened during the night by a major fire which had broken out aboard the *Vanadis*. Fortunately, they were able to untie her lines and push her out onto the lake to save George Knapp's new boathouse. She was a total loss.

Vanadis. Courtesy: Lake George Historical Association.

Sayonara

After his yacht *Vanadis* burned in 1909, George O. Knapp wanted to replace her immediately. He arranged for a new boat to be designed by Tams, LeMoyne & Crane of New York. Again, his new yacht was constructed by George Bates of Caldwell. There was a delay in getting her completed for the scheduled launch in June. The September 12, 1910 Glens Falls Times reported, "Some trouble has been had in getting the craft to the lake shore from the shed near Mr. Bates shop on one of the back streets. It is expected that work on moving the boat will be carried on far into the night in order to get clear of the trolley tracks before tomorrow when there will be extra cars passing enroute for the Warrensburg County Fair." She was finally launched on September 30, 1910, and there were problems again during her launching procedure. Before Mrs. Knapp could christen the boat, the rope broke and *Sayonara* rolled down the ways and unceremoniously launched herself. Mrs. Knapp then christened *Sayonara* on the lake. Rev. Ernest M. Stires blessed *Sayonara* before her maiden voyage two weeks later.

This new yacht was named *Sayonara,* as Mrs. Knapp explained, *Sayonara* is Japanese and loosely translates to "Til we meet again". *Sayonara* was 81 feet long, had a draft of 4 feet 6 inches, a beam of 12 feet 10 inches and was made of East India Mahogany and Andaman Padauk, a rare wood which only grows on the Andaman Islands west

Sayonara ready for launching, September 1910. Courtesy: Lake George Village Historian.

Sayonara at George Knapp's estate beneath Shelving Rock. Author's Collection.

Crusader, Scioto and *Sayonara* at Bolton House dock. Notice *Fanita* at Green Island in background. Courtesy: Bob Benway.

Sayonara and *Mountaineer* in Lake George, 1938. Courtesy: Bob Benway.

Sayonara, 1956, Alden Shaw's Marine Industries dock. Courtesy: Dick and Mary Kowell.

SAYONARA — CAPACITY 80 PASSENGERS
PARADISE BAY and ISLAND CRUISE
TWO TRIPS DAILY
Leave 10 A. M.   Return 12:30 P. M.
Leave 2 P. M.   Return 4:30 P. M.
Fare $2.50 (incl. tax)
Paradise Bay Trips Will Continue Thru October 12
Evening Cruise 1½ Hours
Leaves 7 P. M.   Fare $2.00 (incl. tax)

1956 Schedule. Courtesy: Dick and Mary Kowell.

Sayonara with pilot house, Paradise Bay, 1969. Courtesy: Dick and Mary Kowell.

of Malaysia. The Knapp family had her built for style and comfort, not speed.

Her 150 hp triple expansion steam engine and Roberts tubular boiler were powerful. On one occasion, a tug-of-war was arranged between the *Sayonara* and a Model T Ford. The *Sayonara* won the contest which was stopped just before the auto was pulled into the lake. She was also the boat which held the officials during the Gold Cup Speedboat Races on Lake George during the 1930s. Photos and old newsreel footage of the races in Bolton Bay show the *Sayonara* in the middle of the race course.

As the years passed by, the *Sayonara* changed hands several times. Lynn Goodness of Saratoga says George Knapp sold his father, Paul Goodness, the *Sayonara* around 1940. Young Lynn worked on it as a deck hand. Unfortunately, World War II, the need for gas stamps and a decline in passenger service caused Paul to sell the boat back to George Knapp, who then re-sold it to Harm Burton and Alden Shaw of Marine Industries in Lake George Village. Shaw raised the pilot house during the 1960's and operated tourist rides with it along the Beach Road.

According to my co-worker Captain Darrell Finlayson of the Lake George Steamboat Company, who once worked for the Warren County Sheriff's Patrol during the 1960's, the *Sayonara* was nearly lost on one occasion when a wayward boy untied the boat, started the engines and headed down the lake. Owner Shaw chased after him in a speedboat. The boy jumped out and the *Sayonara* headed directly toward Tea Island with nobody aboard. Fortunately, Alden Shaw was able to pull alongside and rescue the boat in the nick of time.

Ownership changed again from Burton and Shaw to Peter Smith—then to Wilbur Dow of the Lake George Steamboat Company who gave it back to the Knapps in 1973. Captain Bill Huus took her on her last trip. The Knapps pulled it into their shore-side barn behind Fourteen Mile Island with the intent to restore it, but that never happened.

Knapp caretaker Ralph Stiles allowed me to tie up my 1938 Chris-Craft *Alli* anytime I wanted to go visit the *Sayonara*. My young daughter Allison often accompanied me; she loved to explore inside it. By 1986 the Knapp family became concerned that the boat had deteriorated beyond repair. A man was hired to remove all hardware and dismantle the boat, but once he had the mahogany he wanted, he never returned to complete the job.

Ralph Stiles asked my uncle, Robert A. Gates of Bolton, to help him complete the job. They drove a back-hoe through the side of the barn and through the side of the boat to remove the two Chrysler Hemi engines and the Kohler generator. I helped Ralph and my uncle remove all of the remaining hardware. We also brought home the two large brass propeller struts and many of the vertical mahogany window posts. When my uncle died, he left all of these items to me.

On May 7th, 1988, with permission from the Environmental Conservation Department and the Fort Ann Fire Department, Ralph burned the *Sayonara* and her barn on the Knapp Estate shoreline. All that remained were two iron tracks located just beneath the water's surface. Today, these are also gone. A new home and boathouse have just been constructed on the old barn site this year.

Clockwise, *Sayonara's* barn on Knapp Estate. Photo by author.
Sayonara's Name Board. Photo by author.
Sayonara's Wheel, 1960's. Courtesy: Dick Dean. Clock & Barometer. Courtesy: Chris Shaw.
This author, Bill Gates, with my uncle Bob Gates removing remaining hardware from *Sayonara*, 1988. Courtesy: Ralph Stiles.

Elizabeth

The steam powered *Elizabeth* had a comfortable cabin and was owned by Fred Brown. She was 60 feet long, 8 feet wide at her beam and could carry forty people. After the turn-of-the-century, she was owned by Schemerhorn Construction which was based in Lake George Village, operating from the pier at the Lake House Hotel. *Elizabeth* was last known to have sunk in Ticonderoga Creek.

Steam yacht *Elizabeth* in Gull Bay.
Courtesy: Ed and Beth Becker.

Naomi

Naomi at Roger's Rock Hotel Casino.
Courtesy: Dr. G. Peter Cook.

Advertisement, 1900.
Courtesy: Kam Hoopes.

In 1874, the Rogers Rock Hotel was built on the high peninsula that extends into Lake George at the northern end of Rogers Rock Mountain. Originally named Bald, the mountain was renamed in 1758 for Major Robert Rogers who commanded his famous Rogers Rangers here during the French and Indian War's historic Battle on Snow Shoes.

Owning over a mile of lake shore which included the mountain, the hotel enjoyed a wonderful view of the northern end of the lake. To bring new guests from afar, a large steamboat landing was built which still exists today.

In 1903, the Rogers Rock Hotel was purchased by a man named David Williams who renamed it the Rogers Rock Club. Along the shore, there was a large casino where the guests enjoyed swimming, billiards, bowling and entertaining. From here they could charter for $10.00 per day, the hotel's small steamer *Naomi* piloted by Captain George O. Cook who also doubled as the hotel's caretaker. *Naomi* was 25 feet long, 7 feet wide at her beam and could accomodate 15 passengers.

Sagamore

The Lake George Steamboat Company had the steamboat *Sagamore* built at Pine Point in Caldwell to replace *Ticonderoga* (I) which burned the previous year. Modeled after Lake Champlain's steamboat *Chateaugay*, the *Sagamore* was originally 203 feet long, sported an extended beam of 57 feet 6 inches and drafted 7 feet 3 inches. With her new hull of three watertight compartments constructed by the Hollingsworth Shipbuilding Company of Wilmington, Delaware, she was the first steel-hulled steamboat on Lake George. At a cost of $150,000, she could carry up to 1,500 passengers and was capable of speeds up to 20 miles per hour powered by 850 hp W. and A. Fletcher steam engine #184. With her steam powered steering gear, electric lighting and 14 inch search light, she was an efficient and well equipped vessel.

The launching of her hull was held on April 23, 1902 with one of the largest crowds in Caldwell history in attendance. Schools were closed, trolleys arrived overflowing with passengers, a

Sagamore launch day, April 23, 1902.
Courtesy: Lake George Historical Museum.

special train arrived bringing the curious from afar, and the Mohican (I) brought passengers from all the landings along the lake to witness the grand event. By 1:00 pm, over 3000 people had gathered on Pine Point to witness the launching of the *Sagamore*, whose name, like the *Horicon's*, was derived from James Fenimore Cooper's novel, "Last of the Mohicans".

As the 1,125 ton Sagamore began to slide down the ways, Miss Catherine R. Burritt, granddaughter of General Manager Rushlow, christened her bow with the traditional champagne bottle. The *Mohican* (I) then towed her hull over to the main pier where final construction was completed by July 1st. Her first Captain was Elias S. Harris who retired a few months later after having served on Lake George for 59 years. During the christening ceremony, Captain Harris carried on her deck a small anchor, a memento from all of his years on Lake George. This anchor had been with him on the *John Jay* and the *Minne-Ha-Ha*.

For a fare of $1.50, the *Sagamore* departed from Caldwell down the lake, stopping at all hotels and landings. For an additional $1.00, a fine meal was served in the dining room. By fall it became evident that the boat was top heavy and too wide for her length so she was hauled out at Baldwin, cut into two sections and extend-

Sagamore launching. Courtesy: Lake George Historical Museum.

Sagamore's hull at Pine Point. Courtesy: Bolton Historical Museum.

ed 20 feet, making her now 223 feet long. This seemed to solve her difficulties. 1906 was an excellent season for business. That August, the *Sagamore* carried her record crowd of over 1,500 passengers on one voyage. In 1912, the *Sagamore* with 200 passengers aboard, became stuck on the sand bar at Hague for thirty-six hours. Eventually, the *Horicon* was able to pull her off. One of her early passengers was young Franklin D. Roosevelt whose father, James Roosevelt, once served on the board of the company.

Sagamore.
Length, 223 ft.
Beam, 57 1/2 ft.
Draft, 7 ft. 3 in.
Weight, 1,125 tons.
Speed, 20 mph.
Horsepower, 850.
Captain, E.S. Harris.

Author's Collection.

On Friday, July 1, 1927, the *Sagamore* left the Baldwin pier for her regular morning run. Captain John L. Washburn soon experienced visibility problems due to a quickly thickening fog after he left his first landing at Roger's Rock. Forced to run completely by using the compass, the fog thickened even further to such a density that he was unable to see the end of his own bow 75 feet ahead of him. Judging by the clock and listening to the paddlewheel revolutions echoing off Anthony's Nose Mountain, the ship turned left intending to enter Blairs Bay and the Glenburnie dock. She had turned too soon;—she struck the end of Anthony's Nose and split her steel hull severely. Water began pouring in. Captain Washburn immediately realized the seriousness of the situation. The boat was beginning to sink in 170 feet of water. He

STEAMER "SAGAMORE"

Built in 1902, is a magnificent side-wheel steamboat; hull of steel, 224 feet long over all, fitted with Morgan type patent feathering wheels, lighted with electricity, including searchlight, heated and steered by steam; is a model of shipbuilders' art. Large dining cabin is located aft on deck. Price of dinner, $1.00. Passenger capacity, 1,500.

The new steamer "Horicon" will displace the "Sagamore" on the through line in July, 1911.

Ad, Effective June 25, 1911. Courtesy: Dick and Mary Kowell.

ordered matresses to be stuffed into the holes and quickly steamed the final mile to Glenburnie. After passengers and mail were evacuated, he brought the *Sagamore* around to the shallow water north of the pier where the *Sagamore* quickly sank in 18 feet of water.

Three weeks later on July 21st, the *Sagamore* was refloated and towed to Baldwin. Unfortunately, the drydock was not ready to handle the *Sagamore*. After many months of work and $35,000, the railway was ready; she was finally hauled out on December 5th. Extensive repairs were made to the hull and to all of her first deck woodwork which had suffered water damage. All of her hazelwood, cherry paneling, mirrors, carpeting and gold leaf had to be replaced, costing over $30,000. During the remainder of that 1927 season, the *Mohican* (II) and *Horicon* (II) modified their schedules to accommodate the passenger service.

The *Sagamore* was repaired and back in service in May of 1928. She continued her service until 1932 when she was retired. She was a successful enterprise for over three decades. After spending 5 years tied up at Baldwin, the *Sagamore* was finally dismantled in 1937.

Photo 1, *Sagamore's* record breaking crowd, August 1906. Author's Collection.

Photo 2, *Sagamore* sunk at Glenburnie, July 1, 1927. Courtesy: Bill Dow, Lake George Steamboat Co.

Photo 3, *Sagamore* at Glenburnie. Courtesy: Bob Benway.

Photo 4, Spoon from steamboat *Sagamore*, "Sagamore LGSC". Courtesy, Sandi Aldrich.

Photo 5, 1911 schedule. Courtesy: Dick and Mary Kowell.

Distances.	LANDINGS	HORICON Daily	SAGAMORE Daily except Sunday	SAGAMORE Sundays July 9 to Aug. 27		Distances.	LANDINGS	HORICON Daily	SAGAMORE Daily except Sunday	SAGAMORE Sundays July 9 to August 27	
		AM	PM	PM				PM	AM	PM	
0	Lake George......Lv	9.40	4.00	4.30	......	0	Baldwin......Lv	1.20	7.30	1.00	......
4	Antlers............				......	1	Rogers Rock......	1.30	7.35		......
5	Assembly Point....	9.55	4.20		......	4	Glenburnie........		7.50	s 1.15	......
6	Cleverdale........	10.00	4.30		......	6	Hague............	1.45	8.00	s 1.25	......
7	Rockhurst.........	10.05	4.35		......	8	Glen Eyrie........		8.15		......
7	Trout Pavilion.....	10.10	4.40		......	10	Silver Bay........	⸹ 2.00	8.25		......
10	Marion...........	10.25	4.50	s 5.00	......	11	Uncas............	2.05	8.30		......
12	Pilot Knob.......	10.35	5.00		......	12	Sabbath Day Point.	2.10	8.40	s 1.45	......
15	Bolton............	10.50	5.15		......	14	Huletts...........	2.20	8.50	s 1.50	......
15	Sagamore........	11.00	5.20	s 5.20	......	19	Paradise Bay......				......
18	Pearl Point.......	11.15	5.35	s 5.30	......	21	Pearl Point......Ar	2.50	9.20	2.20	......
19	Paradise Bay.....				......	21	Pearl Point......Lv	2.50	9.20	2.20	......
24	Huletts...........	11.50	6.05	s 6.05	......	23	Sagamore.........	3.00	9.35	2.40	......
26	Sabbath Day Point.	12.00	6.15	s 6.10	......	23	Bolton............	3.10	9.40	2.50	......
27	Uncas............	12.10	6.25		......	26	Pilot Knob........	3.20	9.50		......
28	Silver Bay........	⸹12.15	6.35		......	29	Marion...........	3.30	10.00		......
30	Glen Eyrie........		6.45		......	31	Trout Pavilion.....	3.50	10.20	s 3.15	......
32	Hague............	12.30	6.55	s 6.30	......	32	Rockhurst.........	3.55	10.25	s 3.20	......
34	Glenburnie........		7.10		......	32	Cleverdale........	4.00	10.30	s 3.25	......
37	Rogers Rock......	12.55	7.25		......	33	Assembly Point....	4.10	10.40	s 3.35	......
38	Baldwin........Ar	1.10	7.30	6.55	......	34	Antlers...........				......
.....	Baldwin, D. & H.Lv	1.15	PM	PM	......	38	Lake George.....Ar	4.40	11.10	4.00	......
.....	Ft. Ticonderoga, D&H Ar	1.30 PM			......			PM	AM	PM	

Top, *Sagamore* at the Baldwin dry-dock for repairs.
Courtesy: Don Cornell.

Middle, *Sagamore's* relaunching at Baldwin. Courtesy: Bill Dow, Lake George Steamboat Company.

Bottom, *Sagamore* Officers and Crew, 1931. Courtesy: Bill Dow, Lake George Steamboat Co.

Harris Houseboat

My brother Bud and I accompanied our grandmother, Nettie G. (Harris) Gates, and our Aunt Zilpha to a large Harris family reunion at Harris Bay on Lake George in the summer of 1952. Although I was only 7 years old at the time, I instantly fell in love with Russell and Isabelle Harris's old houseboat a few doors away. The whole concept of living on the water appealed to me then and still does today.

There were only a few houseboats on Lake George at the beginning of the twentieth century. They were originally built for hunters and to house the men who logged the mountains around the lake during the lumbering era. Being mobile, they could be towed to any shoreline location, giving these men easy access to their current work site. Later, a few were built strictly for pleasure.

The Harris houseboat is a rare 1903 survivor of that bygone era. When the lumbering era ended on the lake, lumberer Gerome Lapham's son Byron hired the Schermerhorn Brothers Construction Company of Bolton and Lake George to upgrade the houseboat into a summer cottage. The Lapham family previously had a cottage in the Narrows on Phantom Island. When the State of New York claimed the island, the Laphams moved onto their houseboat and moored it nearby at Big Burnt Island. They used their small steam (later converted to naptha) launch for towing and daily transportation.

It was (and is still) 65 feet long and 18 feet wide. The original hull was barge shaped with flat ends and made of oak; today the barge is removed and it rests on 50 stilts in 4 ∏ feet of water. There originally were 4 bedrooms and a kitchen; today two bedrooms have been converted

Top, Harris Houseboat, Big Burnt, 1903. Courtesy: Byron & Joan Lapham
Bottom, Harris Houseboat today. Photo by Author.

into a living room. The original porch roof was canvas; today it is metal. Today the bathroom has a chemical toilet, and bathroom facilities have been constructed into a shoreside building. It still has the original railings around the three-sided first deck porch with three hinged railing bars for easy access to a boat.

In 1915, it was sold to Beecher Clothier, a county attorney. He "ring and cabled" it to two trees on shore in Harris Bay in that same year and it has never been moved since. In the early 1940's, it was placed on stilts. Beecher was quite a sight to young H. Russell Harris who recalls that Beecher had only one good eye and always smoked cigars on the porch. Beecher's wife didn't like boats so he built for her the small cottage that still stands behind it today. Perhaps she had a premonition because Beecher fell out of his Chris-Craft speedboat in 1951 and drowned. His wife immediately sold the speedboat but remained attached to the houseboat. After some coaxing, Russell and Isabelle Harris bought it in 1952.

Russell first saw the houseboat in 1915 when he would go swimming near it after working all day in the hay fields. Isabelle first saw it in 1927 when she and Russell were married. She loved it and hoped to someday own it. People thought she was crazy to have such notions since she had never learned to swim. She "just liked to be near the water." Twenty four years later, her wish came true. When they bought it, they said they would enjoy it forever–and they have.

A houseboat has problems of a different kind. In 1985, the stilts were raised one foot. To quote my cousin Peggy, their daughter who was raised there every summer with her sister Connie, "We got tired of getting our feet wet! Every time a boat would race by, the waves would come through the house!" Isabelle told me about the time a family of beavers began living beneath the boat–"All night long they rolled and thumped the hull." Isabelle thought she could disturb them into moving away by thumping the floor throughout the night with a hammer every time they woke her up, but Peggy said, "She made more noise than the beavers!"

While visiting with my relatives in the houseboat a few summers ago, we all were transported back in time by our surroundings and by the pleasant constant lapping of Lake George beneath our feet. Russell began talking of Moses Harris and our first Harris ancestors to the region. They had seen the lake during the Revolutionary War and vowed to settle here afterwards. Moses Jr. owned from what is now Top-of-the-World to far beyond the Washington County line, including all of Harrisina. Russell then spoke of ancient family steamboat Captains Leander, Walter, Elias, and Stephen Harris and our longtime tradition of being associated with the lake's history. Of the houseboat, Russell said he had no idea back when he was making 35 cents an hour that he could ever own such an enjoyable thing. He's proud that four generations of the family enjoy it now.

While looking out the windows at the sunset over Harris Bay, I felt the happy spirits of everyone who has been associated with this houseboat for its past magnificent one hundred years.

Above, Houseboat. Old Lake George Postcard. Author's collection.

Right, Old Houseboat on Lake George. Rare photo of a hunting party. Courtesy: Dawn Gates Macey.

Scioto

Scioto at LG Village. Fred C. Thatcher photo. Courtesy: The Thatcher family.

At the beginning of the 20th Century, there were numerous mid-sized steamboats plying the waters of Lake George. They belonged to the lake's many wealthy mansion owners or to enterprising individuals who sold tickets for sightseeing excursions around the lake. The *Scioto* was one of these boats. She was 75 feet long with a 12 foot beam. The enclosed aft-cabin was constructed of mahogany with interior benches covered with green seat cushions. She was originally powered by a Seabury engine.

Her first owner was a summer cottager from Bolton named Gilbert who sailed her for his private enjoyment around 1903. Later, during the World War I years, she made daily trips to the several small hotels in the Kattskill Bay region as a member of the Kattskill Bay Line fleet under Captain Frank Hamilton, owner. By 1922, *Scioto* was sailing to Paradise Bay from Shepard Park dock in Lake George Village.

Her final owner was Paul Goodness who rebuilt her during the late 1930's to accommodate 75 passengers. He also installed twin oversized gasoline engines for his daily trips to Kattskill Bay at 10:30 AM and 7:30 PM. His Paradise Bay and scenic coves trip departed at 2:00 PM. Goodness hired an announcer named Clark Lord to speak into a new amplifier for announcing information enroute. Paul's son Lynn told me that when he was young, he would sit on his father's lap and help turn the big wheel. Scioto's last dock was behind the present Lake George Post Office, now Kurosaka Lane.

In 1949, the tired old *Scioto* (sometimes dubbed *Sciota*) was stripped of all her hardware and towed out near the Canoe Islands where her hull was lanced with several swings of an ax before she settled to the bottom of the lake. Lynn still owns the brass wheel with walnut handles and the brass binacle with kerosine side lantern which his father removed from the *Scioto* before she was scuttled.

Less than one year later, in August of 1950, Paul Goodness was gone, too. He was struck by a car and killed while crossing the street in Lake George Village in front of Kurosaka Lane, near where the *Scioto* also spent her final hours.

Good for ONE
SPEED BOAT RIDE
WALTER P. HARRIS
No. 380

Two generations of Harris have been Pilots and Captains on Lake George continuously for ninety years.

Scioto ticket donated by John Hilton. Courtesy: Bolton Historical Museum.

KATTSKILL BAY LINE
The new steam yacht
SCIOTO
Capacity 50 passengers

Will leave the Lake House and the D. & H. R.R. dock daily at 9:45 a. m. via East shore returning via West shore, arriving at Lake George station at 12 m.

2:30 p. m. via West shore; returning via East shore arriving at Lake George station at 5 p. m.

7:55 p. m. or on arrival of D. & H. train via East shore; returning via West shore arriving at Lake George station at 10:00 p. m.

Sundays an extra trip is made leaving Lake George at 5 p. m. via West shore, returning via East shore arriving at 6:30

Fare for round trip 50c   Between ports 25c

FRANK HAMILTON, CAPTAIN.

1915 *Scioto* Ad.
Courtesy: Lake George Historical Museum.

Scioto's remains on bottom of Lake George. Courtesy: Bob Benway & Bateaux Below, Inc.

Scioto and *Sayonara* at the July 12, 1927 $10,000 swim marathon. Photo by J.S. Wooley. Courtesy: Jim Shaughnessy.

Watrous & Lake George Monster

Harry Watrous of Hague. Courtesy: John and Betty Barth.

In 1904, the one of the most famous practical jokes in Lake George history was played by Hague's Harry Watrous on his best friend, Colonel William D'Alton Mann, owner of the *Saunterer* mentioned earlier. The two men had engaged themselves in a private contest to determine who was the best fisherman. Several days later, Colonel Mann pretended to catch a real trout which might have weighed 30 pounds if it hadn't been made of wood. Watrous was easily fooled for awhile since Mann was some distance away in his own boat. Not to be outdone, Harry Watrous conjured up an idea that would make history. Watrous, who had once been a sculptor, carved a wooden monster from a log, painted it green and black and attached two green elecrtical insulators for eyes. Watrous rigged the monster beneath the lake's surface on an elaborate pulley system which allowed the monster to appear and quickly disappear. Colonel Mann was so surprised when the monster appeared before him that he fell out of his boat. This story spread quickly around the lake and soon it appeared in the New York Times.

Lake George Monster.
Courtesy: Walter Grishkot.

The monster was discovered in 1919 on the Watrous estate and later it found its way to the Virgin Islands. It was rediscovered in 1971 by Shirley Armstrong and Walter Grishkot and was displayed at the Lake George Historical Society. During the summer of 2001, the monster once again made the headlines. During a mock trial at the old Warren County Courthouse, it was decided that the monster would forever be shared by the Hague, Bolton Landing and Lake George Historical Societies. The monster was paraded down the lake from Lake George to Bolton and finally to Hague in a wonderful procession of antique boats. Interestingly, we all fell for another great Lake George Monster hoax that day. An exact duplicate was secretly made for the day-long journey to insure the safety of the original. None of us in the procession realized it until we reached Hague and the two monsters were displayed for us side-by-side.

July 7, 2001. Lake George Monster delivered to Hague. Left, Lake George Historical Society in *Pamelaine*. Photo by author. Middle, Bolton Historical Society in *19+*. Courtesy: Brian Granger. Right, Hague Historical Society. Photo by author.

Forward

William K. Bixby of Bolton Landing owned The American Car & Foundry Company in Saint Louis. His son Harold later financed Charles Lindberg in 1927 on his famous flight to Paris in the Spirit of St. Louis. Bixby, who owned several boats, owned the *Forward* in 1906. An August newspaper that summer mentions that the *Forward* was used for a family wedding. The wedding couple was "met at Lake George and conveyed to Bolton in W.K. Bixby's new launch *Forward* and taken back to Lake George later in the day." *Forward* was 45 feet long and was powered by twin 30 HP engines. She was sunk during the 1930's without any written account. In 1989, *Forward* was rediscovered in 40 feet of water east of Diamond Island. The dive site, overseen by Bateaux Below, Inc., became the first Submerged Heritage Preserve in New York

Forward. Courtesy: Ted Caldwell.

Wininnish

The "Auto-Boat" *Wininnish*, sometimes referred to as the *Winnish*, was owned by LeGrand C. Cramer of Cramer Point on the Lake George to Bolton Road. LeGrand was the son of George Cramer, one time President of the Rensselaer and Saratoga Railroad which later became the Delaware and Hudson. She was a Consolidated Speedway, built by Charles L. Seabury and the New York Gas and Power and Electric Company. With a powerful Standard engine, Cramer used her for Penant Racing. Her top slid up from the sides over brass bows, a system known then as a "Navy Top". On August 17, 1907, *Wininnish* won the Sagamore and Broesel Cups while racing in the Lake George Club Regatta.

Wininnish.

Above, Courtesy: Bob Benway.

Left, Courtesy: Lake George Village Historian.

Kiowa

In 1907, the Horicon Lodge comissioned Captain Hiram Hyde of Sandy Hill (Hudson Falls) to construct the *Kiowa* to be hired by guests for excursions. *Kiowa* was 40 feet long, 5 feet 8 inches wide at the beam and was powered by a 14 HP Fay & Bowen engine. Made of white oak and mahogany, her estimated speed was 14 mph. George A. Ferris was her captain.

Frank Bushbaum and Harvey Niemer bought *Kiowa* in the late 1920's and used her briefly for charters to the Narrows and other hotels. Soon thereafter, she began to deteriorate rapidly and was scuttled.

Courtesy: Fort Edward Historical Museum's Jim Cronkhite Collection.

Grace

Grace was a 30 foot naptha launch owned by Charles and Emma Ervien. She was built on Lake George sometime before 1907 by a man named Tuttle. The Ervien's first vacationed on Lake George at the Pearl Point Hotel in the Narrows. Soon after, they began renting an East Indian bungalow owned by Delavan Bloodgood on Hen and Chickens Island. That same bungalow stands today on Watch Point. Later, they purchased a parcel of lakeshore property in Northwest Bay, just south of today's Adirondack Park Motel. When Charles died, the property was sold and subdivided. Grace was sold before Charles died, sometime between 1910 to 1915. Charles' grandson, Bob Ervien of Assembly Point, is the proud owner today of several mementos from the Grace.

Grace with Charles and Emma Ervien in Northwest Bay, Lagoon Manor in background.
Lantern and Flag were on Grace. Flag depicts the family Coat of Arms. Courtesy: Bob Ervien.

Grace (another Grace)

Another Grace at a regatta at Baldwin. Photo, Author's collection.

Mohican (II)

When the wooden hulled *Mohican* (I) began showing signs of age in 1906 after only twelve years of service, the Lake George Steamboat Company decided to replace her with a new steel hulled vessel as was done with the Sagamore in 1902. The finest marine architect in the nation, J.P. Millard of New York City, was hired to design her. It was decided that the T.S. Marvel Shipbuilding Company in Newburg, New York would build her. The hull was bolted together first in Newburg and inspected. It was then dismantled and shipped to the Baldwin Shipyard on Lake George near Ticonderoga where it was reassembled and completed throughout the summer of 1907. She was launched at 11 AM on Saturday December 14th of that year and was christened by Miss Louise Loree, the daughter of the D&H Company's

Mohican (II) built at Baldwin, Fall 1907. Courtesy: Bill Dow.

President, Mr. L.F. Loree. The *Mohican* was almost named *Uncas* after the hero in James Fenimore Cooper's "Last of the Mohicans", however she was christened *Mohican* because she was close in design to the beloved *Mohican* (I) which was scheduled to be dismantled.

Mohican (II), also depicted on front cover, launched 1907. Author's collection.

Mohican (II), 1910. Author's collection.

Her specifications were reported as:— length 117 feet, beam 26.5 feet, displacement 198 tons, and powered by "two inverted, direct-acting Fletcher-built compound steam engines, with a high pressure cylinder of ten inches in diameter, low pressure cylinder 21 1/2 inches, and 16 inch stroke with two water tube boilers providing steam", as quoted from the Glens Falls Star. *Mohican* (I) had only a single screw; *Mohican* (II) had twin 58 inch propellers bringing her speed up to 15 mph. The main deck had a freight space forward capable of carrying a Model T Ford, a purser's office was on the rubber tiled quarter deck, and lunch counters and officer's quar-

Mohican (II) at Lake George Steamboat Company, 1950. Courtesy: Dick Kowell.

ters were also aboard on the quarter deck. A carpeted ladies cabin was provided aft on the main deck featuring cherry and butternut, finished to show the natural wood.

Under the command of 66 year old Captain Wesley Finkle, the new *Mohican* began her duties in 1908 by taking over the Paradise Bay cruises and by running opposite the other steamers to provide better service. Mr. Finkle had been a pilot for 20 years and a captain for 14 years when he took command of the *Mohican*.

The Great Depression and World War II hurt the tourist business on Lake George to the extent that by 1945, the only boat owned by the Lake George Steamboat Company was the Mohican. At that time, the small struggling company was purchased by admiralty lawyer Wilbur E. Dow Jr. At the end of 1946, Mr. Dow directed *Mohican* Captain Walter P. Harris to deliver the boat to its drydock where it was converted from steam to diesel power under new design plans by Sparkman & Stevens of New York. Olin Stevens supervised the sleek remodeling of her looks which included the installation of four General Motors 671 engines. Captain Harris retired in that 1947 year and was replaced by new Captain George Doane.

Mohican (II) Ad, June 1946. Courtesy: Bill Dow.

Mohican (II) showing sleek new look, 1950. Courtesy: Dick Kowell.

The *Mohican*'s flawless record was interrupted briefly in the dark of the night on August 7, 1965. With a charter of 340 people aboard, she was sailing off the shores of Huletts Landing when she struck Whaleback Rock on her starboard side tearing off some plating and damaging her starboard shaft and propeller. The captain quickly and safely disembarked the passengers at the Hulett's dock. Realizing that the pumps were unable to keep up with the incoming water, he brought the boat into the beach to the north and let it safely settle in shallow water. With assistance the following morning from her sister ship *Ticonderoga*, she was brought to the drydock, repaired and was back in service in only 7 days.

In 1967, she was remodeled again from plans designed by Tiedeman & Sons of New Jersey. The sleek 1946 hull style was totally replaced back to her original traditional steamboat look which she still has today. In 1998, her engines were replaced with two Caterpillar diesels totaling 760 hp. During 2001, the *Mohican* underwent another restoration overseen by John Gilbert & Associates of Boston, prominent marine architects. Steamboat Company Engineers John Meyer, James Bessett and welder Hank Overbeck brought her up to Coast Guard "K-Boat" Standards which includes removal of all portholes, adding two additional water-tight bulkheads (giving her now a total of 7 water-tight walls), new wiring and plumbing and new inclining (stability) standards. Even the pilothouse has been beautifully refinished in mahogany by carpenter Mike Curri.

Open stern, 1950's. Courtesy: Dick Kowell.

Most of us alive today grew up with the *Mohican*. We think of her with the same affection we bestow on any of our loved ones. Like an old tree in the mountains, we could easily take her for granted because she has been here all of our lives. I had no idea when I was a youngster growing up in Bolton Landing that I'd be piloting her today. Captains

```
            FROM
        TICONDEROGA
          M/V MOHICAN
       (July 2nd thru Sept. 5th)
       (Daylight Saving Time)
              LEAVE
  Ticonderoga Landing *      10:00 AM
  Hague                       10:20
  Silver Bay                  10:45
  Huletts Landing             11:05
  Bolton Landing              11:50
              ARRIVE
  Lake George Steel Pier **   12:30 PM
              LEAVE
  Lake George Steel Pier       4:40
  Bolton Landing               5:20
  Huletts Landing              6:05
  Silver Bay                   6:25
  Hague                        6:40
              ARRIVE
  Ticonderoga Landing          7:00
  ROUND TRIP FARE    .   $3.00 (Including Tax)
```

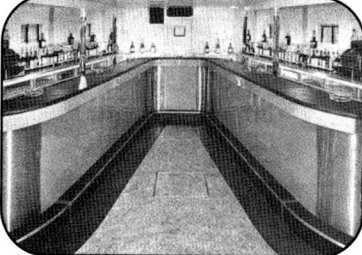

Mohican (II), 1950's Lounge and Snack Bar. Author's collection.

1950's *Mohican* (II) Schedule. Author's collection.

Mohican (II) towing skiers, 1960's publicity photo. Courtesy: Bill Dow, L.G. Steamboat Co.

Tom Conerty and Ed Stanilka contacted me back in 1987 and hired me aboard. I've piloted the "*Mo*" and the "*Saint*" since then, every season. There are literally hundreds of wonderful stories that can be told of our adventures on the *Mohican* throughout the years. Current Captains Tom Conerty, Ed Stanilka, Darrell Finlayson, Lee Taber, Don Cornell, Ray Mound, George LaPoint and I each have our own unique *Mohican* stories to tell –great stories.

History continues to be made on the *Mohican* every day as she heads off for her full lake Discovery Cruise or her regular Paradise Bay trips. New passengers are totally amazed to see the *Mohican* enter Paradise Bay. Often she is chartered for an

Baldwin Drydock from *Mohican* (II).
Photo by Author.

Mohican (II) on Baldwin Drydock, 2001.
Courtesy: Brian Granger.

Mohican (II) in 14 Mile Island channel.
Photo by Author.

Mohican (II) entering Bolton Bay, 1999.
Photo by Author.

evening, for a wedding or a corporate party. No two days on her are ever alike. Every day brings the unexpected and we all love the tradition of stopping at Bolton Landing and Baldwin. Whenever you see her out on Lake George, you can be certain that our crew is having as much fun as our passengers.

On February 2, 2002, the *Mohican* made history once again. For only the second time in 100 years, Lake George failed to freeze over. Like a group of anxious school boys, ten of us decided we would do something that had never been done before in the entire history of the Lake George Steamboat Company since it was formed in 1817. We took one of our big boats, the *Mohican*, the entire length of the lake, to Baldwin and back—in February! It was a COLD trip, but we all had a great day.

Recently, Steamboat Company Owner and President Bill Dow began the paperwork to place the *Mohican* on the National Register of Historic Places. While we discussed the boat's new improvements and colorful history in Bill's office recently, Bill turned proudly toward the *Mohican* out his office window and remarked,—"There's no reason now why she can't be around for another hundred years". We all hope she will be.

Mohican (II) Pilothouse, 1999. Photo by Author.

February 2, 2002 after *Mohican* (II) took historic "no ice" winter trip to Baldwin and back. Photo: Author's collection.

Apperson Canoe

Morris canvas-covered wooden canoes were first built at Veazie, Maine around 1882. In fact, they were the first canvas-covered canoes ever to be advertised, appearing in Field and Stream magazine in 1887. B.N. Morris sold his canoes in four models, ranging in length between 12 to 20 feet. In 1920, his factory was totally burned by an arsonist. After the fire, Morris continued to build his boats on a limited scale up into the late 1930's in his small shop.

John S. Apperson (1882-1963) was a regular friend and customer in my parent's diner, Bill Gates Diner in Bolton Landing, which is now at the Adirondack Museum in Blue Mountain Lake. John was a very quiet, interesting and determined man. He began living in Schenectady in 1900 and quickly adopted Lake George for enjoyment and preservation. He began a life-long obsession with the lake at that time and left a legacy for all of us who enjoy the lake today.

John Apperson began coming to the lake every week all year round beginning in 1907. He was impressed by the Narrows and the natural beauty

John Apperson, West Dollar Island, 1920's. Courtesy: Tom Apperson.

of the mountains and islands. In 1909, he became concerned that the Dollar Islands were beginning to erode, so he began "rip-rapping" them with rocks along their shoreline for protection. Over his lifetime, he helped to preserve over 50 islands and encouraged New York State to begin taking over this job in 1917. This same great man purchased Dome Island after hearing that it might be sold for development. He kept Dome preserved throughout his lifetime until he turned it over to the Nature Conservancy for preservation. Apperson also was appalled during

Tom Apperson delivering his uncle John Apperson's Morris canoe to the Bolton Historical Museum, Fall 2000. Courtesy: Ted Caldwell.

the 1920's when he was told that the new highway over Tongue Mountain might be cut along the shoreline of the Narrows. His relentless lobbying against that plan was successful which is the reason our Narrows still has its original natural charm. John, who never married, once explained, "Lake George is my wife, and the islands are my children."

Although John Apperson had a motorized boat, he did most of his exploration of the lake in his Morris canoe. John also entered it in the 1921 American Canoe Association regatta which was held from his property in Huddle Bay which was located on the site of the old Lake View Hotel. This well known canoe was kept by John's relatives after John died in 1963 and was rarely used. In September 2000, John's nephew, Tom Apperson, paddled this canoe on its final voyage from Huddle Bay to Rogers Park in Bolton where it is now on displayat the Bolton Historical Museum.

Mountaineer (II)

New *Mountaineer* (II), 1912. Courtesy: Bill Dow, L.G. Steamboat Co.

The Lake George Steamboat Company's *Pampero* was assigned to transport passengers to a series of small piers along the southern end of Lake George in 1910. By 1911, it became evident that a larger vessel was needed to accommodate a growing number of passengers.

Alexander McDonald of Mariner's Harbor in Staten Island, N.Y. was hired to construct the *Mountaineer* along the most modern of designs. Her size was limited by the railroad clearances, since a train would be transporting her to Lake George Village. She was 70 feet in length, carried a 12 foot 6 inch beam, drafted 3 feet 9

Mountaineer (II). Courtesy: Esko Virta.

inches and was constructed of White Oak. An enclosed cabin ran practically the entire length of the yacht. Her single engine was a six-cylinder model of 125 horsepower which could push her to speeds of 15 mph.

The new 75 passenger *Mountaineer* was launched on June 8, 1912 at Staten Island and was christened by Irma Williams, niece of the late W.H. Williams, who had been the company's vice president.

After her christening cruise, her raised structures and stack were removed for easy transport north. She was towed up the Hudson and loaded onto a train for the trip to Lake George. The railroad maintained a submerged track for boat launchings at Lake George Village. It is still visible today on a calm clear morning, slightly east of the Lake George Steamboat Company's Steel Pier.

Her schedule was to leave Lake George Village at 10:00 AM, 3:00 PM, 5:00 PM and 8:00 PM, stopping at all the small landings along the southern end of the lake. Later, her evening trips went north as far as the Sagamore Hotel.

The *Mountaineer* was removed from service in 1918 due to World War I, and she continued to rest on shore at the Baldwin drydock until 1920, when she was once again put into service.

One foggy morning, while on a trip to Paradise Bay, she struck the rocky reef and was totally lifted out of the water. Fortunately, no passengers were injured and the *Mountaineer* received only minor damage.

By 1922, she was becoming obsolete and her costs to operate efficiently were quite high. The decision was made to remove her from service. She lay idle until 1927 when she was sold to Mr. O.R. Mitchell of Glens Falls who converted her into a houseboat. She lasted into the late 1930's when she finally disintegrated along the shore of Warner Bay.

Mountaineer runs aground.
Top left, courtesy: L.G. Village Historian.
Top right & bottom left, courtesy: L.G. Historical Museum.
Bottom right, new spray rail. Courtesy: L.G. Village Historian.

Horicon (II)

By 1908, *Horicon* (I) had aged to a point where major expenditures were required to put her back in first class operating condition. Rather than spend forty thousand dollars on a thirty three year old ship, the Lake George Steamboat Company decided to build a new one. *Horicon* (II) was designed by J.W. Millard & Brother of New York. In 1909, her construction contract was awarded to the W. & A. Fletcher Company of Hoboken, N.J. who installed engine serial #206 and sublet the hull construction to the T. S. Marvel Shipbuilding Company in Newburgh, N.Y. She was constructed at the Baldwin Shipyard on northern Lake George throughout 1910 at a cost of $210,000 with joiner work done by carpen-

Top, *Horicon* (II) under construction at Baldwin, November 17, 1910.
Bottom, hull stuck on the ways at launching, December 1, 1910. Courtesy: Lake George Historical Association.

ters of the Lake George Steamboat Company. Her was launching at 11 AM on Thursday December 1st during inclement weather. Mrs. Clarence S. Sims, wife of the General Manager and Vice President of the D&H Railroad, broke the traditional champagne bottle during the *Horicon*'s christening ceremony.

Able to carry more than 1,500 passengers, she was the longest, fastest and best equipped of all the vessels ever built to sail on the lake. The twin boilers were of the lobster tubular return type and the stroke of the piston was ten feet, producing 1280 horsepower. She was 230 feet long and 59 feet wide across her beam. Her 1175 displacement tons drafted 7 feet 5 inches, and she traveled at speeds reaching 21 miles per hour under her first Captain, John L. Washburn. Her patent feathering wheels were twenty-two and one half inches wide and had curved steel buckets. *Horicon* (II)'s elegant dining room seated 100 guests and was paneled in butternut with cherry trimming. Her saloon deck allowed for several small parties to be held simultaneously in the several small cabins which had been built here. During the 1920's, she was modified to carry small automobiles between landings on her first deck stern. Horicon left Lake George at 10:00 AM, arriving at 1:00 PM at Baldwin. She returned to Lake George at 4:30 PM.

When the new highway was completed over Tongue Mountain in the late 1920's, the number of steamboat passengers dropped off significantly. In 1933, Senator Frederick Kavanaugh, who

Horicon (II) construction at Baldwin, March 17, 1911. Courtesy: Lake George Historical Association.

Horicon (II) carring record crowd of 1,560 passengers. Courtesy: Mike DeLarm.

Horicon (II), 1931, Officers and Crew. Courtesy: Ed Stanilka.

lived north of town in Bolton, leased the Lake George Steamboat Company with the idea of importing well known bands to draw customers. From 1933 to 1938, the *Horicon* became known as the "Show Boat" due to her popular evening dance cruises every summer, Wednesday through Sunday. My father once told me that he and his friends would often go down to the shoreline at night to listen to the dance music of Howard LeRoy's orchestra flowing across the water as the *Horicon* (II) passed through Bolton Bay.

By 1937, she was making two 2 1/2 hour trips daily at a cost of $1.00 per passenger under Captain Alanson A. Fisher. She never sailed once during 1939 due to the effects of the Great Depression and the approaching World War II. That fall she was sold to a Troy scrap iron company for $5,000 and was dismantled at Baldwin where she began her life 28 years earlier.

Horicon (II). Courtesy: Lake George Historical Association.

Passengers aboard *Horicon* (II). Courtesy: Lake George Historical Association.

As with most old ships which were dismantled, parts of *Horicon* (II) still live on today. Her helm was actually two large wooden wheels with a drum in the center for the steering cables to wrap around. One of those original wheels is now part of a wall display on the Lake George Steamboat Company's *Lac du Saint Sacrement*, and the other is still in use today in the pilothouse of the *Minne-Ha-Ha* (II). Although it was not known at the time, she was to be the last of the great sidewheelers to be built for Lake George.

Horicon (II) Dining Room and staff. Courtesy: Mike DeLarm.

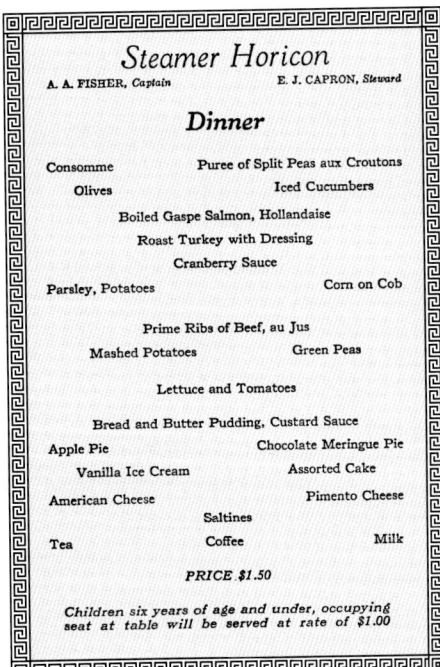
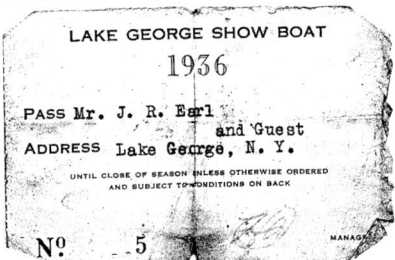
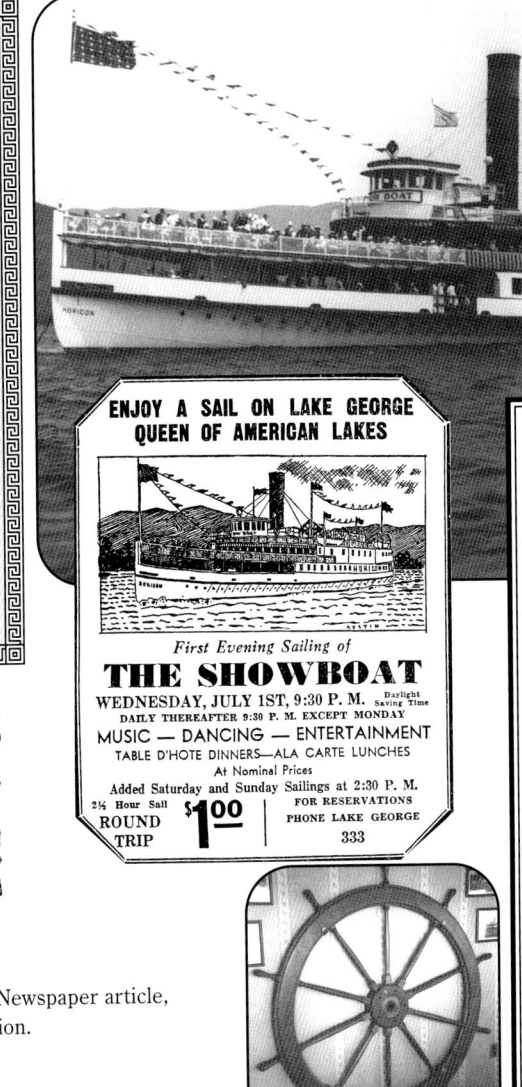

Horicon (II) Menu, 1936 Showboat Ad and Newspaper article, courtesy: Lake George Historical Association.
Showboat photo, author's collection.
1936 Pass, courtesy: Wayde Earl.
Horicon (II) wheel aboard *Lac du Saint Sacrement*. Photo by author.

Show Me III

W.K. Bixby of St. Louis, owner of the boats *Forward* and *St. Louis*, raced a fast boat in 1906 when the Lake George Regatta Association sponsored their first Lake George races. Bixby raced in the *Show Me II* at speeds up to 20 mph for six years until she capsized. *Show Me III* used that same 1911 Van Blerck six-cylinder engine, now equipped with electric starter, up to 32 mph speeds. Bixby once raced *Show Me III* in a 15 mile race with only 29 minutes of elapsed time.

Show Me III, 1911. Courtesy: Henry Caldwell.

86

Ankle Deep (1914 Gold Cup Races)

Lake George has attracted many interesting and talented individuals to its shores during the past 200 years. One of the most flamboyant was Count Casimir S. Mankowski. Tallwoods, his home on Lake George, was located north of Bolton Landing where the Contessa Restaurant is located today. The Count's wife came from wealthy California stock and wasn't the only young American woman who traded her fortune by marrying for a title.

The restless Count raced a small boat named the *Gem* in some local races and decided to indulge himself into fame by entering the world famous American Power Boat Association's Gold Cup Speedboat Challenge Race in 1912. These races had been dominated since they began in 1904 by the Columbia Yacht Club of New York City and the St. Lawrence River contenders.

Ankle Deep. Author's collection.
Count Casimir S. Mankowski.
Countess Clara Mankowski.
Courtesy: Wauneata Waller.

The 32 foot boat he ordered was named *Ankle Deep,* and was powered by a 300 hp engine. *Ankle Deep* arrived from Detroit directly to the Thousand Islands race course in 1912 at the last possible moment–the day of the race! The only practice the Count had in piloting it was the distance from his dock in Clayton to the starting line. During the race, the Count lost control of his unfamiliar new boat; he and his mechanician rolled it over and sank it to the bottom of the St. Lawrence..

The following year was a totally different situation. This time Count Mankowski was prepared for Alexandria Bay's 1913 Gold Cup Races, once again in the Thousand Islands, and the support from his Lake George sponsors and fans was overwhelming. The Count would not let them down. On the first day of the big event, *Ankle Deep* raced from a poor last place start to win the 30-mile first heat. After winning again on the second day, there was a strong fear among his Lake George fans that the Count's luck wouldn't last. To everyone's amazement, *Ankle Deep* achieved international fame by winning the 1913 Gold Cup. Horns blasted and wild fans screamed. Celebrations lasted for days afterward, especially when the Count selected his hometown of Bolton Landing on Lake George as the site for the Gold Cup Races in 1914.

The actual 1913 winner's cup went to the Count's sponsor, the Lake George Regatta Association. The Count received an embossed certificate stating, on the: "1st day of November–from the Secretary of the American Power Boat Association to Hydroplane *Ankle Deep*–Gold Cup Winner–sanctioned by the Thousand Islands Yacht Club–31 July to 12 August, 1913–Elapsed time 2 hours, 22 minutes, 25 seconds–Course 87 nautical miles–Speed 36.66 nautical miles per hour–5 competitions–(signed by) Mooris M. Whitaker." I own this original framed certificate. It came to me through my two uncles, Walter "Smokey" Gates and

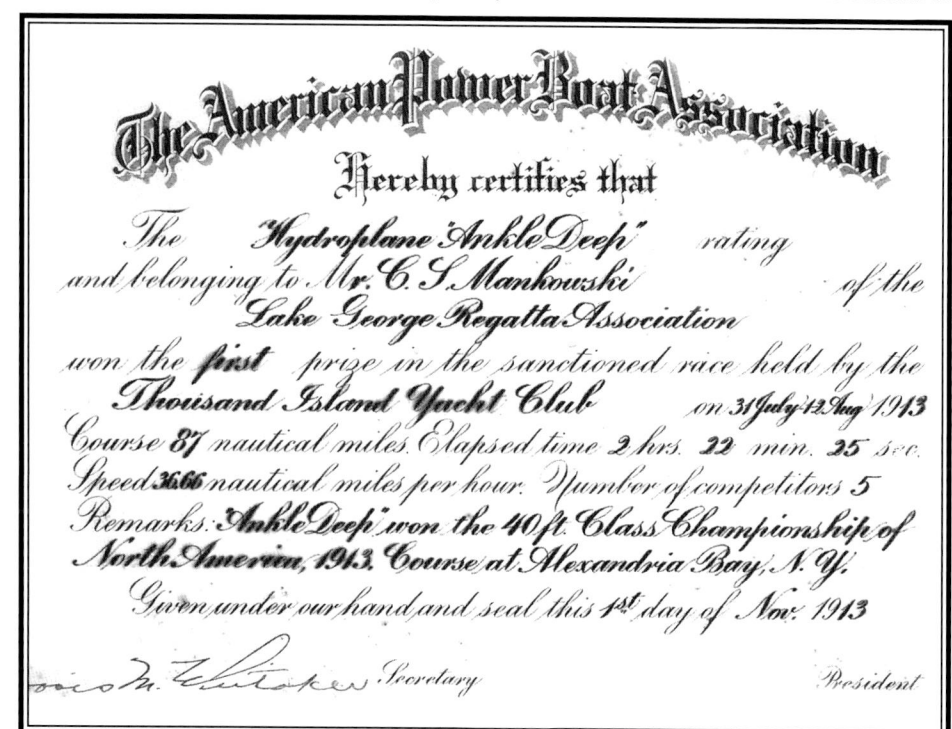

Ankle Deep's original 1913 embossed certificate in collection of author.

87

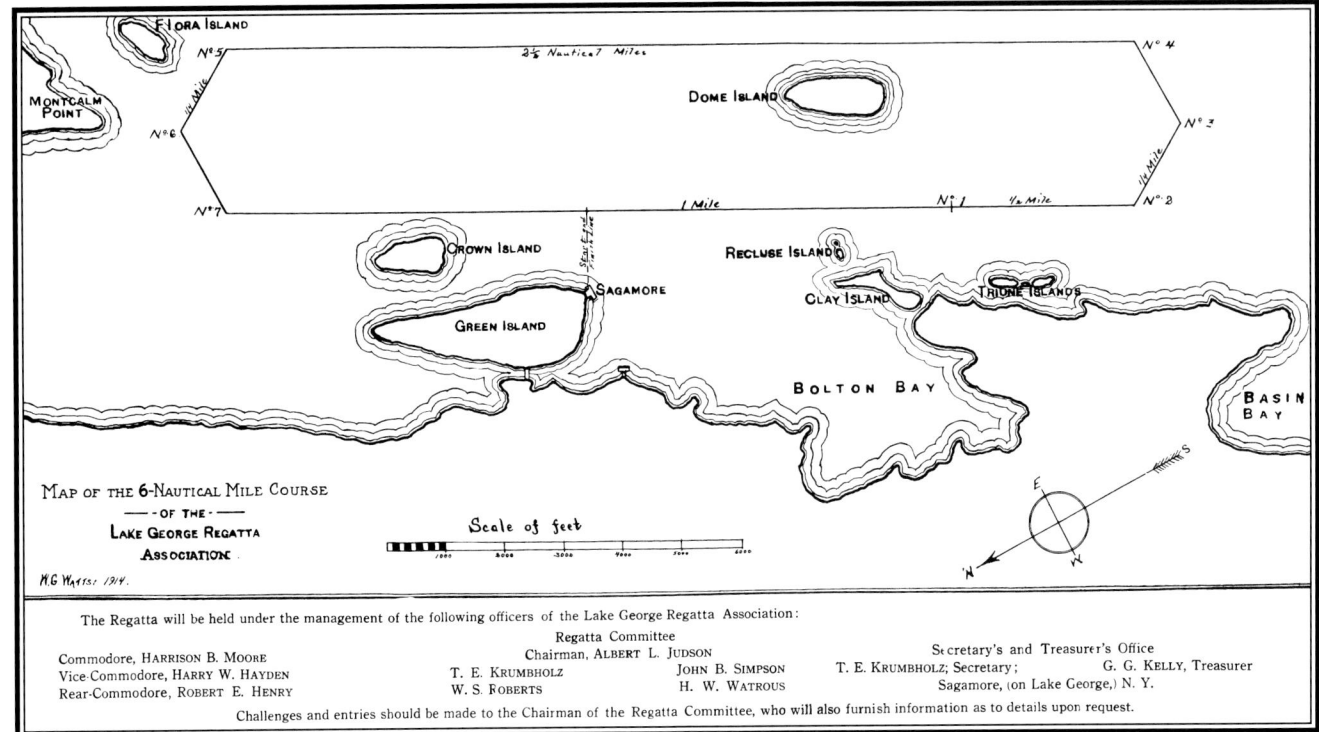

1914 Gold Cup Race Course, Bolton Landing. Courtesy: Henry Caldwell.

Robert A. Gates, who were closely associated with Gold Cup speedboat racing during the 1930's.

1914 was a difficult year for Bolton Landing. The Sagamore Hotel was to be the focal point for the race festivities, but it burned down on Easter Sunday. Green Island was closed off to automobiles for the season, however a grandstand was constructed on the steamboat pier in front of the burned out hotel. The steamboat *Horicon* (II) was moored in the middle of the six-mile course so its passengers could get a 360 degree view. The races were to be held from Wednesday July 30th to Friday August 1st, however all events were moved ahead a day due to poor weather on Wednesday. The race course was elliptical in shape, running from Montcalm Point, past Dome to the Triuna Islands and back, with the start and finish lines at the Sagamore Hotel. The course was 5 miles long and was to be circled 6 times for a total race of 30 nautical miles.

Ankle Deep was off to a roaring start during the first two days of racing. *Ankle Deep* appeared to be off to a second win when her propeller shaft broke from the strain during the second race and she coasted to a disappointing stop. On the final day, with only four boats still in the race and victory nearly in his grasp, the shaft snapped again, throwing the Count and his mechanic into the lake. *Ankle Deep* was defeated by *Baby Speed Demon II* which went on to win the Gold Cup. The Regatta Ball that evening was held at the

Count Mankowski (center) with drivers and judges at Sagamore Hotel, 1914. Courtesy: Bolton Historical Museum.

Before 1914 races, Bolton Landing.
Courtesy: Bolton Historical Museum.

Fort William Henry Hotel in Lake George Village. During the final circuit race that year in Buffalo on the Niagara River, *Ankle Deep* caught fire and was badly damaged. The Count and his mechanician, Frank Grenon, had to swim for their lives. Grenon was badly burned and *Ankle Deep* would never race again. The boat was shipped back home to Tallwoods in Bolton Landing where it further deteriorated in the yard. Old locals around Bolton say it was eventually placed into an old shed that was accidentally destroyed when brush was being burned nearby. There was nothing left.

After attempting to race again in later years in the *Hawk Eye* and *Ankle Deep Too*, the unsuccessful Count abruptly disappeared. He left the Countess behind and never again returned to Lake George.

Oval, *Ankle Deep* at Sagamore, courtesy: Bolton Historical Museum. Racers, author's collection. Sterling engine, courtesy: Henry Caldwell. Broken propeller, courtesy: Wauneata Waller. Trophy, courtesy, Henry Caldwell.
Mankowski boathouse showing *Hummer* (right) and the Count's small launch. Courtesy: Bolton Historical Museum.

Left, *Ankle Deep's* last pleasure run on Lake George before heading to Buffalo, 1914.
Courtesy: Ike Wolgin.
Above, *Ankle Deep* at Buffalo, NY, preparing for her final race before she burned, 1914.
Courtesy: Wauneata Waller.

Ankle Deep Too

Count Mankowski was deeply discouraged when his beloved *Ankle Deep* burned in 1914. Immediately following *Ankle Deep's* destruction at Buffalo, the Count soon commissioned for the construction of the 26 foot long *Ankle Deep Too*. Powered by twin 250 hp engines, it could reach Mile-A-Minute speeds, burning 40 gallons of fuel per hour. *Ankle Deep Too* was designed by Fred Chase of Tams, Lemoyne and Crane.

The Count in California.
Courtesy: Wauneata Waller.

Baby Speed Demon II

When Bolton Landing's Gold Cup winner *Ankle Deep* brought the Gold Cup races to Lake George for the first time during the last three days of July 1914, *Ankle Deep* was the favorite to win. There were nine other boats competing in that event including *Hawk Eye*, *Baby Reliance V*, *Harpoon*, *Tech Jr*, *Peter Pan VI*, *PDQ IV*, *PDQ V*, *Buffalo Enquirer* and *Baby Speed Demon II*.

Baby Speed Demon II was sponsored by the

Baby Speed Demon II. Author's collection.

Motor Boat Club of America of New York City, owned by Paula H. Blackton and was driven by Bob Edgren. Mechanician was Jack Beebe. The "*Demon*", as she was called, was 20 feet long, 7 feet wide across her beam and was powered by an eight cylinder 150HP Sterling engine featuring four stack pipes extending 24 inches skyward above the hull in front of the two racers aboard.

The 6 mile race course on the main body of the lake circled Dome Island outside Bolton Bay and was to be completed 5 times on the first fair weather day of competition which began at 5:15PM. Several boats got off to a bad start in this first event because crews held back too long trying to "lie back" for better position. Peter Pan shot into the lead right away with *Buffalo Enquirer* only three boat lengths behind. All boats held their relative positions throughout the first lap. *Baby Reliance* then secured the first position and held it to the end. Excitement was high in the third lap when *Ankle Deep* charged ahead from her fifth place position to overtake *Buffalo Enquirer*. J. Stewart Blackington's *Baby Reliance*, sponsored by the Atlantic Yacht Club, finished first that day with a timed speed of 32.81 minutes. *Ankle Deep* finished a distant fifth due to a poor start. Ironically, second place was captured by *Baby Speed Demon II*, owned by the winner's wife, Mrs. Paula H. Blackington. *Hawk Eye*, another Lake George boat which was sponsored by the Lake George Syndicate, finished in a disappointing last place.

In the racing events which followed over the next two days, *Baby Speed Demon II* remained strong and dependable while local favorites *Ankle Deep* and *Hawk Eye* failed to finish due to mechanical difficulties. With one of the largest crowds ever to view this event watching from boats and along Bolton's shore, *Baby Speed Demon II*, pilot Bob Edgren and mechanic Jack Beebe made Lake George history, and racing history, by winning the 1914 Gold Cup at Bolton Landing.

Baby Speed Demon II after winning race. Courtesy: Bolton Historical Museum.

Baby Reliance V

Above, *Baby Reliance V* racing at Bolton Landing, 1914, sponsored by the Atlantic Yacht Club. Courtesy: Bolton Historical Museum.

Left, *Baby Reliance V* and *Baby Speed Demon II* between races, powered by Sterling 180HP engine. Fenimore Hotel dock in background. Courtesy: Bolton Historical Museum.

Tech Jr.

Tech Jr. was sponsored by the Corinthian Yacht Club of Cape May. She was built by Adolph Apel for owner Mr. Coleman du Pont. She was 19 feet 11 inches long, 8 feet wide at her beam and was powered by an 8 cylinder 180 horsepower Sterling engine. Her helmsman was Francis V. du Pont and her mechanician was Brady Wiley.
Engine photo, courtesy: Wauneata Waller. *Tech Jr.* photo, courtesy: Henry Caldwell.

Peter Pan

Peter Pan, 1914 Gold Cup racer at Bolton Landing. Sponsored by the Columbia Yacht Club of New York. Built by Reliance Motor Boat Company. Owned by James Simpson. 19 feet 11 inches long and 6 feet wide. Powered by an 8 cylinder 150 hp Van Blerck engine. Helmsman was H.W. Patterson. Mechanician was John A. Screfer.

Courtesy: Henry Caldwell.

P.D.Q. V.

P.D.Q.V., 1914 Gold Cup racer at Bolton Landing. Sponsored by the Thousand Islands Yacht Club. Built by Fred Adams. Owned by A. Graham Miles. 26 feet long and 6 feet 8 inches wide. Powered by a 12 cylinder 300 hp Van Blerck engine. Helmsman was owner A. Graham Miles. Mechanician was builder Fred Adams.

Courtesy: Henry Caldwell

Harpoon

Harpoon, 1914 Gold Cup racer at Bolton Landing. Sponsored by the Colonial Yacht Club of New York. Built by Kretzer Boat Works. Owned by Wilbur H. Young. 26 feet long and 5 feet 6 inches wide. Powered by an 8 cylinder 95 hp Van Blerck engine. Helmsman was owner Wilbur H. Young.

Courtesy: Henry Caldwell.

Hawk Eye

When the Gold Cup races came to Lake George in 1914, it was decided that a secondary raceboat would be entered by the Lake George Syndicate, under Chairman A.L. Judson, in the event that *Ankle Deep* was unsuccessful so as to further the chances that Lake George might hold on to the races for another year. *Hawk Eye*, a one-step hydroplane sponsored by the Lake George Club, was designed and built by John L. Hacker at his Watervliet facility. She was 26 feet long, 7 feet wide at her beam and was powered by a 300 hp Van Blerck engine. Helmsman was Frederick G. Peabody, mechanician was Henry Pohl. Bolton's William Kneeshaw assisted Pohl with much of the dockside maintenance. Unfortunately, *Hawk Eye* suffered two serious breakdowns and was not able to complete the race. On both occasions, her chain drive had broken. This was replaced after the races with a gear drive which helped *Hawk Eye* race at speeds approaching 50 mph.

Hawk Eye. Top photo, William Kneeshaw and Henry Pohl. Courtesy: Bolton Historical Museum.
Left photo, courtesy: Bolton Historical Museum. Right photo, courtesy: Henry Caldwell.

Simplex XV

Simplex XV was a very popular and successful raceboat which has nearly been totally forgotten in Lake George boating history. She was originally owned by Herman Broesel of Bolton Landing. When Broesel died, the boat was purchased from his estate by J.P. Randerson of Albany who had a home on the Bolton Road, six miles north of Lake George Village. (Randerson was not satisfied by the slow speeds of his old boat which his son's continued to race, renaming it *Dart II*.)

Simplex XV was 39 feet 6 inches long, 4 feet 7 inches wide and was powered by a 75 hp Sterling engine producing 1,110 rpm. Made entirely of mahogany, she could reach speeds up to 27 mph.

Simplex XV winning a cup race.
The fastest boat on Lake George for several years at 27 mph. Author's collection.

Simplex XV was luxurious and fast in her day. Launched in 1908, she beat LeGrand C. Cramer's *Wininnish* in an endurance race which went the entire length of the lake and back with *Wininnish* having a head start handicap of 4 minutes and 14 seconds. In 1908, she also won the LaGrand C. Cramer Cup in the Glens Falls Regatta, and in 1911 she won the Fort William Henry Cup, racing against a young George Reis in his *Mignon* and G.W. Stebbins in his *Carol II*.

Whip-Po-Will

Albert Judson owned a summer home on Green Island adjacent to the Sagamore Hotel. As Commodore of the Lake George Regatta Association, Judson enjoyed the sport of Penant Racing on Lake George at the Lake George Club. His own personal turn-of-the-century craft named *Whip-Po-Will* was somewhat similar to his friend LeGrand C. Cramer's *Wininnish*. Both were long, narrow and black, and both displayed the unusual convertible top with metal tubular top bows. Both were "Gentleman's Racers" used both for club racing and pleasure rides. *Whip-Po-Will*, however, had an upswept bow and rounded stern, noticebly different from *Wininnish's* stern and bow.

Whip-Po-Will owned and raced by Albert Judson. Courtesy: Ike Wolgin.

Whip-Po-Will Jr.

Commodore Al Judson of the Lake George Syndicate was in charge of organizing the Gold Cup races on Lake George in 1914. The Syndicate was disappointed when *Ankle Deep* failed to complete the race and they were further disappointed with the poor performance of their back-up racer *Hawk Eye*. In 1918, the Syndicate, which included William K. Bixby of Bolton Landing and H.B. Moore of Heart Bay, decided to build a new racer with the intent of winning back the cup in the Detroit races and returning the event to Lake George. *Whip-Po-Will Jr.* was designed and constructed by the Beebe brothers who had been trained by Chris Smith, the builder of Chris-Craft boats. Gar Wood had entered two boats in the races, *Detroit II* and *Detroit III*. Wood's strategy was to push *Detroit II* hard and force *Whip-Po-Will Jr.* to overextend her engine until it broke down, leaving the race open for *Detroit III* to win. Soon, *Whip-Po-Will's* engine caught fire and she was forced out of the race. Riding mechanician James Kneeshaw was successful in extinguishing the fire, and driver George Reis would eventu

Whip-Po-Will Jr. Above, racing on the Detroit River, 1918. Below, at Detroit River race, 1918. Photos, courtesy: Bill Morgan.

ally achieve Gold Cup fame three times on his own in his *El Lagarto* during the mid 1930's.

Whip-Po-Will Jr. went on to race in the Thousand Islands, Minneapolis and on Lake Ontario. In 1920, she was shipped to England to compete for the Harmsworth Trophy. The racer caught fire during a practice run. George Reis and Jim Kneeshaw leaped into the ocean to save themselves and were immediately rescued. *Whip-Po-Will Jr.* was totally destroyed.

Barge Races

Regattas of all kinds were very popular before and after the turn of the Twentieth Century. Barge races were organized for competitions between clubs, hotels and towns around the lake.

At right is the barge sponsored by the Worden Hotel in Lake George Village. Author's collection. Below right is the barge from Bolton Landing. Courtesy: Bolton Historical Museum.

1911

Soloman   Prosser   Burton   Hawley   Sullivan

1914 medal won by Al. M. Seaman of Bolton Landing. This actual original medal has been in my family collection for decades. Author.

1914

Roy Potter   John R. Stickney   Allen M. Seaman   Sherman Durrin   George Truax

Photos by Fred C. Thatcher.

Nellita

Nellita. Courtesy: Lake George Village Historian.

Resolute

Eber Richards first brought young Duane Irish to Pilot Knob in 1902 to operate the steam yacht *Theta* as engineer. Over the years to follow, Duane purchased Victoria Lodge, operated a general store, sold ice and did all kinds of handy work. During the 1920's, there were many more summer residents along the southern lakeshore who required Duane's ice, milk and supplies. Duane then used his boat *Resolute* to make daily deliveries. As business increased, he hired George Flieshmann and Lew Canney to make the deliveries for him in the *Resolute*.

Duane Irish in *Resolute* at Pilot Knob, 1920's. Courtesy: JoAnn Irish Mahoney.

Winogene

Winogene was also owned by Duane Irish. With others running his boat delivery operation, Irish was now free to manage his small fleet of launches for hire. Every Sunday morning, he would transport passengers in his *Winogene* from Pilot Knob to the small church on the East side of Cleverdale.

Winogene at Pilot Knob. Courtesy: JoAnn Irish Mahoney.

Jolly Roger

Frank Fielding and *Jolly Roger* in Dunham's Bay, 1928. Courtesy: Steve Lapham.

When John L. Hacker designed and built the Gold Cup racing boat *Miss Mary* in 1926, (later renamed *El Lagarto*), he built another similar Gold Cup racer named *Jolly Roger* for Jonathan Moore of Heart Bay. In the 1930's, Moore traded *Jolly Roger* to Henderson's Boat Livery who sold it to Frank Fielding, owner of a beautiful, yet small, stone summer mansion which looked northward towards the main body of Lake George. Their home still stands;–it is visibly incorporated into today's Dunham's Bay Lodge. At that time, there wasn't any bridge over the wetlands to connect Frank's property to Bay Road as there is today. To access his property, they had to use Ridge Road to Cleverdale and pass Assembly Point to his estate. His estate was where the road ended.

The Fieldings had a boat house in the bay and a large apple orchard behind their home along the wetlands. (Frank's brother Fred also owned a large apple orchard in Cleverdale. Fred's barn adjacent to the Rockhurst turn has been restored by owner Robin Inwald and has an acknowledgement to the Fielding's painted in black on the corner of the barn.)

Frank Fielding's *Jolly Roger* continued as a "gentleman's racer". Its Liberty 225 Horsepower 6 cyl. engine was only one number apart from the original engine in George Reis' famous *El Lagarto*. The *Jolly Roger* was 26 feet long, 6 feet 6 inches wide across her beam and capable of reaching speeds approaching 60 miles per hour.

Frank and his son George measured a one mile race course on the winter ice from an old tree which once leaned over the lake at Assembly Point to a large boulder on the east side of Dunham's Bay. When the ice melted in the spring, their goal was to achieve the incredible racing speed of 1 mile in 1 minute (or 60 mph). According to Ralph Lapham, George's young friend who witnessed the event, *Jolly Roger* wasn't quite able to hit the 60 mph mark.

As the years passed, Frank lost interest in speed and in a boat that consumed 60 gallons of gasoline very rapidly. He then split the boat in half, widened the beam, cut down her length at the stern and raised the freeboard, converting the *Jolly Roger* into a day-cruiser so it could accommodate a larger number of people on trips to the Narrows and around the lake. Finally, he installed a 4 cyl. engine. Renamed *Jolly Roger II*, she was too narrow and too top-heavy for comfortable excursions. Soon after, she caught fire, sank and was forgotten until she was recently rediscovered and photographed on the bottom of the lake.

Jolly Roger II. Courtesy: Steve Lapham.   Underwater photos, courtesy: Bob Benway and Bateaux Below, Inc.

Flying Boats

George McGowan and Harry Rogers brought the Flying Boats to Lake George during the 1920's. Harry Rogers was a former "Barn Stormer" who later became a pioneer in aviation. He personally planned and flew the original air routes to South America in a time when it took a week to get there. Rogers and his partner George McGowan operated Aeromarine Flying Cruisers and had one of the first contracts to fly mail outside the United States during the early 1920's. They flew mail from Miami and Key West to Havanna, Cuba. They soon sold their mail business to Juan Tripp, founder of Pan American Airlines. Their next brief venture was to fly a small commuter business which ran flights from Manhattan to Long Island Sound

Curtis Flying Boat at Lake George in the 1920's. Fred C. Thatcher photo. Courtesy: Dick Kowell.

and Newport, Rhode Island. They met many celebrities while in the flying business such as Howard Hughes and Charles Lindbergh, and they once flew Al Capone from Bimini to Miami. Important friends also visited them here at Lake George such as B. Frank Mahoney who built "The Spirit of St. Louis" for Charles Lindbergh, Major M.K. Lee who financed the first non-stop flight from New York to Miami, Duke Shiller the famous Canadian flier who rescued the survivors of the ill-fated German Flying boat *Bremen* when it made a forced landing and crashed off of Newfoundland, and George Rummell of Saranac Lake who was the first pilot to fly night patrol in a seaplane for the US Navy during World War I.

In 1923, Rogers and McGowan began the Flying Boat business here at Lake George during the summer while operating trips from Miami in the winter. They purchased four planes, one built by Curtis, the others were Air Yachts built by Grover Loning. The Curtis was purchased in Cuba from the "US and Cuban Mail Service". Each plane, requiring two pilots, was a double-wing model with Liberty engines, and each plane could carry up to six passengers.

On one occasion, one of the planes here on Lake George caught a cross draft while landing and struck the end of the Lake George

Flying Boats, Pergola in background. Courtesy: Dick Kowell.

Steamboat Company pier. Fortunately, there were no injuries. The primary concern here at that time wasn't the danger—it was the loud noise from the unmuffled Liberty Engines which powered the planes. By the early 1930's legislation was introduced which prohibited the use of aircraft for commercial operation and the Flying Boats disappeared from the lake.

George McGowan first leased, then purchased the Sky Harbor Restaurant which once stood on the corner of Canada Street and the Beach Road. Sky Harbor burned in 1973. George McGowan died in 1984. Harry Rogers died on Lake Mead when the plane he was landing struck a small unseen obstruction in the water.

Aviator George McGowan at Lake George. Courtesy: George McGowan Jr.

Top, seaplane on Lake George. Courtesy: Fort Edward Historical Museum. Bottom, seaplane at Pilot Knob. Courtesy: Roy and Jeanette Hunt.

Rainbow IV

Boat racing is as old as boating itself and Lake George has been fortunate to have been the racecourse for many kinds of competitions including four Gold Cup Speedboat Races sponsored by the American Powerboat Association in 1914, 1934, 1935 & 1936. A direct result of these competitions here on our lake is that there is still a strong interest in these early racers. The few racers that still exist have been beautifully restored and many lost boats such as *Rainbow IV* have been completely recreated from the original plans.

Rainbow IV, 1924 ditchburn racer. Author's collection.

Commodore Harry B. Greening of Canada's Royal Hamilton Yacht Club had enjoyed Gold Cup competitions in three *Rainbow* racers without achieving a Gold Cup win. For the 1924 races he hired Herbert Ditchburn Boats of Gravenhurst, Ontario to build *Rainbow IV* (G-71) designed by eminent boat designer George Crouch. She was 27 1/2 feet long, 6 1/2 feet wide and had 11 approved hydroplaning clinker-built "steps" across her hull to help reduce friction and drag by 12%. She was powered by a 200 hp Packard Engine. I find it interesting to note that there even were sleeping quarters for three inside the hull for the race crew when they were away for races.

Above, *Rainbow IV* at 1984 Green Island, Lake George Boat Show. Photo by author.
Right, steering aparatus. Courtesy: Jack Binley.

The August 30, 1924 Gold Cup Races were held at Detroit, Michigan. With top speeds of 60 mph on the straights and an average speed of 46 mph overall, *Rainbow IV* easily beat favorites *Baby Bootlegger* and *Miss Columbia*. A major protest and deliberation followed with the judges disqualifying *Rainbow IV* because of her controversial 11"steps" which the Commodore claimed were legal lap-strakes. The win, however, was eventually awarded to *Baby Bootlegger*.

Ready for a new challenge, Commodore Greening installed a 400 hp Gar-wood Liberty engine in 1925 and established a new world's endurance record of 1,218.879 miles in twelve daylight hours/day for 24 hours at an average speed of 50.78 mph.

Without a Gold Cup win, *Rainbow IV* was sold to Samuel S. Dunsford of Concord, N.H. in 1926. He painted her bright green and raced her on Lake Winnipesaukee where she won the James R. Irwin Cup in 1926 and placed third in the Massachussets Gold Cup Regatta in 1927.

Rainbow IV was retired in 1929 and replaced by the John L. Hacker designed *Scotty*. In 1932, my two uncles, Walter "Smokey" Gates and Robert A. Gates, mechanics for Bolton Landing race driver George Reis, traveled to Lake Winnipesaukee to bring her engine to Bolton. Together, they installed the engine in the soon-to-be-famous El Lagarto (G-18) which would soon make world, and Lake George, Gold Cup history.

Rainbow IV's fate thereafter is still a mystery. Perhaps she eventually was scrapped—or—perhaps she still exists somewhere out there in some unexplored shed or barn. I'd like to think she's still in hiding and waiting to be discovered. Fortunately for all of us Gold Cup fans, there is Bill Morgan of Morgan Marine at Silver Bay on Lake George. Bill built an exact replica of *Rainbow IV* for Jack Binley of Hague in 1988. Many times I enjoyed seeing her on our lake and at boat shows. Today she is in storage. Unfortunately, many of Lake George's classic boats have gone to other lakes, so I know I'm not alone in my wish that replica *Rainbow IV* remain on our lake where it can continue to offer us a glimpse into the great Gold Cup years here on Lake George.

Pippa II

The story of *Pippa II* is deeply entwined with the history of Cannon Point. Although it is commonly believed that the point received its name because it was used as staging area for cannon by the British during the Revolution, there isn't any documentation for this theory. There is, however, an obscure little poem which was written and published by J.P. Sweet in 1863 about a family named Cannon who resided in this area during the mid 19th century. It reads:–"The Cannon Point lies near our destin'd way; Just on the north of this the last-named bay, from old Phil Cannon it derived its name, Who had five children, and a simple dame."

The point passed through a series of owners through the 1800's and early 1900's. In 1912, Cannon Point was sold to two sisters, Louise and Anna Stebbins of Springfield, Mass. The Stebbins sisters, who never married, loved world travel and could easily afford to do so every year because their father was a wealthy mill owner. The great summer cottage on the point was constructed for them during 1908-1909 by the Schermerhorn Brothers Construction Company of Lake George Village. The sisters loved Lake George and stayed here every summer with the exception of 1925 when they traveled to Europe. That summer, their cottage was rented by United States Supreme Court Chief Justice Charles Evans Hughes who was born nearby in

Glens Falls.

The first boat owned by the Stebbins sisters was named *Pippa*. All that is known of it is that it was a 22 foot double ended launch, possibly a Fay & Bowen. The name *Pippa* was derived from Robert Browning's classic prose "Pippa Passes", and means, "God is in his heaven, All is right with the world."

We do know that *Pippa* was replaced in 1917 by a new 30 foot Fay & Bowen Golden Arrow named *Pippa II* which was stored and cared for at Hall's Boat Company in Lake George Village. *Pippa II* was purchased from Walter Harris' Fay & Bowen dealership. Walter Harris received three identical 30 footers that year, *Pippa II*, his own boat *Snuff* and *Great White Dragon* owned by Dr. Peterson of Hulett's Landing. Each of these boats rolled from the assembly line together and carried serial numbers only one number apart.

When Louise Stebbins died in 1928, Anne became the sole owner of the property and *Pippa II*. In 1929, Anne

Pippa II. Courtesy: John Hilton.

had the original Fay & Bowen 6 cyl. engine removed from *Pippa II* and replaced it with a 6 cyl. Scripps Rainbow purchased at the NYC Boat Show, This engine helped *Pippa II* achieve local fame here on Lake George winning the Davis Cup on more than one occasion.

Upon Anne's death in 1939, ownership passed on to her heirs. They, in turn, sold everything to a niece named Frances and her husband, Charles Wallour of Massachusetts. *Pippa II* was still stored at Hall's. Wallour then gave *Pippa II* to Activities Manager Loftheimer at the Lake George Club in 1969 after he sold Cannon Point to Cyrus Woodbury of Diamond Point and Herman Muller of New York City. *Pippa II* was bought by John Hilton in 1985 for his 40th birthday present and is still owned by Hilton today.

Falcon V

Falcon V and Jonathan Moore, late 1920's. "Worden Trophy, 1st prize, 10 Mile Speed Boat Race, won by *Falcon* V, August 27, 1927." Courtesy: Mary Chester Flagg.

Harrison Bray Moore of Brooklyn owned the speedy *Pampero* at Heart Bay in 1877. In 1888, the *Pampero* raced the *Dandy* in one of the most action packed races in Lake George history. H.B. Moore's son Jonathan inherited his father's interest in fast boats and racing and later owned his own racer named *Jolly Roger*. The story goes that racing driver George Reis bought his *Miss Mary*, later renamed *El Lagarto*, with the intention of beating Moore's *Jolly Roger*. Once that feat was accomplished, Moore, who had owned a series of boats named *Falcon*, commissioned John L. Hacker to build the *Falcon V* so as to out race

Miss Mary. The *Falcon V* was a 30 foot single step hydroplane and had a powerful V-12 Liberty engine producing 450 hp which could reach 60 mph speeds. After more steps were added, this fast boat out raced *Miss Mary* and thus the friendly rivalry continued. Reis then commissioned a new boat to be constructed named *El Lagartito* which was fast, but not a strong contender. It was then that George Reis rebuilt *Miss Mary* into the *El Lagarto* and the rest is history. The *El Lagarto* went on to make Gold Cup history and the *Falcon V* was soon forgotten. Jonathan Moore, President of the Theodore Crane Company in the Erie basin, continued his interest in fast boats up into the 1930's. He eventually traded both *Falcon V* and *Jolly Roger* to Henderson's Boat Livery. Unable to sell her, Henderson removed *Falcon V*'s engine and hardware and cut the boat up for firewood. *Jolly Roger* was sold to Frank Fielding at Dunham's Bay.

Jonathan Moore, 1937.
Courtesy: Mary Chester Flagg.

El Lagartito

El Lagartito with George Reis and Dick Bowers. Author's collection.

Gold Cup speedboat racing first appeared and disappeared on Lake George all in the same year of 1914, with Bolton Landing's *Ankle Deep* achieving worldwide fame. There were many schemes afterward for returning racing to our lake. George Reis of Bolton Landing had witnessed the fame and glory heaped on Bolton's Count Mankowski and his *Ankle Deep* during those 1914 races. Actually, George as a youngster raced in his own racing outboard *Krazy Kat* in some races that very same year. He won the Fort William Henry Loving Cup twice, allowing him to keep the trophy, and won the Mirror Cup for traveling at speeds reaching 32 miles per hour.

During 1918, 1919 and 1920, Reis raced the *Whip-Po-Will Jr.* at other racing events and locations for Al Judson, Commodore of the Lake George Racing Association. When the *Whip-Po-Will Jr.* burned, George became determined to race a boat of his own.

From 1903, when the American Power Boat Association was formed, to the early

El Lagartito, George Reis and Smokey Gates at Pilot Knob. Courtesy: Bill Morgan.

1920's, racing boats took on many shapes and styles, and with a fairly accurate handicap rule, every hull design raced against the others;- displacement hulls actually competed against the new hydroplanes. In 1921, the rules were changed. Hydroplanes were eliminated from Gold Cup competition permitting only the "gentleman's racers", the graceful displacement hull types such as the ones designed by Chris Smith, Gar Wood and John L. Hacker. The Purdy Boat Company at Port Washington, New York designed and built for George Reis the *El Lagartito* (not to be confused with Reis' later John L. Hacker designed *El Lagarto*).

El Lagartito and George Reis. Courtesy: Bill Morgan.

The *El Lagartito* (G3) was a welcome sight on Lake George during the 1920's. My father often spoke of this sleek mahogany craft because it offered the exciting possibility of returning the Gold Cup to Lake George and our hometown Bolton Landing. Powered by a 1M-621 Packard engine, George and his racing friend Anderson "Dick" Bowers of Pilot Knob, would practice their racing strategies between Bolton Bay and Lake George's Long Island. Ironically, Reis already owned his future winning *El Lagarto* which was then called the *Miss Mary*. At the time he believed the former racer's career was over, so he used the *Miss Mary* as his personal pleasure craft.

The *El Lagartito* was a strong contender but never succeeded in being a winner. In the 1930 Gold Cup at Red Bank, New Jersey, *El Lagartito* finished 5th in a field of 7 contenders. George decided to retire her and with the assistance of his racing mechanic, my uncle Walter "Smokey" Gates, they converted the *Miss Mary* into the successful *El Lagarto*. The *El Lagartito* was sold a few years later to Edmund Guggenheim of Saranac Lake and renamed the *Miss Saranac*. The *Miss Saranac* appeared in the racing competition for the President's Cup races in September of 1934 on Lake George. Seven boats were entered. *Miss Saranac* finished an impressive 3rd. *Miss Saranac* was a popular favorite every year in the races sponsored by the Saranac Boat and Waterways Association on Saranac Lake, as well.

Although *Miss Saranac* never again raced for the Gold Cup, she appeared annually for the Presidents Cup challenge event and in 1936, she competed for the American Speedboat Championship race for the Hearst Trophy at Lake George. During the race she was clipped by another boat and lost the port side of her bow. Badly damaged, she continued to race and succeeded in winning the third place award.

It was always told to me by my father, my two racing uncles and Bill Morgan of Silver Bay, –that while practicing on Saranac Lake, New York during the late 1930s, *El Lagartito* (*Miss Saranac*) caught fire, burned, sank and never was recovered.

El Lacayo

George Reis of Bolton Landing, best known for his Gold Cup winning racer *El Lagarto,* also owned a pleasure boat he would use for his personal family enjoyment. *El Lacayo* is a 28 foot Gar Wood that Reis purchased new in 1929. She is the "sister ship" to the *Black Swan* owned today by the Gabriel's family on Green Island. I have many memories of the *El Lacayo* from my youth because my Uncle Walter "Smokey" Gates worked for George as his boat mechanic. I have several old photographs of *El Lacayo* in my collection showing George, his wife Mary and their large black dog Tuffy aboard *El Lacayo*.

El Lacayo and Reis's dog Tuffy. Reis home and boathouse in background. Author's collection.

Twice, Reis was known to be involved in collisions with *El Lacayo*. In one situation during a dark moonless evening, Reis's son ran the boat up onto Elizabeth Island. The damaged boat was pulled off the next morning by a group from Pilot Knob. On another occasion, at 11:30 on a Saturday night in July of 1956, Reis collided with an 18 foot launch owned by a John O'Bain of

Diamond Point. O'Bain and his four guests were not injured and Reis pulled them aboard before their boat sank in 70 feet of water near Tea Island.

After George died in the early 1960's, his boat was purchased by Joe Smith of F.R. Smith & Sons in Bolton Landing. Joe used *El Lacayo* for both commercial and personal pleasure rides. Locals in Bolton will always remember Fred Smith Junior's wake at Roger's Park in May of 1999 when *El Lacayo* carried Fred's casket to the ceremony.

El Lacayo today. Photos by author.
Courtesy: Scott Anderson, Garth Monroe, Brian Cassidy, and Joan Baldwin.

Scotty-Too

The first *Scotty* was a 1928 racer built by John L. Hacker for Sammy "Scotty" Dunsford of Lake Winnipesaukee, NH. She was 26 feet long, 5 feet 5 inches at her beam and powered by a Packard IM-621 300 hp engine. Entered in only one race in that same year, her 65 mph performance was totally unsatisfactory. Dunsford immediately commissioned *Scotty-Too* to be built. The engine was removed from Scotty (I) and interestingly, another engine was never installed in her. *Scotty* (I) lay idle throughout the remainder of Dunsford's life.

The new *Scotty-Too*, built in 1930, was 26 feet in length and 6 feet 6 inches at the beam. She raced every year from 1930 to 1934. Racing in the Gold Cup, president's Cup and the National Sweepstakes, she was only able to win one second place Gold Cup trophy. *Scotty-Too* was a unique racer sporting a mahogany deck and spruce sides. There were three steps on the bottom and an external rudder which was a new idea attracting much interest.

When "Scotty" Dunsford died, Samuel Rogers of Lake Winnipesaukee acquired the boat from his estate and later sold it to Edward A. Larter Jr. of Dunstable, Mass. for use at his summer home on Lake George. Mr. Larter enjoyed running *Scotty-Too* the full length of Lake George every summer morning when the weather permitted. *Scotty-Too* still apears at many of our Lake George Boat Shows.

Top, *Scotty-Too* racing, 1930's. Courtesy: Bill Morgan.
Scotty-Too in Bolton Bay, 1980's. Photo by author.

El Lagarto

Gold Cup speedboat racing has been synonymous with sportsmanship since Gold Cup speedboat races began back in 1904 when the Columbia Yacht Club of New York City was first presented with the trophy by the American Power Boat Association. The winning boat every year had the privilege of taking this trophy to its home waters and having its name engraved on the Gold Cup. The competition to develop speed and dependability on water directly and positively influenced the development of boat design and boating as we know it today, and experimentation with length, hull designs, hydroplaning and engines led to many significant rule changes every year as the sport developed.

Miss Mary, later renamed *El Lagarto*. Courtesy: Bill Morgan.

By the 1920s, advanced developments occurred so frequently that boats became obsolete after only a few racing seasons. This became the fate of Edward C. Grimm's, 1922 John L. Hacker designed *Miss Mary* (G-2). Grimm owned the Peerless Motor Company in Buffalo. Following three unsuccessful seasons from 1922 to 1924, she was sold to racing driver George Reis of Bolton Landing for use as his personal pleasure boat when he was not racing his *El Lagartito* (G-3). Not even George Reis himself realized at the time that his sleek old pleasure boat would rise to world fame a decade later.

The earliest racing boats relied on their narrowness to reduce friction and to attain speed, where today's wider boats rely on their ability to hydroplane on top of the water to achieve the same goal. A significant

Above, George Reis and Dick Bowers in *El Lagarto*. Courtesy: Bill Morgan.
Below, 1935 Gold Cup Race Course. Author's collection.

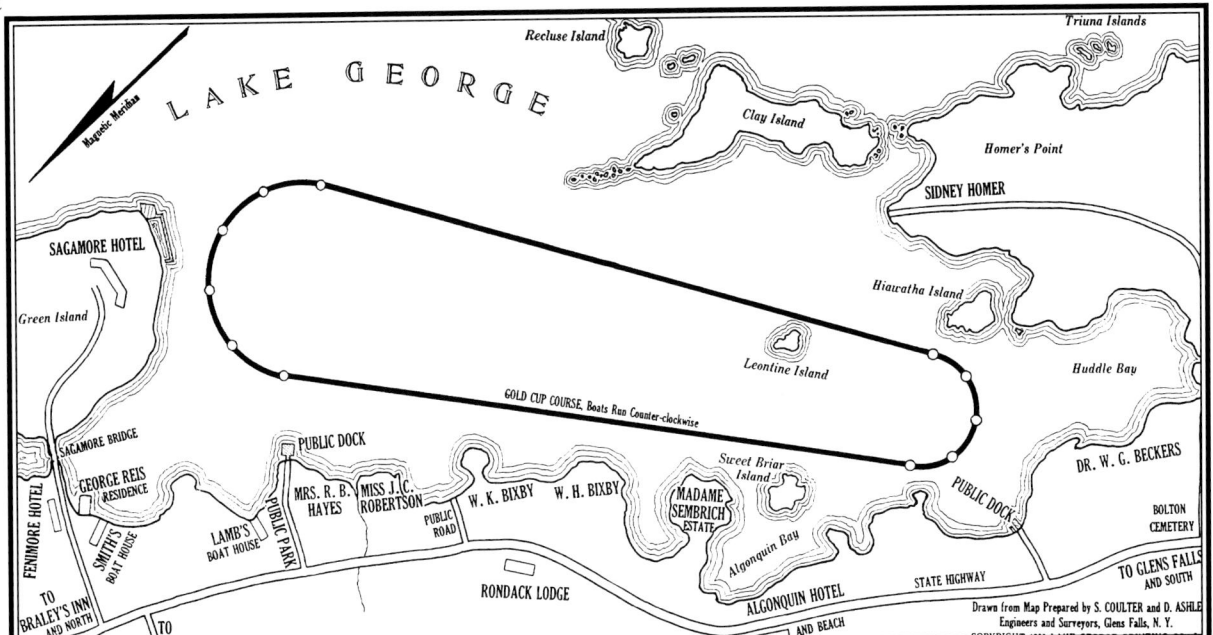

El Lagarto (G-18) overtakes *Californian* (G-2) and *Louisa* (G-23). Courtesy: Bill Morgan.

point to keep in mind during the 1930s is that these were the "in-between" years when boats were still in the transition stage towards hydroplaning. With the goal of reducing friction in mind, George Reis began looking at his *Miss Mary* with a renewed interest. He designed a series of steps, or elevation changes, which could be incorporated into the hull of the boat which would cause it to leap out of the water. To continue the propulsion forward while the boat was at the high point, the Monel metal propeller shaft was extended deeper downward into the water. The boat he chose to experiment with was his old *Miss Mary*. With the help of his mechanic, my uncle Walter "Smokey" Gates, the result was astonishingly successful—so much so that George set aside his *El Lagartito* (G-3),– renamed the *Miss Mary* to *El Lagarto* (G-18) and entered her in the August 16, 1931 Gold Cup races at Lake Montank Long Island powered by Packard's 1M-621 engine No. 1 which had been used in *Baby Bootlegger* to win the 1925 Gold Cup. *El Lagarto* was the oldest boat in the race and she was powered by an old engine but her performance was remarkable. She finished in second place attaining the fastest single heat record of 57.31 mph. The newspapers delighted her fans by nicknaming her "The Leaping Lizard".

The 1933 races were held on the Detroit River. My Uncle Smokey continued to race with George in many of the prelimi-

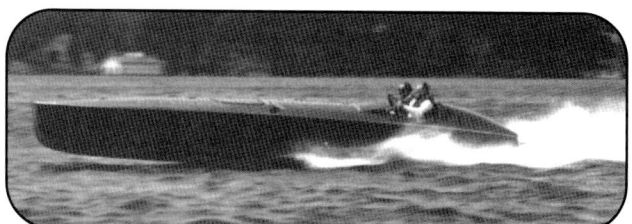

El Lagarto in Bolton Bay. Courtesy: Bill Morgan.

El Lagarto wins at Bolton. Courtesy: Bill Morgan.

Reis and Bowers after a win at Bolton Landing. Courtesy: Bill Morgan.

nary races throughout the early racing seasons, but during the Gold Cup races, George would invite his summer friend from Pilot Knob, stockbroker Anderson "Dick" Bowers, to ride along with him. *El Lagarto* won the National Sweepstakes, President's Cup and the 1933 Gold Cup bringing the 1934 races to Bolton Landing on Lake George. To the delight of all the local fans, *El Lagarto* won again, and Reis and Bowers repeated their win in July of 1935 as well, attaining a record speed of 70.2 mph. The trophy, valued at $17,000, was displayed at the home of his sponsor, the Lake George Club.

Although she lost the 1936 race due to the failure of her new Reis-Menaco M-728 engine, *El Lagarto* won other competitions that year. On September 7th, George and Smokey won the Lake Winnipesaukee Sweepstakes. Although her racing days ended in 1937, she had won a significant place in racing history winning eight major trophies, and she garnered an unforgetable place in the history of Bolton Landing and Lake George, as well. Following Smokey's retirement, my uncle Bob Gates cared for *El Lagarto* up until George died in the early 1960s. George's will stated that his ashes were to be spread upon Lake George in Bolton Bay from the *El Lagarto*, and his wishes were carried out. My uncle Bob didn't have the heart to start *El Lagarto* after George's death so George's ashes were spread from the *El Lagarto* as it was being towed by the *El Lacayo*.

George Reis and Dick Bowers win Gold Cup. Courtesy: Bill Morgan.

Repairing *El Lagarto* in Reis boathouse after colliding with *Delphine IV* in 1935. Courtesy: Bill Morgan.

El Lagarto showing five steps on bottom and newly added "bustle" on stern deck. Courtesy: Bill Morgan.

Most of us who grew up in Bolton can tell wonderful stories of hearing her engine roaring out on the lake every spring and fall, and a rare few of us can tell of the time George took us for a ride, but the best ending for this story is that George Reis provided in his will for all future generations to experience the *El Lagarto* whenever they visit the Boat Building at the Adirondack Museum in Blue Mountain Lake. The voice you will hear on the video monitor describing El Lagarto during her racing years is Bob Gates. Before Bob died, he gave the museum *El Lagarto*'s original steering wheel which is now back on the boat.

Top row, Smokey Gates and *El Lagarto*, 1930's. Author's collection. Guy Lombardo and George Reis at Reis boathouse, 1950's. Courtesy: Bill Morgan.

Middle row, George Reis and Smokey Ferris Gates, 1930's. Author's collection. Trophy, "Presented to Ferris Gates, Riding Mechanic in *El Lagarto*, Winner of Lake Winnipesaukee Sweepstakes, Sept. 7, 1936." Courtesy: Smokey's grandson, Jeff Lawrence. Clock from *El Lagarto* in author's collection.

Bottom photo, George and Mary Reis and dog "Tuffy" in El Lagarto at Reis home in Bolton. Courtesy: Bill Morgan.

Happy Times

Above, Bill Morgan in *Happy Times* on Lake George. Courtesy: Bill Morgan.

Left, *Happy Times* at 1984 Boat Show on west side of Green Island in Bolton Landing. Photo by author.

Happy Times is an exact replica of *El Lagarto* built in 1969 by Bill Morgan of Morgan Marine at Silver Bay. *Happy Times* is 26 feet long with a 6 foot beam and is a five step hydroplane as was *El Lagarto*. She is powered by a 550 hp Chrysler Hemi engine which propells *Happy Times* over 72 mph.

Californian

Californian setting Gold Cup lap speed record of 63.64 mph against *Hotsy Totsy*. Right, 16 cylinder 620 Miller engine. Courtesy: Bill Morgan.

When I first saw *Californian* in the mid 1980's, she was unrecognizable. I was visiting Bill Morgan of Morgan Marine at Silver Bay with my two boat racing uncles, "Smokey" and Bob Gates, when Bill told us to walk out to his upper barn for a look. Just inside the door and to the right sat the burned out rotting remains of a boat with all of her sun dried ribs exposed—a sorry sight. Bill told us that he had searched for her in California where she had originated in the late 1920's and found what remained of her at Long Beach. Although she had been left outside next to a shed, exposed to all of the elements for many years, Bill purchased her and brought her to Lake George.

Californian (G2) was originally owned and driven by Dick Loynes of Long Beach, California. She first competed in the Gold Cup races on August 16-20, 1930 at Red Bank, New Jersey racing against *Hotsy Totsy*, *Scotty-Too*, *Miss Philadelphia*, *Imp*, *Red Banker* and George Reis's *El Lagartito*. Powered by a highly modified 16 cylinder 620 Miller engine, *Californian* set a Gold Cup lap record of 63.64 mph before bending her propeller shaft strut which forced her to retire from the race which *Hotsy Totsy* went on to win.

The August 16, 1931 Gold Cup began at Lake Montauk, Long Island featuring their home winner from the previous year, *Hotsy Totsy*. *Californian* was among a field of 10 racers which included George Reis's new Hacker contender *El Lagarto* (G18), reconstructed from Edward Grimm's 1922 racer *Miss Mary*. After the starting gun was fired, *El Lagarto* shot into the lead for the first 10 laps. *Californian's* Miller engine was not running well and by the second heat her engine failed completely during the final lap. In the final heat, her engine died in the first lap allowing *Hotsy Totsy* to win the competition a second year in a row. *Californian* never again raced for the Gold Cup.

At this time, the "gentleman's racer" *Californian* was relegated into use as a pleasure craft, a fate which fell to most of these retired old racers. Her life is mostly undocumented from the 1930's to the mid 1980's when Bill Morgan found her and brought her to Lake George. Morgan Marine, which specializes in the construction of the 1930's Hacker Crafts, undertook a total

Californian burned during race. Courtesy: Bill Morgan.
Californian II (replica), 1990's. Photo by author.

reconstruction of the boat. Bill never installed a new engine in it nor did he ever intend to; today, 15 years later, she is still without an engine, intended for display only. As I write this, the restored original *Californian* is on exhibit for an unknown length of time at the Clayton Antique Boat Museum in Clayton, New York at the Thousand Islands. A replica of *Californian* named *Californian* II often is on display at our Lake George boat shows.

Hotsy Totsy

Hotsy Totsy 1930 & 1931 Gold Cup race winner. Courtesy: Bill Morgan.

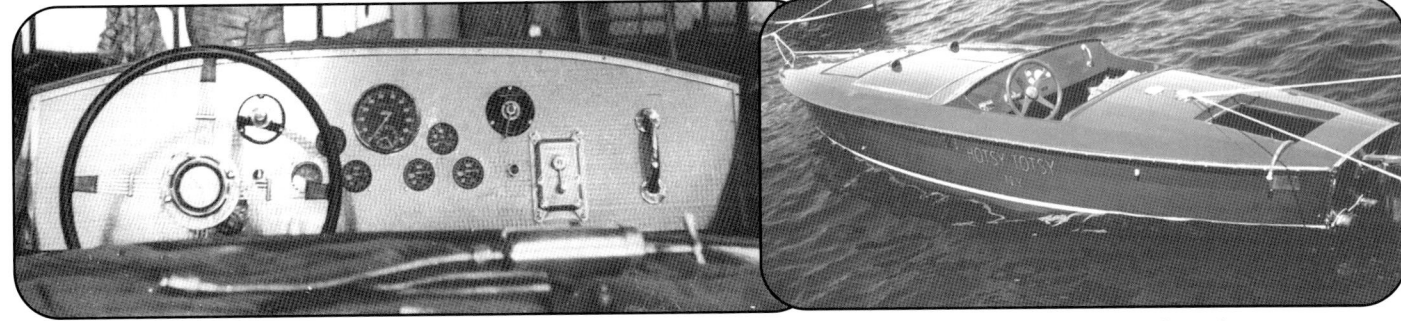

Hotsy Totsy's instrument panel, 1930's. Courtesy: Bill Morgan.　　　　　　　　　　　　　　*Hotsy Totsy*, 2000. Photo by author.

Owner and driver Victor Kliesrath of the South Bend, Indiana Yacht Club purchased *Hotsy Totsy* (G4) in 1930 prior to the racing season and immediately added 5 steps to the bottom. With the help of his powerful 625 Wright engine, *Hotsy Totsy* won the 1930 Gold Cup in red Bank, New Jersey at 56 mph with Scotty Too a close second. George Reis came in fifth in *El Lagartito*. Kliesrath repeated this same feat the following year at Lake Montank, Long Island at 54.9 mph with *Miss Philadelphia* coming in second. Reis finished sixth and last in his new racer *El Lagarto* due to the failure of a valve. Later, there was a *Hotsy Totsy* II and III with *Hotsy Totsy* III winning the Gold Cup in 1940 driven by Sidney Allen.

Baby Bootlegger

I've been around old mahogany speedboats my whole life and I love them. Growing up around the *El Lagarto*, former 1930's Champion, I thought that no other boat could stir my passion as much. When I attended the First Antique Gold Cup Regatta on Lake George in August of 1977, the field of only 8 vintage racers on parade was a stunning sight. One of these boats was unrestored and displayed on an old trailer. I learned that the boat's name was *Baby Bootlegger* and it had raced under the designation (G5). At the time, I was most interested in the boats that had been restored, the ones that were in the water and running. I had no idea then that the partially burned ugly duckling *Baby Bootlegger* would soon become a beautiful swan, perhaps the most beautiful swan of them all.

At the beginning of the 20th Century, the Europeans were the first to place engines into boats. These "auto-boats" as they were called, put the Europeans far ahead in engine development from the beginning. The British Harmsworth Trophy became the first international prize offered for speed on water. The

Top, *Baby Bootlegger*, 1977. From 1977 Antique Gold Cup Regatta Program. Bottom, at Silver Bay Boat Show, early 1980's. Photo by author.

Gold Cup was offered soon afterward in 1904 in America by the American Powerboat Association to encourage competition between the sportsmen here at home.

From 1904 to around 1910, these first racers all carried displacement hulls which plowed through the water. Designs began changing through the next decade when racers were experimenting in hydroplaning, lifting their hulls out of the water to reduce friction and drag. One way they were able to improve in this area was to move the engines further back on the hull to reduce bow weight. At this same time, the racers were highly expendable with owners racing new boats every year and discarding the old ones. Thus, very few of these boats remain today.

By 1922, thinking changed again. Designers thought it would be more appropriate to produce "gentleman's racers" which could be used for enjoyment after their brief racing days were over. They had to be at least 25 feet long, yet not extend beyond

40 feet at the waterline. Engines were limited to 625 cubic inches and were required to be concealed beneath hatch covers. Exhaust pipes were moved down to the water level, seats for two additional passengers were required and operating running lights installed.

This new breed of racer was exactly what suited millionaire Caleb S. Bragg of Sands Point, Long Island. Bragg had raced automobiles against the famous Barney Oldfield and was looking for a new challenge. In 1924, he hired successful designer and Navy architect George F. Crouch to build his new "displacement-planing" racer at the Nevins Boat Company on City Island, NY. After installing a Hispano-Suiza V-8 engine in the completed 29 foot, 10 inch *Baby Bootlegger* won the 1924 Gold Cup. In 1925, Packard's 621 engine #1 was installed as an experiment and she won again and she was ahead in 1926 when her engine blew up. The fans, the press and even the other drivers all loved *Baby Bootlegger*. Not only was she a winner, but she was absolutely beautiful.

Baby Bootlegger disappeared from racing, and public life, in 1926. During the many decades which followed, even her whereabouts became lost information. She was soon forgotten altogether. Those that might have read something about her racing days assumed that she had been destroyed along with most of the others a long time ago. Mark Mason of Detroit, Michigan, a passionate wooden boat enthusiast, became determined to discover the end of the story for this exotic champion, so determined that those of us here at Lake George will forever associate Mark P. Mason with the boat.

Mark spent years researching and trying to track down *Baby Bootlegger*. Libraries, journals, traveling, leads, someone who thought he saw her once— dead ends. The last time she was seen was in 1950, yet Mark refused to stop searching. One day Mark received a letter from a man who said the boat's last owner was a C. W. Wragge from the Toronto area. After finding Wragge in Florida after a long search, Mark was told the boat had burned long ago, however Mark wanted proof, so Wragge sent Mark to a scrapyard in Quebec where the burned boat was discarded many decades ago. Through an interpreter, the yardsman was asked about "*Le Bebe' Contrabangier*". The man responded excitedly by saying, "I knew you were coming. I have saved the boat for you. I did not think that you would take so long!" The boat and original trailer had been sitting there in a shed for 26 years.

Mark now focused on restoring *Baby Bootlegger* to perfection—and he certainly did just that. When I first saw the restoration at Silver Bay in the early 1980s, she was absolutely flawless with each of her exposed brass screws lined up like soldiers. She stopped the show. Mark has cared for this boat wonderfully, but apparently the time has arrived for them to part. Mark recently sold *Baby Bootlegger* for a very sizable sum to a man in Michigan.

Delphine IV

Delphine IV, 1932. Courtesy: Bill Morgan.
Delphine IV, replica. Photo by author.

Delphine IV, designed by George F. Crouch and built by Horace E. Dodge, was originally christened *Solar Plexis* in 1925. In 1932, Dodge changed her name and added 5 shingled steps beneath her hull. She was 25 feet 4 inches long, 6 feet wide at the beam and powered by a Packard 3M-621 Gold Cup engine. In the skilled hands of Bill Horn and Charles Graflin, she won the President's Cup, then the Gold Cup at Lake Montank, Long Island in 1932.

There were other *Delphine*'s. *Delphine VI* experienced a name change to *Impshi*. With Benny Hill as driver, her name was then changed to *Hornet*, and then back to *Impshi* again with a new driver named Kaye Don. After her engine was supercharged, she raced on Lake George for the 1936 Gold Cup and won against the *El Lagarto* and seven others. *Delphine VII* was of lap strake construction. In 1979, Bill Morgan built a replica of *Delphine IV* which is owned today by John Skinner of Pilot Knob. This replica frequently appears at many of our Lake George Boat Shows.

Delphine VI became *Impshi* and won the Gold Cup on Lake George in 1936 for the Detroit Yacht Club.

Courtesy: Bill Morgan.

Delphine VII featured lapstrake construction, unusual for a Gold Cup racer.

Courtesy: Bill Morgan.

Ethyl-Ruth IV

When the *El Lagarto* won the Gold Cup in 1933, George Reis brought the races back to Bolton Landing on Lake George for the first time since Count Mankowski and *Ankle Deep* brought the races here in 1914. The races were held during the first week in August of 1934 with a field of 6 racers competing: *El Lagarto*, *Delphine IV*, *Imp*, *Hornet*, *Scotty-Too* and *Ethyl-Ruth IV*. There was a series of these *Ethyl-Ruth* boats; all were fast racers.

When *Ethyl–Ruth III* was retired, her replacement, *Ethyl-Ruth IV* (G7), was different in design than her earlier sisters. Designed by John L. Hacker for her owner John Shibe of Philadelphia, she was considered to be a serious contender here on Lake George. An interesting characteristic about her was that she rode absolutely level on the water, making it easier for her driver, Armand Pugh, to see ahead.

Top, Ethyl-Ruth III. Courtesy: Bill Morgan.
Middle, Ethyl-Ruth IV in her shop. Courtesy: Bill Morgan
Below, Ethyl-Ruth IV racing in 1934 Gold Cup on Lake George. Author's collection.

Imp

Imp was a strong contender on the Gold Cup circuit from 1930 to 1934. In 1934, she raced in Bolton, finishing in third place in the skilled hands of owner-driver Jack Rutherford of Port Washington, Long Island. Her 625 Wright engine never faultered.

Author's collection.

Miss America IX

Miss America IX was designed, built and driven in 1930 by the great Gar Wood. She is a 30 foot Single Step Hydroplane with an 8 foot 2 inch beam. Gar Wood drove her to victory in 1930 and 1931 in the Harmsworth International Trophy Races with the help of his riding mechanic Orlin Johnson. Originally twin Packard V-12 powered, she was the first boat to exceed 100 mph. Today she is powered by two 427 Chevy L-88's.

Miss America IX at Bolton Boat Show, 1980's.
Photo by author.

Gold Cup Drivers.
(Left to Right)

Bill Horn of *Delphine IV*.
Benny Hill of *Hornet*.
Dick Loynes of *Californian*.
George Reis of *El Lagarto*.
Vic Kleisrath of *Hotsy-Totsy*.

Courtesy: Bill Morgan.

Betty III & V

Top left, *Betty III* (*Black Betty*) in Northwest Bay. Top right and above, *Betty V* in Bolton Bay. Author's collection.

Much has been written about Mankowski and Reis, Lake George's own racing champions, but we had a third local champion who is remembered today by only a few and he needs to be recognized by the masses, and as with Mankowski and Reis, he also spent his summers in Bolton Landing. Young W. Melvin "Mel" Crook, fresh out of college, owned the racer *Betty III*, nicknamed *Black Betty*, and raced her successfully in the 1933 National Sweepstakes, but he did not win. The following year, he had a new single-step hydroplane named *Betty V*. (*Betty IV* was his pleasure boat.)

Betty V was an unusual boat in her time, built especially for the Sweepstakes Class, not the Gold Cup. She was a 29 foot hydroplane built by Walter Buskee of Dover, NJ. and was powered by a 12 cylinder Packard 3A-1500 aero engine, producing over 600 hp at 2500 rpm. She was easily capable of speeds around 80 mph. Mel entered her in the Governor Lehman Trophy Race in 1934 against *Delphine IV* driven by Bill Horn, *Chief II* owned by Senator F. B. Kavenaugh and driven by George Reis, and two Chris-Craft runabouts. Crook took an easy win and continued his winning streak at the National Sweepstakes in Baltimore averaging a record speed of 57.107 mph.

During the American Speedboat Champion Race, *Betty V* competed against *Miss Saranac*, formerly *El Lagartito*, and beat her, setting a new lap record of 64.3 mph. Only the day before, Crook put *Betty V* through the one mile trial runs and set a new American single-engine hydroplane record of 82.759 mph. He went on to win the National Sweepstakes again the following year in 1935. At the Red Bank National Sweepstakes Regatta in August of 1936, Mel and *Betty V* won the race for the third year in a row. In these mile trials, he achieved another new record by hitting 85.511 mph.

Ironically, it was not these races that would provide Mel Crook with enduring recognition. Mel became one of the best and fairest power boat officials ever involved in the sport. Although a Certified Public Accountant by profession, he also became a writer and wrote about power boat racing for national magazines for the next forty years.

During his racing years, Mel practised racing *Betty V* over a one mile course measured out in North West Bay and he positively influenced many young boating enthusiasts around the lake, such as Bill Morgan who became a racer himself. My uncle's Smokey and Bob Gates were always talking about boats with Mel, as was my father, Bill. Mel gave my dad wonderful photos of *Betty's III* and *IV*, and somehow, my uncle Bob ended up with *Betty V*'s extended trailer made from a Packard automobile frame, a yard trailer that I now own today.

MORE RACERS

There have been many Antique Boat Regattas on Lake George in the past few decades. These well organized events help to keep our boating history alive. Occasionally, our well attended regattas feature vintage racers, such as these below. Photos by Author.

My Sweetie

Baby Horace III

Wilverne

Verne Hovey of Basin Bay ordered a new 28 foot 1930 Chris-Craft Model 117, Hull #3116. On April 29 of 1930, it was delivered to Lamb's Boat Company in Bolton Landing. Hovey named his new craft *Wilverne*, a combination of the names of his two sons, Will and Verne. Eventually, he sold it to Henry Wright across the lake who changed the name to *Adeleda IV*, a combination of his two daughter's names, Adeline and Aleda. When Henry died, the boat went to his daughter Adeline and her husband. Today it belongs to Tom and Judy Moynihan of Cleverdale and is renamed *Big Momma*.

Wilverne at Verne Hovey's home in Basin Bay, 1930's. Courtesy: Kam Hoopes.

Lady of the Lake

Of all the wonderful Hacker's ever to ply the waters of Lake George, *Lady of the Lake* was the longest at 39 feet. *Lady of the Lake* was named for the English classic poem by the same name, written in 1902 by Sir Walter Scott. She was purchased by a family from Schroon Lake named Bofinger who once used her large cabin to give Franklin D. Roosevelt a tour of that lake. During the 1950's, *Lady of the Lake* was purchased by Alden Shaw for his boat charter business in Lake George Village, Marine Industries, Inc. Shaw removed her cabin and added her to his fleet of *Miss Lake George* charter boats. She passed through a series of Lake George owners, the LaFort's and the De Lucca's, and she is now gone from Lake George.

Lady of the Lake at Bolton Landing, 1980's. Photos by author.

Early Cabin Cruisers

Chris-Craft "Clipper", late 1930's model, in Paradise Bay.   Courtesy: Dick Dean.

There were only five or six of these late 1930 Chris-Craft "Clipper's" ever on Lake George. Each had Model "K" 95 hp engines, a sink, ice box and a head. One was owned by the owner of Mannis Oil Heat, the Water Bug was owned by Rachael Brandt of Cleverdale, Beckwith's of Assembly Point owned one and later sold it to Ed Kennedy of Cleverdale, Walt VanDuesen of Lake George Garage owned Van-Ann named for his wife, and John Hilton of Pilot Knob owns one today. Some had inside steering and others steered from outside. Each had a round porthole on the cabin and an open rear deck.

1930's Cruiser at Paradise Bay.
Postcard, author's collection.

Cachalot

Cachalot was built for Ted Culver by his neighbor and friend Art Stewart at the Pilot Knob Boat Shop. Culver and his dog loved to pilot along in this Lyman engine powered 20 foot cruiser at about 5 mph to troll for trout.

Cachalot owned by Ted Culver of Pilot Knob.
Courtesy: Roy and Jeanette Hunt.

Roamer

In 1931, John E. Lindsay of the Lindsay Boat Company on Hub Island in the Thousand Islands received an order for a 48 foot long, 12 foot beam, 60 passenger boat from a prospective Canadian buyer. After the basic hull was completed at their facility near Clayton in the Thousand Islands, the buyer backed out, citing financial difficulties related to the Great Depression. The Lindsay's stored the inverted boat and finally completed it six years later, then sold it for $10,000 to Alden Shaw and Walter Harris of Lake George. The *Roamer* was equipped with twin 6 cylinder Chris Smith gasoline engines and weighed 9 1/2 tons.

Roamer on the road to Lake George, November 1937. Courtesy: Dick Kowell.

On November 10, 1937, the *Roamer* was piloted to Fisher's Landing on the St. Lawrence, was hauled onto a cradle with two pairs of wheels attached and was slowly towed over 200 miles to Lake George. Alden Shaw's father, Ralph, ran a boat rental business between 1910 and 1920 renting canoes and rowboats in the area known today as Shepard Park. His son Alden expanded the business during his tenure between the late 1920's and the 1940's. Later, Alden's son "Tink" (Ralph) operated it from World War II to 1970 when he sold Lake George Marine Industries, Inc. to Pete Smith.

Roamer on Lake George. Photo by Art Knight. Courtesy: Lake George Historical Museum.

The *Roamer* was only one of many boats owned by the Shaw's, others being the *Barge Boats*, the *Ranger*, the *Sayonara*, a Float Plane for rides and lessons and the fleet of *Miss Lake George* speed boats. They began using the *Roamer* in 1938 for Paradise Bay cruises out of Lake George Village. They owned the *Roamer* for 33 years before they sold her to Peter Smith, current owner of the East Cove restaurant. From 1970 to 1973 Pete ran one-hour cruises with her to the Antlers Hotel, across to Assembly Point, into Dunham's Bay, and back to the village. The boat was sold to the Lake George Steamboat Company in 1973. Until 1980, she sailed from the pier at Rogers Park in Bolton Landing under Captain Kev Conerty, father of Tom Conerty who is the current Senior Captain and General Manager of the Lake George Steamboat Company. I came aboard at Bolton several times so Kev could give me a look-around. I remember vividly the *Roamer*'s large bus steering wheel mounted on an almost vertical shaft.

In the spring of 1981, Wilbur Dow of the Steamboat Company sold the *Roamer* to the Mid-Lakes Navigation Company on

ROAMER
1 HR. SHORELINE CRUISES

Leave 11 A. M.	Return 12 Noon
Leave 1 P. M.	Return 2 P. M.
Leave 2:30 P. M.	Return 3:30 P. M.
Leave 4 P. M.	Return 5 P. M.

Fare $1.25 (incl. tax)

All Points of Interest Announced on All Trips

Roamer Ad. Courtesy: Dick Kowell.

Roamer Ticket. Courtesy: Chris Shaw.

Skaneateles Lake near Syracuse. She was hauled out of Lake George by crane at the Lake George Steamboat Company's Steel Pier and placed onto a trailer. In April of 1981, the *Roamer* was towed through the town of Skaneateles Lake, New York.

Renamed the *Barbara S. Wiles* after the owner's late mother, on January 5th, 1982, the *Barbara S. Wiles*'s cradle mysteriously slid down into the icy lake and washed ashore causing $20,000 in damage. Severe winds, high waves and blocks of moving ice slowed rescue efforts considerably. Fortunately, she was finally rescued and repaired.

Our old *Roamer* still makes daily cruises around the north end of the lake. Several years ago, I drove out there to take a ride on her with my friend from Syracuse at the wheel, Captain Dick Kowell. She had just been varnished, painted and fitted with new twin diesel engines. Although I am a bit saddened that this classic old boat no longer plies the waters of Lake George, it is also a pleasure to know that the old *Roamer* is still in service—with a new name—on a new lake—enjoying a new life.

Roamer interior, 1940's. Courtesy: Chris Shaw.

Patricia, *Roamer* and *Sayonara*, 1969. Courtesy: Dick and Mary Kowell.

Arriving at Skaneateles, April 1981. Courtesy: Dick Kowell.

Washed aground in rough water, January 5, 1982. Courtesy: Dick Kowell.

Barbara S. Wiles (*Roamer*) rescued by Peter Wiles Sr., January 6, 1982. Courtesy: Dick Kowell.

Barbara S. Wiles (former *Roamer*) next to the *Judge Ben Wiles* at Skaneateles, early 1990's. Photos by author.

Miss Lake George Boats

Following World War II, Ralph A."Tink" Shaw operated a fleet of rental 14 boats, a business that was begun by Harm Burton. All were named *Miss Lake George*, followed by a Roman numeral. These were Hackers, Gar-Woods, Higgins, a few were Chris-Crafts, and each had a Native American name, as well. They were named by Alden Shaw's wife Waneta who was part Native American. By the time Dick Willmen purchased this part of the business in 1957, there were 7 boats in the fleet, and all of them were stored for the winter in Towers Hall. Some of the boat names then were: *Nee-Wah, Hawk, Dat-Me, Skip-It, Who-Dat, Gotta Go* and *Miss Lake George*. They all continued to operate with the *Miss Lake George* logo. There were 26 foot Chris-Craft's, a 30 foot Sea Lyon and a 23 foot Hacker. Miss Lake George was a 39 foot Hacker which was sold and became *Lady of the Lake*. She was powered back then by two Kermath engines. Willmen owned the business for 20 years until 1976. He sold the business to Jim Quirk who owns Shoreline Cruise Line.

Both photos, courtesy: Lake George Historical Association.

Ticket. Courtesy: Chris Shaw.

Courtesy: Wayde Earl.

Advertisement. Courtesy: Dick and Mary Kowell.

Miss Lake George docks. Courtesy: Gary Miller.

Ranger

After the World War II, there was an increase in demand once again for sightseeing rides on Lake George. The US Navy's Elco PT Boats, made famous by John F. Kennedy's exploits on PT 109, were originally built for use in the Pacific Islands. These PT Boats were fast because the hulls were constructed of lightweight plywood. After the war, they often found themselves being converted to passenger use on lakes and rivers around the country.

Alden Shaw and Harm Burton of Lake George Marine Industries, Inc. purchased one of these boats in 1946, valuing its hull at $75,000, with conversion costs planned to reach $50,000. The 40 ton, 80 foot long, 21 foot beam, 150 passenger *Ranger* was towed here up the Hudson River from Bayonne, New Jersey to the Champlain Barge Canal's Lock 4 between Fort Ann and Whitehall. She was strapped to the same cradle on which she was built and dragged ashore by two bulldozers and a crane. With

Ranger out at Barge Canal, 1946. Courtesy: Chris Shaw.

her superstructure removed, she was paraded through the streets of Glens Falls on June 26, 1946 on her way to Lake George where she would be stored and rebuilt over the next year in a large Quonset hut at the railyard behind the D&H train station. Three new 225 hp General Motors 671 diesel engines were installed to thrust her three large propellers. The 40 foot glass-enclosed mahogany interior was capable of transporting up to 150 passengers.

P T Boat *Ranger* in Glens Falls, June 26, 1946. Courtesy: Chris Shaw.

Quonset Hut at D&H Station. Courtesy: Gary Miller.
Right, *Ranger* emerges, 1947. Courtesy: Chris Shaw.

Ranger launching at Lake George. Courtesy: Gary Miller.

Construction for all the work was directed by George A, "Art" Granger of Lake George Village.

The completed boat was lowered down the marine railway to the edge of the lake for the christening ceremony which was held on May 31st, 1947. There was an excited crowd because it had been 35 years since a large boat of this size had been launched on the lake. The traditional champagne bottle was struck by Beverly Burton, the lovely sixteen year old daughter of Harm Burton, company treasurer. The boat was christened the *Ranger,* a familiar name to those who know of Major Robert Rogers and his Rangers in our local French and Indian War history. She then slid down the ways into Lake George and was

Ranger, 3 propellers and 3 rudders.
Ranger christening May 31, 1947.
Courtesy: Chris Shaw.

towed across the bay by *Miss Lake George III* where her final construction would be completed in time for the summer season. With George Doane as her first captain, the *Ranger* could easily reach speeds up to 20 mph. Her schedule took her on $2.60 cruises the entire length of the lake, departing at 11 AM and returning at 3 PM. She also ran a $1.50 evening cruise from 7PM to 8:30 PM which ran to Bolton Landing and back. Those of us who were here during the *Ranger*'s lifetime remember that she created a tremendously large wake. By the mid 1950's, the *Ranger*'s plywood hull began to suffer significant dry-rot. She was pulled up onto the shore where the present Boardwalk Restaurant is located in Lake George Village. There, she was cut up and burned at the waters edge on May 18th, 1957.

Ranger launching, May 31, 1947. Courtesy: Chris Shaw.

See The Entire Lake
On Board the New, Luxurious
"RANGER"

Capacity 150 Passengers   Lectured Tours

You will cruise thru the beautiful islands and see many of the exclusive homes along the shore

The Ranger is designed exclusively for sight-seeing and has individual seating for your comfort.

ENTIRE LAKE TRIP — $2.60
(Inc. Tax)
Leaves 11:00 A. M.   Returns at 3:00 P. M.

EVENING TRIP — $1.50
(Inc. Tax)
Leaves at 7:00 P. M.   Returns at 8:30 P. M.
Passing by Bolton Landing, Sagamore Hotel and Kattskill Bay

LIGHT LUNCHES ARE AVAILABLE ON BOARD

(All Times Listed Are Eastern Daylight Time)
LAKE GEORGE MARINE INDUSTRIES, Inc.
BEACH ROAD, REAR SKY HARBOR
For Reservations Phone 549

Top row, *Ranger* launched at marine railway. Courtesy: Chris Shaw. *Ranger* towed by *Miss Lake George III*. Courtesy: Tom Hirchburg. Middle row, Three 671 Detroit diesel engines installed. *Ranger*, Roamer ticket booth with Sky Harbor in rear. Courtesy: Chris Shaw. Bottom row, *Ranger* schedule, 1947. Courtesy: Dick Kowell. *Ranger's* bow. Courtesy: Tom Hirchburg.

Ranger on Lake George, 1950's. Courtesy: Tom Hirchburg.

Ranger being scrapped in Lake George Village at site of the present Boardwalk Restaurant on May 18, 1957. Courtesy: Chris Shaw.

Float Plane

After World war II, "Tink" Shaw began a Float Plane business at Lake George Marine Industries which he operated up until 1960. He gave flying lessons and was available as a charter service to fly passengers to other nearby lakes and locations.

Courtesy: Chris Shaw.

Barge Boats

From the late 1930's into the 1940's, Alden Shaw at Lake George Marine Industries, Inc. had a small fleet of Barge Boats which were available for rental. They were powered by small inboard engines and were quite stable in rough wate, although they were not very pretty to look at. With hulls made out of only plywood, very quickly they began leaking. Soon. they began to show serious dry-rot and were then abandoned.

Courtesy: Chris Shaw.

State Barges

They've been out on Lake George for many decades. Their green and yellow hulls with the long ramp on the bow send a dull signal to our brain –"There's a State Barge". Thinking back, I suddenly realized that they have been around all of my life. Frank Leonbruno, former head of the New York State Conservation Department on Lake George, informed me that these are the original 9 barges brought here immediately following World War II. They were Army Surplus units, built to be fastened together end-to-end, to become makeshift floating bridges across waterways in a war zone.

New York State Army Surplus Barge, 1946 to present. Photo by author.

Once they arrived here at Lake George after the war, state workers cut out each stern to accommodate an outboard motor and added the bow ramps. Their original outboard motors were 25 & 30 hp Johnson's and Evinrude's. Two men have always been assigned to each barge for safety reasons and to assist with any lifting involved. One of the two men is usually "in training" while the other acts as instructor. Each barge works a 5 day schedule per week.

For dock assembly in the spring, men use chain falls and a crank on the barge to lift each 10 foot dock section into place. Leroy Ryder, the current head of the DEC, says that barges are also used to build and repair tent platforms, outhouses and stone fireplaces. Whenever a tree blows down, the men are on the site immediately to cut up the wood and make repairs. Garbage pick-up and pumping of holding tanks is also on their work list.

Today, 7 barges are in use and 2 are in storage on Green Island. More than once a barge is caught in a storm heading to Bolton Landing from the Narrows and is nearly swamped from waves washing over the side. The men who work on them work hard and in very hot weather. Occasionally they would meet in a pleasant location after their work is completed for a quick swim. Once, back in the 1960's, I was surprised and amused to see one of the happy workers water skiing on a small piece of plywood behind a barge behind an island in the Mother Bunch Islands.

These barges are also utilized from mid June to November to transport Washington County Correctional Facility prisoners out to the state lands to assist with maintenance and repairs. It is easy to recognize when prisoners are aboard because each wears an orange life vest at all times.

The barges measure an overall length of 37 1/2 feet, breaking down as follows: a 30 ft. hull, plus a 2 ft. transom board with a 5 1/2 ft. ramp attached to the bow which helps the barges access a campsite without using a dock and without disturbing the occupants. The vessel approaches shore bow first and the ramp provides easy access to land.

Powered today by powerful 125 hp Mercury and Chrysler Force engines, these old green and yellow work horses still have many years of life still in them, and they will be out on Lake George for many years to come.

Ticonderoga (II)

The Great Depression and World War II took a negative toll on the tourist business here on Lake George. Following the war, the *Mohican* (II) was the only vessel owned by the Lake George Steamboat Company. Wilbur Dow purchased the company in November of 1945, and by 1949, he believed that the increased passenger possibilities warranted a new second vessel.

Following an extensive search, a retired Navy ship, *LCI (L) 1085*, was purchased from a moth balled fleet at the Brooklyn Navy Yard. She was originally built for the U.S. Navy in 1944 by the Defoe Shipbuilding Company in Bay City, Michigan. The ship served our country proudly as a member of Cincpac,

LCI (L) 1085 (Ticonderoga II). Courtesy: Bill Dow.

Ticonderoga's bow crossing D&H tracks between Champlain Canal and Lake George. Courtesy: John and Betty Barth.

Flotilla 23, Group 69, Division 138 in the final year of World War II, sailing through the Panama Canal to the Hawaiian Islands and Leyte Gulf in the Philippines while carrying out support missions. After the war, she carried men and supplies to Okinawa and Japan before she ended her career by sailing the eastern U.S. coast until the summer of 1947. She was then ordered to return to Com 3 at Newport, Rhode Island, then to Brooklyn Navy Yard where she was retired at anchor on 16 July 1947 and placed up for sale. On 30 September 1947, she was sold to the McAllister Brothers of New York City.

Left, the *"Ti"* in Ticonderoga. Courtesy: Don Cornell.
Above, the bow in Ticonderoga. Courtesy: Dottie Taber.

After Mr. Dow purchased her from the McAllister's in 1949 for $11,000, Captain George Doane sailed her up the Hudson and through the Champlain Barge Canal to Ticonderoga where she was cut into four sections and trucked five miles away to the Lake George Steamboat Company's Baldwin drydock at the northern end of the lake, passing through the town of Ticonderoga. At a cost of $250,000, she was reassembled and launched in October of 1950 experiencing extensive difficulties during the launching procedure. She was christened M/V *Ticonderoga* at Baldwin by 16 year old Miss Karlene LaPointe of Ticonderoga, winner of the Miss Ticonderoga Contest, sponsored by the Chamber of Commerce to determine who would christen the vessel.

For the first time since 1933, round trip service was restored to Lake George for the 1951 season aboard this refitted vessel christened *Ticonderoga*. Originally she was painted a very light blue color which made her difficult to see under unfavorable conditions so she was quickly painted white with a bright blue trim. The *Ticonderoga* was 168 feet long, 25 1/2 feet wide across the beam and carried a displacement of 360 tons. Twin Diesel engines totaling 900 horsepower pushed her along at an average speed of 14 miles per hour.

The *"Ti"* at Baldwin, winter 1949-1950. Courtesy: Dottie Taber.   The *"Ti"* at Baldwin, August 1950. Courtesy: Dick Kowell.

The new *Ticonderoga* (II) on Lake George, 1951. Photo by Art Knight. Courtesy: Lake George Historical Association.

The *Ticonderoga* was loved by thousands of Lake George fans who either rode her every season or watched her wind her way through the Narrows on her full length lake tour. I have a few clear memories of my own,

Marine Lounge and Marine Restaurant aboard the *Ticonderoga*. Courtesy: Lake George Village Historian.

Ticonderoga, my sister Jeanine, and me at age 12, on Bolton Pier, 1957. Author's collection.

riding her from Bolton Landing to Ticonderoga and back with my brother Bud. She experienced a few changes over the years–new windows were added, an upper canopy was installed, her first deck stern was enclosed and her pilot house was

LANDING PASS
Must Be Surrendered Upon Landing

TICONDEROGA Excursion Rate Ticket
Round Trip Through Lake George from Lake George and Return

This ticket constitutes the entire contract of carriage between the Lake George Steamboat Company and the buyer. It is expressly agreed that the Lake George Steamboat Company does not undertake to be liable for injuries, arising from the negligence of its servants, agents or employees or from any other causes.

Fare ...... $3.50   P N⁰ 5981

Lake George Steamboat Company, Inc.
Lake George, N. Y.
(Please Sign on Back)

Pass, 1960's. Courtesy: Darrell Finlayson.

M/V TICONDEROGA SCHEDULE
(All times listed are Daylight Saving Time)

LEAVE	June 11th through Oct. 22nd	June 11th through Sept. 10th
Lake George	10:40 AM	4:00 PM
Bolton Landing	11:20 AM	4:40 PM
Sagamore Hotel	11:26 AM	4:46 PM
Huletts Landing	12:03 PM	5:13 PM
Silver Bay	12:20 PM	5:30 PM
Hague	12:38 PM	5:48 PM
ARRIVE		
Ticonderoga	1:00 PM	6:10 PM
LEAVE		
Ticonderoga	1:05 PM	6:15 PM
Hague	1:25 PM	6:35 PM
Silver Bay	1:41 PM	6:51 PM
Huletts Landing	1:58 PM	7:08 PM
Sagamore Hotel	2:37 PM	7:47 PM
Bolton Landing	2:43 PM	7:53 PM
ARRIVE		
Lake George	3:23 PM	8:30 PM

The TICONDEROGA connects with the morning train from Albany, the afternoon train to Albany and the afternoon train from New York.
ROUND TRIP FARE (Including Tax) $2.60.
Children 5 to 12, half fare. Children under 5, free.
June 25th Through Sept. 17th

M/V MOHICAN SCHEDULE

14-Mile Island Cruise	11:00 AM to	12:30 PM
Paradise Bay Cruise	1:30 PM to	4:00 PM
Eastern Shore Cruise	4:30 PM to	6:00 PM
Sunset Shoreline Cruise	7:00 PM to	8:30 PM
Moonlight Sail Cruise	9:00 PM to	11:00 PM

(Saturdays and Sundays, July and August through Labor Day only).
All Cruises $1.25 (Tax Included) Except Paradise Bay, $1.50 (Tax Included).

Schedule, 1950's. Courtesy: Bill Dow.

raised, but she was still the *Ticonderoga* that we all loved.

In 1989, the new *Lac du Saint Sacrement* was built to replace the *Ticonderoga*. From 1989 to 1993, the tired old ship lay across the end of the Steel Pier in Lake George Village where she was used primarily for storage and quarters for our crew members. By 1993, the "*Ti*" as she was affectionately called, was beginning to deteriorate to the point where something had to be decided about her fate. The decision was painfully made. The "*Ti*" would be dismantled and her steel sold for scrap.

  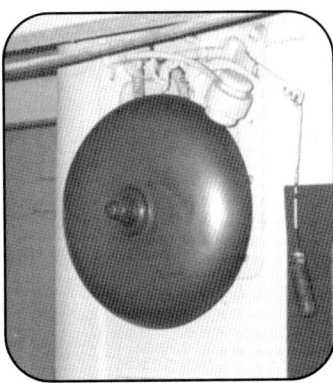

Ticonderoga (II) in storage at Steel Pier, 1991. Pilothouse. Engine. Alarm Bell.
Compass binacle and alarm bell are now on display at the Bolton Historical Museum. Photos by author.

Minne-Ha-Ha (II), *Mohican* (II), *Ticonderoga* (II) and *Lac du Saint Sacrement* at Steel Pier in Lake George Village, 1992.
Courtesy: Bill Dow, Lake George Steamboat Company.

The *Ticonderoga*'s Last Voyage.

In every person's lifetime, a few significant events occur that continue to live on within our vivid memory forever. The final voyage of the Lake George Steamboat Company's M/V *Ticonderoga* was one of those memorable historical events. People become very attached to boats. Vessels are given birthdays, christenings, names—and they live unique lives of their own. They become a significant and proud member of the "family" who sailed upon her. Company owner Bill Dow and managers Ted Kalisz and Tom Conerty decided that the *Ticonderoga* would sail proudly under her own power to our Baldwin dry-dock at the northern end of the lake for her final voyage on Wednesday, October 13th, 1993.

The weather was partly cloudy— cool winds pressed steadily out of the north. A large crowd had gathered on the Steel Pier by 10 a.m. Too many people wanted to ride so the policy was made that only the Dow family, (Bill, son Luke and sister Lynn), captains, engineers and a handful of invited quests would ride along. All lines were released at 11 a.m. sharp. Horns were sounded—people applauded—and the Star Spangled Banner was played. Cameras and photographers were everywhere—on land, in boats and aboard. So many boats followed us up the lake that we looked like a whale with its pilot-fish alongside.

Every captain on board took turns piloting the boat during her final voyage—Bill Dow, Ted Kalisz, Tom Conerty, Bill Wilson, Ed Stanilka, Tom Curri, Don Cornell and me. Our engineers aboard were Wayne Anderson, John Meyer, Kim Staats and Bill Meyers. We weren't in any hurry to end this nostalgic voyage. A trip that could have ended in 2 1/2 hours ran from 11 a.m. to sunset. We covered a lot of lake that day. The "*Ti*" passed closely to every one of her old steamboat stops on her final voyage. Our only docking along her old route was at the Bolton Landing pier. Many onlookers had gathered –a small music group from Bolton Central School played drums and clarinets for us–and a wonderful photo was taken of all the captains aboard lined up on the Bolton pier. After we landed at Baldwin, we celebrated the historic occasion with a brief champagne toast. The very next day, the Ticonderoga was lifted up onto our dry-dock and the dismantling was begun. Here she was, being scrapped on the very same drydock where she was assembled and launched 43 years before.

LCI (L) 1085, M/V *Ticonderoga*, registration PV-NY7865AF is forever gone, but parts of her can still be found around the lake. The captains and engineers each have one of her brass portholes–(Mine is proudly displayed in my home.) Her engines are in a tugboat on the Champlain Canal, and the Steamboat Company's old Lake George Train Station displays artifacts and proud photographs of her. Mark Curri of Bolton was given her anchor, and the Bolton Historical Museum has her compass binacle and alarm bell. In our fondest memories, the M/V *Ticonderoga* will always sail gracefully upon the beautiful waters of Lake George.

Left to right: Bill Wilson, Bill Gates, Tom Curri, Bill Dow, Ted Kalisz, Tom Conerty, Ed Stanilka, Don Cornell. Bolton Pier, October 13, 1993.

Pilothouse scrapped, 1993. Courtesy: Dick Kowell.

Above, *Ticonderoga*'s anchor. Courtesy: Mark Curri.

Left, *Ticonderoga* scrapped, 1993. Photo by author.

"MY LAST TRIP"
by Dr. Richard Garrett, Sr.
October 13, 1993.
<u>The *Ticonderoga* 'speaks' of her life on Lake George.</u>

Something there is 'twixt men and ships' that makes
A bond of kinship known to those few
Who build, and steer their course on seas and lakes,
And span the years dividing old and new.

Five years have passed while I lay at my berth,
And younger sisters came and took my place.
My engine heart, so strong and built to serve
Deprived of service, idly filling space.

My pilot house has stared with vacant eyes
Across the waters to that busy shore,
Whence came the throngs aboard with cheerful cries,
Those joyful souls my decks so proudly bore!

With deck plates longing for the pulse of life,
In patient silence have I spent the years
With memory's echoes of the sounds of strife
Of men in battle, ling'ring in my ears.

I served my country well in time of war,
In south Pacific seas, in Navy gray
I carried troops, and landed them ashore
In hostle lands so very far away.

Today my engine heart awoke! Once more,
With men aboard who know me, and who care,
I greet the wind and waves just as before,
And breathe the clean and chill October air!

My work is done. I sail to meet my fate,
And leave this blessed lake I love so well.
For men and ships alike, death sets the date,
And life must end. Let poets toll the bell!

Outboard Racing

Outboard racing began in the early 1920's with those first competitors reaching speeds of 25 mph. Through experimentation, it was discovered that mixing of fuels and engine modifications could create higher speeds, and it was later discovered that mixed alcohol fuels produced the greatest speed. By 1975, the fastest racing outboard achieved a speed of 115.547 mph with speeds even higher today.

Under American Power Boat Association rules, Stock Outboards must be run without the benefit of modifications; their engines must be run as they are right off the assembly line. Competitive stock racers depend instead on keeping the engine properly tuned, keeping weight to a minimum, having the exact engine height and angle, and having the right propeller for the surface of the water you are racing in.

Outboard racing began here during the mid 1930's. By the 1950's and 1960's, we had wonderful "90-mile Marathon" outboard races here on Lake George at Hague, sponsored by the Northern Lake George Regatta Association. When I was in high school, I traveled by boat to attend many of these races with my friend John Babe. The 1961 winner was Johnny Johnson of Kenosha, Wisconsin. In 1962, the race was won by Harry Smith of Pomeroy, Pa.

By 1963, over 100 entries came from all over the United States and Canada. Two generations of Hague's own Henry family participated in many of these races in both the A and D classes. The 90-Mile Marathon was raced on Sundays over a 5-mile course, which was run 6 times. It began at Hague, went south to Silver Bay and back north

"WHOOPEE" GOING STRONG. Dan Winchester leading, awakening machine-gun-like echoes from tne Lake George shore.

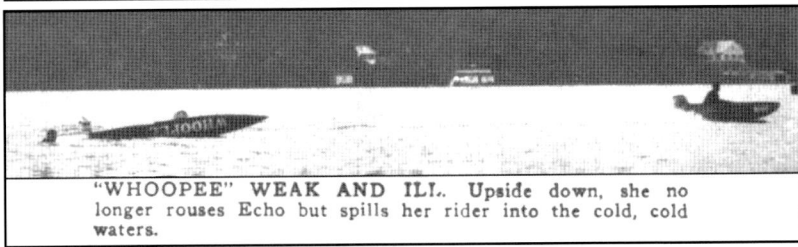

"WHOOPEE" WEAK AND ILL. Upside down, she no longer rouses Echo but spills her rider into the cold, cold waters.

STILL "WHOOPEE" BUT VERY LITTLE WHOOPEE. Dan Winchester, wet and cold, towed in after the ignominious upset.

Above photos, Outboard Racing, 1930's. Courtesy: Bolton Historical Museum. Below, Outboard racers at Hague, 1950's.

to Ticonderoga. In previous years, rough water forced many boats to the sidelines. On more than one occasion, John and I saw racers flip over or drivers flying out of their boats while racing at high speeds, however, each time the racer emerged safe and well. The fastest time for the Marathon was in 1957 when Eddie Tom of Fort Wayne, Ind. Ran the course in—1 hour, 59 minutes, 46 seconds.

On Saturday in 1963, an "Aquarama" was held featuring a parade on the lake and an afternoon water show. In the parade was a Chinese Junk named the *China Star*, a pint sized boat named *Little Toot*, a swimming automobile, and a kite flying demonstration by the internationally known sky skier, Alvara Duarte of Columbia, South America. In addition, a team from Chic's Aqua School in Bolton Landing named the Mad-Cat Maniacs performed their antics with Chic himself demonstrating the art of barefoot skiing.

Outboard racing at Hague, 1960's.

On June 14 and 15 of 1975, stock outboard races appeared once again on Lake George at Bolton Landing, sponsored by the Bolton Landing Chamber of Commerce. A series of nine races were held over the two day event with both Runabouts and Hydro's competing.

The Henry's of Hague still own their *Gingerly* and a second vintage racer, and a few others still exist around the lake today.

Racer being hoisted into Lake George at Hague, early 1960's.
Photo by author.

3N at Hague, 1960's.
Courtesy: Pat Steele, Historian.

Miss Mystery at Silver Bay, 1980's.
Photo by author.
Courtesy: The Larter's.

V-30 belongs to Buzz Lamb at NO-RO-WAL Marina in Bolton Landing.
Photo by author.

Ice Boating, by Sail

There are several possible explanations for the creation of the first ice boat–each is a fanciful yarn. One old legend suggests that a full-skirted lady and her skating partner were suddenly surprised by a strong gust of wind which propelled her swiftly across the ice. Her escort immediately saw the possibilities for combining skates, wind and a blanket into an ice sailing device, (later to be called Skate-Sailing). Another old tale is of a Norseman skiing along with a blanket over his arm when suddenly the wind caught his blanket and swiftly increased his speed while decreasing his effort.

One fact is certain–that the first true ice boats were built by the Dutch who used them as work boats along the Baltic coasts and throughout the Netherlands. The earliest recorded plans exist on an engraving dated 1768. The Dutch brought ice boating to the United States when they began settling the Hudson Valley in 1790. In 1871, the 140 mph "Icicle" and "Zephyr" raced the New York-Chicago Express train–and won.

The heydays of ice boating came to an abrupt halt on the Hudson in 1902 when ice-breakers began opening up the waterway for commercial navigation in winter, however, the successful "Hudson River" design continued in popularity up into the 1930s. Racing was a serious business, and interstate and international rivalries pushed ice boat experimentation towards an exact science. The Great Depression caused the paid professional crews to fade away–to be replaced by the mechanically inclined local builders who worked their creativity on a low budget to achieve speed and adventure on ice.

The earliest record of ice boating on Lake George dates back to the mid 1800s when Captain Sam Patchen of Sabbath day Point attached a sail to his sleigh, and using a pitchfork as a rudder, began sailing a full load of grist towards the mills of Bolton. Under the influence of too much rye, Captain Sam approached Vicar's Island at a rapid rate of speed, believing he might successfully jump the island. His judgement was as impaired as he was. His sleigh was demolished and Sam was deposited into a snow-drift.

Capt. Sam Patchen. Drawing by S.R. Stoddard, 1870.

Ice boating by sail as we know it first appeared on Lake George in Hague in the early 1900s with a craft built and piloted by a man named Lee Palmer. John Boulton Simpson of Bolton Landing also had one, but it received little use because he was primarily a summer resident. Ice boats began appearing in larger numbers by the early 1930s. Life-long family friend Charles "Juddy" Peer of Bolton Landing built one of the first ones. "It was a bow-steerer, constructed from whatever materials were available for me to use", says Juddy. "Its speed depended on what the wind was offering at the time, but it often reached speeds of 100 mph."

Nature didn't always provide the best ice for ice boating. Very smooth ice was required–ice without much snow or deep drifts. The best opportunities arose immediately after the ice froze and before the first snow. Another opportune time was when the ice melted and refroze–and there had to be a wind, too, of course. There were only a handful of days every year that fit these requirements so the ice boats and their captains had to be nearby and always ready. Often, the ice boats were on the lake the very same day the lake froze over.

J.B. Simpson's ice boat, 1907.
Courtesy: Bolton Historical Museum.

After World War II, ice boating by sail on Lake George began to grow in popularity and number. By the late 1950s and early 1960s, it reached its peak with annual race competitions held from the sheltered bay in front of Canoe Island Lodge at Diamond Point. The established course was 30 miles long and from a half-mile to four and a half miles wide.

Granville A. Beals of Assembly Point, once President of the Lake George Club, raced his ice boats on Lake George for years. His first was a large stern-steerer; his last two were of the International Skeeter Class. His son, John Beals, now of Pilot Knob, built and raced many ice boats, including those of the Yankee I Design. During the 1960s, John reached speeds, "three and four times greater than the velocity of the wind." He once crossed Lake George diagonally in 40 seconds from Lake George Village to Assembly Point, and piloted it regularly in excess of 100 mph on the straights. John explains, "The reason these boats can travel 4

Silver Bay, 1929. Courtesy: Silver Bay Association.

times faster than the speed of the wind velocity is that they are propelled by both the rear wind and the second wind forces created by the forward motion of the boat. When a boat is sailing at right angles to the wind, the combination effect of these forces, called Apparent Wind, is always somewhat greater than the speed of the boat, and increases as the boat goes faster."

Other competitors during those race years 40 years ago were: William C. Busch Jr, Vice President of the Bolton Chamber of Commerce, Richard Chase, Principal of Lake George Central School, Dr. Clinton Lawrence of Warrensburg, Albert Schumaker of Lake George, the Lamb brothers of Bolton Landing (Norman, Robert and Walter), Ned Pitcairn of Diamond Point and Philadelphia, Joseph Scully of Lake George, Don Quigan and two other ice boats from the Northern Lake George Yacht Club in Hague. By 1962, there were over ten ice boats of sail in the Adirondack Ice Yachting Association on Lake George—6 Yankee, 3 Skeeter Class boats and some Renegade's.

While growing up in Bolton, I can clearly remember these swiftly moving ice yachts sailing on the lake at incredible speeds. They were long–dark–sleek–and silent, almost mysterious. The cockpit at the stern could

"Juddy" Peer, 1936. Courtesy: "Juddy" Peer.

Top, Ice Boat racing at Canoe Island Lodge, 1960's. Courtesy: Walter Grishkot.
Left, Dick Chase's Ice Boat, 1960's. Courtesy: Darrell Finlayson. Right, Joe Scully's *Renegade*, 1960's. Courtesy: Joe Scully.

hold two people, but almost always the pilot sailed alone. Bill Busch often took his dog "Prince" along which was a novel sight to see. Once, my pals and I put skiis on an old door, rigged up a small sail and tried our own novice hands at the sport. We soon discovered that we were unable to steer it—and we also discovered that it wouldn't tack back home without the essential blades which would hold it onto the ice. We were forced to tow it back to Bolton all the way from Log Bay, but we never stopped dreaming and scheming about how to create our own ice boat.

During the mid 1960s, the fast ice yachts began disappearing from Lake George's frozen horizon. There suddenly were too many people, snowmobiles and fishermen out on the lake. The primary reason that this sport had diminished is that our ice conditions have not been favorable for decades. This past January of 2003, however, excellent black-ice conditions once again appeared on Lake George, and many of us dusted off our old ice boats and sailed all over the lake for the first time in decades. The small, convenient and popular Lackley "Skimmer's" made by Lockheed Martin Aircraft were seen everywhere. Of the slightly more than a dozen larger hulls once on lake George, only a few remain. Most of them have been dismantled or were scrapped in favor of the snowmobile, but this year of 2003, ice boats of all models appeared once again in all of their glory. Today, it is the wish of many that the once popular "Hard Water Sailing" days will once again return to Lake George.

Clockwise, Bill Busch and John Beals, 1960's. Photo by Walt Grishkot. *Ticonderoga* (II) and John Beals. Photo by Walter Grishkot. Rene Brochu and Bill Gates aboard Lockley "Skimmers", 2003. Photo by Mark Ackerle. Zandy Gabriels' ice boat, 2003. Photo by author. Doug Houghton's *Ice Scream*, 2003. Photo by author.

Skate Sailing

Skate Sailing was popular here also during the late 19th and early 20th centuries. Many photographs exist around the region depicting this early sport and speedy mode of transportation. The Bolton Historical Museum has several early photographs and proudly displays skate sails and skates once owned and enjoyed by early conservationist John Apperson. The museum also has another old 1925 skate sail recently donated by Walter Eichler of Lake George. This past January, 2003, John and Debbie Gaddy and their friend Margaret Wallace took advantage of Lake George's excellent black-ice conditions and skate sailed all the distance from Bolton Landing to Sabbath Day Point by sharing the same skate sail.

Skate Sailing at Tea Island, 1890's.
Courtesy: Bolton Historical Museum.

John Gaddy in Bolton Bay, 2003.
Photo by author.

Ice Boating, by Engine

The first "Motor Sled" in this region appeared in Glens Falls as early as 1915. It was owned by R.J. Scoville and Arthur Pike, and was powered by a bicycle motor. One of the early engine-powered ice boats on Lake George was owned by Clarence Shear in 1930, and Charles "Juddy" Peer of the "Huddle" in Bolton built one in the late 1930s. His sleek red three-runner craft

Bob Gates and his red Ice Boat in Huddle Bay, 1950's. Photos by Jack Bryan.

was powered by a recycled Harley-Davidson motorcycle engine mounted high in the stern and was capable of speeds in the 80 mph range. Its frame and runner-plank were constructed of hardwood for strength, while its body was constructed of canvas stretched over a lightweight frame. Each of the three steam-bent skis were ten inches wide for lifting the craft above the snow, and each ski had a thin metal runner-blade for stability on bare ice. The cockpit would hold two people, with the passenger seated behind the pilot.

After World War II, Juddy sold this ice boat to my uncle, Robert A. Gates, also of Bolton's "Huddle". Uncle Bob soon repowered it with a Lycombing aircraft engine which helped to push it close to the 100 mph mark. I both rode in and piloted this ice boat many times during the 1950s. Uncle Bob kept it on the ice all winter along the shore, north of the Huddle Public Dock. Without a mechanical starter, Bob would raise the propeller blade high in the air by hand and snap it downward until the engine roared to life. There wasn't any guard to shield the propeller—safety was always on our minds. Often we would

"Juddy" Peer's second Ice Boat, 1950's. Courtesy: "Juddy" Peer.   "Juddy" and the Gabriels family. Courtesy: Jane Gabriels.

throttle the craft quite high initially to break it free–and off we would go. With the engine only a few feet behind our heads, the roar was deafening. The ride was usually a little rough and sometimes the cold wind was a little difficult to take, but a new wind shield solved that issue. It was always a thrilling experience.

In the quest for more speed and new challenges, Juddy built a second ice boat for himself, and soon Uncle Bob and my Uncle "Smokey" Gates built a larger and faster one also which easily reached roaring speeds over 120 mph. Jack Bryan of Bolton came up with both of Bob's aircraft engines and helped to install them.

The only other engine-powered ice boat at the time was owned by George Reis, famed *El Lagarto* Gold Cup speedboat owner and driver. He had an

George Reis in belt driven Ice Boat. (Where?) Courtesy: JoAnn Irish Mahoney.

enclosed, heated ice boat constructed from the cockpit of an old green and white airplane. Local rumor always said that George was disappointed because it wasn't fast enough for him. What I remember is– soon afterwards, it was gone. Soon, others began appearing. Dick Willmen and Tom Roach each had one.

Today I own both of my Uncle Bob's engine-powered ice boats–the last two still in existence on Lake George. Although these museum pieces have been in storage since the 1960's, it wouldn't take long to get them running again, and I've promised many of my friends that I will do so someday. The thrill of speed on ice and the sound of the roaring engine is reason enough–and if you combine that with the nostalgia of going back to one of the great adventures of my youth here on Lake George–I don't really have a difficult choice at all.

Tom Roach's Ice Boat, 1960's.

Dick Willmen's Ice Boat, 1960's.
Both photos courtesy: Tom Roach and Joe Scully.

Clockwise, John Finlayson's aircraft powered Ice Boat on Upper Saranac Lake, 1960's. Courtesy: Darrell Finlayson.

Darrell Finlayson's small Dragonfly Snow Sled on Upper Saranac Lake, 1960's. Courtesy: Darrell Finlayson.

Bolton Landing Fire Department's new Ice Boat used for rescue on Lake George during winter season. Photo by author.

Horse Racing on Ice

During the early 20th Century, local sportsmen used the frozen surface of Lake George for serious horse racing competitions. Nearly every settlement on the lake had a featured racer. In 1907, the Bolton Horse Race was called off because one of the three horses to race was sick. In 1910, G. Frank Bryant's *Bell Ringer* covered a mile in 2:09 which broke the world record for ice races, giving him the $100 purse. The 1911 and 1912 races at Hague were held at Supervisor R.J. Bolton's hostelry and featured two classes of five horses, each racing for $75 purses. In 1912, races were held at Lake George Village for three days on a "Kite Shaped" course. The 1916 races at Lake George Village required six heats to decide the winner of the first event and four to choose a winner in the second event.

Above, Horse Racing at Lake George Village, early 1900's. Courtesy: John Beals.
Below, Racing at Lake George Village in the 1930's. Author's collection.

Amphicar

Amphicars were built in Germany for the American marketplace from 1961 to 1967. There were 3,800 of them built; 3000 of them were shipped here. Today, only about 500 remain here in America with about 80 remaining overseas. The Amphicar Company spent too much time on engineering and not enough time in marketing their product. Furthermore, it was not a very good performer as either a boat or a car, thus it was not a successful business. They did not have enough power to easily climb hills, but they had great gas milage using only $6.00 in gas over 4 hours, less when in water.

 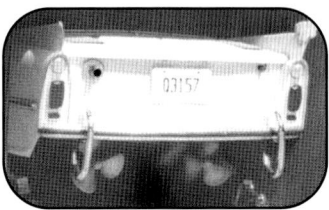

Larry Fueling's 1966 Amphicar entering Lake George at Rogers Rock Campground.
Courtesy: Bud Rawson, Ranger.

Amphicars were powered by a 43 hp Triumph-Herald engine, had a convertible top and featured a bilge pump which only was needed every 4 hours while in the water. Powered by twin propellers, it was steered in the water by the steering wheel, using the front wheels as rudders. It was very stable, but it was not very maneuverable. With their tops up, a group of them once successfully crossed the English Channel in a storm.

During my college years, I remember seeing several of these Amphicars around Bolton, and saw several drive into Lake George at Lamb Brother's Marina and at NO-RO-WAL. A red one appeared at the Bolton Boat Show during the mid 1980's and took a ride around Sawmill Bay, impressing the crowd.

In more recent years, an Amphicar Club camps every summer at Roger's Rock State Campground at Lake George's northern end. Ranger Bud Rawson says he looks forward to this group visiting every summer. Amphicar owner Larry Fueling of New Jersey says he likes not having to deal with a boat trailer, and they are great attention-getters.

Above, an Amphicar at a Bolton Landing Boat Show, 1980's. Photo by author.

Right, Larry Fueling and Bud Rawson cruising Lake George at Rogers Rock. Courtesy: Bud Rawson.

Patricia

The *Patricia* was built in 1965 at the J. Nolan Shipyard in Erie, Pennsylvania, hull number #292688. She was 64.9ft. lond and sported a 17ft. 5 1/2 inch beam. Her gross tonnage of 49 tons was propelled by twin 671 engines producing 350 horsepower. The Nolan Company leased her to a Jack Barnhill in Sault Sainte Marie, Michigan for ferry use in the Straits of Mackinaw.

At the conclusion of her first year, Alden Shaw purchased her and brought her here to Lake George during the winter with the help of his son "Tink". Captain Marty Fisher was at the helm, Earl Barrett was engineer. While on a stop at Buffalo, they picked up Tink's son Chris and sailed onward to Lock 4 at Fort Ann where she was transported to Lake George on January 21st for the 1966 season. She then spent her time making trips for up to 176 passengers to Paradise Bay. Peter Smith of Lake

George Marine Industries purchased the *Patricia* in 1970, and for only $2.50 per person, passengers could cruise from Lake George Village to the Narrows and Paradise Bay. (His Marine Industries also offered cruises on the *Roamer* and the *Sayonara*.)

Her next owner was Wilbur Dow of the Lake George Steamboat Company. In 1973, he trucked her over to Lake Champlain once again where Captain Marty Fisher was to sail her to Florida. On Thanksgiving Eve, Captain Fisher called William Dow (Wilbur's son) from Atlantic City with the message that the *Patricia's* navigation system equipment had become inoperative. Bill Dow, an experienced navigator, left immediately and brought the *Patricia* across the Chesapeake to Norfolk, Virginia where Captain Fisher could then easily proceed down the Inland Waterway to the Saint Petersburg Cruise Lines, owned by the Dows. She was renamed the *Sunshine City*, and there she sailed alongside the *Sun Coaster*, both piloted by Captain Lee Taber of Warrensburg, one of my present day sailing partners and friends at the Lake George Steamboat Company. Lee told me the new *Sunshine City* sailed in Saint Petersburg for two winter seasons. Now under Coast Guard regulations, her passenger capacity was lowered to 126 persons.

The boat sold again in 1975, ironically, to the very same man in Michigan, Jack Barnhill, who had leased her briefly in 1965. Lee Taber told me that Jack loved the boat and wished he had bought and kept her right from the beginning.

To complete the sale, Captain Taber sailed her to New Orleans where she was to be lifted onto a barge in the Industrial Canal. On May 5, 1975, a belt beneath the boat slipped off and she dropped onto her starboard side across the top of the barge. Fortunately, the boat did not sustain major damage, the sale was finalized, and she was renamed the *LaSalle*. In September of 1980, Lee Taber spotted the *LaSalle* in the "For Sale" section of Boats and Harbor Magazine. The Star Line had upgraded her engines to 871GM's at 360 horsepower each. Her passenger capacity was increased to 139 and the asking price was listed at $175,000 firm.

Alden Shaw's *Patricia*, 1967. Courtesy: Chris Shaw.

Peter Smith's *Patricia*, early 1970's.
Courtesy: Lee Taber.

ABOARD THE M.V. "PATRICIA"
Mid-May 'Til Mid-Oct.

2-Hr. 35 Mile Cruise

SHORELINE CRUISE TO THE NARROWS	Lv. 11:30 A.M.
PARADISE BAY CRUISE (2½ Hrs.)	Lv. 2:30 P.M.
EVENING SHORELINE CRUISE	Lv. 7:00 P.M.
MOONLIGHT CRUISE (1½ Hrs. $2.00)	Lv. 9:30 P.M.

$2.50
Children Under 12 ½ fare
Under 5 free

Built in 1965, the Patricia is the newest, most modern vessel that offers you the maximum in safety and comfort while you ride aboard the most maneuverable vessel on Lake George.

- Every morning at 11:30 we leave on a 2-hour shoreline cruise visiting eight communities, over a dozen bays and inlets along with over a score of islands. • At 2:30 every afternoon, we schedule a trip to unsurpassed Paradise Bay — you will be amazed at the beauty of Lake George as your captain eases around the dozens of islands. • In the evening at 7:00, you are offered a cruise along the shoreline under the rising moon, and inspired by soft music and beautifully lit homes. • A moonlite cruise at 9:30 P.M. is a fitting climax to a busy day around the lake. Soft music, the stars and moon relax you as we drift along the shoreline. (Legal Beverages Served)

Amazingly, Lee still had this 20 year old advertisement! My hands were shaking slightly as I dialed the telephone number. I reached one of the three owners, Tom Pfeiffelman, who told me they eventually sold the *LaSalle* to the Sleeping Bear Dunes National Lakeshore at Leland, Lake Michigan where she still makes daily ferry trips to the two North and South Manitou Islands. She now sails under a new Indian name.

To get an idea of the *Patricia*'s appearance, you can view her Nolan sister-ship, the *Defiance*, at Shoreline Cruise Lines in Lake George Village. The only noticeable difference is that the *Patricia* had a raised pilot house.

Many of you out there remember the *Patricia* with very fond memories. I'm certain you are as glad as I am to discover that she is still alive and living an active, useful life.

Patricia reentering Lake Champlain, 1973.
Courtesy: Chris Shaw.

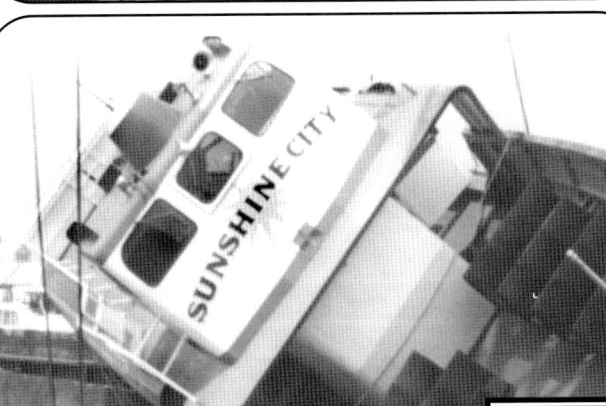

Top right, *Sunshine City* (*Patricia*) at St. Petersburg, Florida.

Sunshine City (*Patricia*) mishap at New Orleans, May 5, 1975.

Courtesy: Lee Taber.

PASSENGER BOAT FOR SALE: Nolan blt. 65' x 17' x 5½' all steel boat. USCG approved for 139 pass. Powered by twin 871 GM engines (360 HP each; new in 1976). Boat in excellent condition & now operating. Hull inspection 1979. Fully equipped: Decca Radar, Radio, P.A., Quality compass, new seating on upper deck. Available after Labor Day. $175,000 Firm. Ordering new boat. Pictures.

LaSalle (*Patricia*) advertisement, 1980. Courtesy: Lee Taber.

Submarines

Baby Whale

Many people have dreamed of exploring Lake George's crystal clear waters in a submarine, and a few have actually tried it. The first research submarine on the lake was to be christened the *Baby Whale*, but the christening never took place. *Baby Whale* was a two-person sub, totally home made, was 15 feet long, weighed 3,700 pounds and was painted bright yellow. She was designed and built over an 18 month period by three local partners; James Parrott, Gerald Root and Art Jones for the purpose of exploring for underwater artifacts relating to the French and Indian War. The sub had only one 12 inch glass porthole on her starboard side to facilitate underwater maneuvering and photography at a maximum depth of approximately 30 feet. On August 2,1960, the $1,500 *Baby Whale* was lifted into Lake George by Del Hammond's large crane at the Lake George Steamboat Pier and was towed to a private dock on the east shore of the lake where resurfacing equipment and an electric motor were to be installed.

During the night of August 4th, less than two days after her launching, *Baby Whale* disappeared and was never found. An extensive search was made at the time on land, by air and under water. She had vanished without a trace.

Bateaux Below, Inc. became interested in the submarine in 1987 when they began exploring the 1758 bateaux recently discovered off Wiawaka. On and off over the years to follow, they began searching for the lost sub by using divers and side scan sonar. During the summer of 1995, the lost *Baby Whale* was discovered and investigated by the Bateaux Below, Inc. research team of Bob Benway and Joe Zarzynski. Her location is still being kept a secret at this time while the submarine is being researched, documented and explored. In the future, it might become another feature in Lake George's Underwater Heritage Preserve.

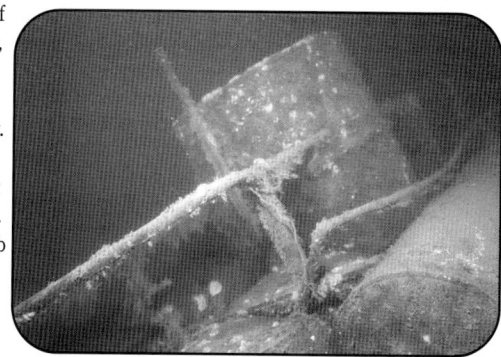

Top photo of *Baby Whale*, 1960. Courtesy: Bob Benway.

Underwater photo, 1995. Photo by Bob Benway of Bateaux Below, Inc.

Porpoise

Bill Dow, owner and President of the Lake George Steamboat Company, once tried his hand on a Lake George submarine, and he nearly lost his life doing so. In 1965, it was suggested that another attempt should be made to have a submarine available for research and rescue. Bill Dow was then sent to Florida for a 5 day training session on a new German built Graf Hagenburg one-man submarine. Bill enjoyed the experience, purchased one named the *Porpoise* and brought it to Lake George. It was displayed in the spring of 1966 by the Lake George Chamber of Commerce at the Fort William Henry Hotel during their annual Adirondack Sports-O-Rama.

Soon afterwards, a man in a rowboat drowned off Diamond Island, and the *Porpoise* went out to search. *Porpoise* was towed out to the site by Bill Dow, Ted Kalisz and Jim Marvel, all from the Lake George Steamboat Company. Bill entered the sub, gradually let the air out and suddenly it "sank like a rock and hit the bottom hard", 90 feet down. With the lead keel driven deep into the mud, Bill was in trouble. He began rocking the hull back and forth as he gradually let air into the floatation tanks. Suddenly, the keel broke free and *Porpoise* rocketed to the surface faster than it had sunk. To the astonishment of Ted and Jim at the surface, the *Porpoise* leaped out of the water and landed with a huge splash. Fortunately, it had not come up beneath the towboat; it had, however, rocketed skyward too close for comfort. Soon thereafter, the *Porpoise* was sold to two men from Buffalo.

Bill Dow's *Porpoise*, 1966. Courtesy: Darrell Finlayson.

Diver's World

In 1982, another one-man submarine owned by Ed Hines, owner of Diver's World on Route 9, appeared here on Lake George. Ed had purchased the sub in Florida. Named *Diver's World*, it could travel at 5 mph and was powered by two 12 volt batteries with a 4 hour underwater cruising capacity. The sub was capable of reaching depths of 300 feet, perfect for Lake George with 200 feet east of Dome Island being its deepest spot.

The hull's yellow walls were quarter-inch fiberglass and featured a transparent bubble conning tower of 1/8 inch clear plastic. It had radio communication for talking with the surface, carried lead for ballast, was 8 feet long, 40 inches wide and 46 inches high. To operate it, Ed would sit on the battery case in his SCUBA gear and descend by pulling a lever which filled the cabin itself with water up to the pilot's chest. Air pressure kept the water from rising further. To ascend, air was again pumped inside through a 6 inch opening to force out the water. The pilot could even land on bottom, use his SCUBA tank to explore and photograph, then reenter the sub, pump out the water and rise again. When Ed first tried it out in Lake George, he was astonished to discover that the steering mechanism worked in reverse order. He later discovered that its first owner was a large man and the only way he could steer it in the cramped cockpit was by crossing his arms. Ed immediately reversed the steering mechanism. *Diver's World* was used every summer in Lake George to explore the bateaux sites and for investigating around the islands in the Narrows up until 1991. In 1993, it turned up missing—it was stolen and resold.

Diver's World submarine, early 1980's.
Courtesy: Karol Hines

Algonquin, de Champlain & Ethan Allen

Jim Quirk, owner of the Shoreline Cruise Company in Lake George Village, began his business here on Lake George by leasing the docks from the Rogue's Roost and the Jolly Roger (now Shepard Park) from 1967 to 1972. By 1974, the business moved to the Village Docks along the Beach Road until he moved to his present location behind Kurosaka Lane in 1979. During the mid 1970's, Jim took his sons to the Thames River in Connecticut to view the Polaris Atomic Submarine. After learning that the tour boat he was riding on was for sale along with two similar vessels, he purchased them immediately with the intention of using them at his other boat rental business on Lake Champlain. In May of 1977, Jim and his crew, which included Bill Huus, Al Dardis, Merle Smith of Diamond Point and four eager crew members, arrived at Groton, Connecticut. The three boats were ready and waiting with all necessary gear stored aboard. "Quirk's Navy" spent six unforgettable days on the

Above, after boats were delivered in 1977. Left, *de Champlain* showing canvas roof. Below, *de Champlain* today. Photos, courtesy: Jim Quirk.

journey northward. When they sailed out of Groton and on into Long Island Sound, the weather was fine, however, as they approached Huntington, Long Island, a strong gale-force wind blew up, totally soaking the crew. On the positive side, Jim now realized that his three new boats were very stable in rough water. Near the end of their northward journey, all three boats passed

Ethan Allen and *Algonquin* today. Photos by author.

through the 8 locks from the Hudson into the Champlain Barge Canal. This 165 foot high lock system is one of the highest lifts by locks anywhere in the world. On the final day, the boats were lifted onto specially built trailers for the 3 1/2 mile journey from Ticonderoga to the northern end of Lake George.

That first year, these boats departed every half hour to Diamond Point, Long Island, Assembly Point and into Harris and Dunham's Bays. Each boat has a 40 foot fiberglass hull carrying a beam of 12 feet with a draft of only 21/2 feet. Jim recently told me that their 50 passenger capacity hulls are actually Herrschoff designed Dyer built sailboat hulls equipped with full length 2 ton keels and large rudders which adds very positive results in handling. Each hull, built in Rhode Island, displaces 10 tons in weight. Recently Jim replaced the *de Champlain*'s old Hercules engine with a new Isuzu 125HP model which efficiently and cleanly uses only 1 gallon of fuel per hour. All three of these boats are extremely quiet in operation, a fact that is greatly appreciated by lakeshore property owners who have had more than their fill of unnecessarily noisy boats. For the first few years, all three boats featured canvas tops until they were replaced recently with solid ones. The heads were removed from the *Ethan Allen* and the *de Champlain*, however, the *Algonquin*'s head is still in use. Since no refuse is permitted to enter our clean lake, the holding tank requires regular pumping.

Operated by Dick Paris, Frank Antos, Bill Perry, Bruce Beck and John Mason, these three boats depart approximately every half hour for one hour narrated cruises around the southern basin, and they run on charter cruises quite frequently, also, with some of them departing from as far north as Bolton Landing, Hulett's Landing and Silver Bay. In addition, the *de Champlain*, *Ethan Allen* and *Algonquin* are used 30 to 40 times a year by the Lake George Association for their educational "Floating Classroom" program. Participants use Secchi disks, plankton nets and other scientific equipment to test and study the water quality of Lake George. Shoreline Cruises has managed to carve a niche for itself in today's market quite successfully with these three boats, along with their *Horicon* and *Defiance*.

Defiance

The *Defiance* was built in 1978 by the J. Nolan Shipyard in Erie, Pennsylvania, and she is a sistership to the *Patricia* which once sailed here on Lake George. The one noticeable difference between the *Defiance* and the *Patricia* is that the *Defiance* has a lower pilothouse. Originally, the *Defiance* sailed on Long Island Sound and was named the *Long Island Queen*. In 1983, the 65 ton boat was brought up the Hudson to Lake Champlain and trucked overland to

Above, *Defiance* removed from Champlain Canal, 1983.

Left, *Defiance* arrives on Beach Road for launching.
Courtesy: Jim Quirk.

Lake George Village where she was launched along the Beach Road with the help of a large crane. She is 65 feet long, has an 18 foot beam and can carry up to 150 passengers. *Defiance* is powered by twin 1000 hp Detroit 8v71 turbo-diesels and can reach a speed of 12 mph. Her first captain was Jim Flowers, followed by Bill Huus and Al Dardis. Today she's run by Dick Paris, Frank Antos, John Mason, Bill Perry and Bruce Beck. Her schedule takes her on evening Happy Hour cruises from 7 to 8:30 Pm, on Paradise Bay runs, on charters and on entertainment cruises when the *Horicon* is out of port.

Today, spring 2003, a plan is being discussed to replace the Defiance with a new 400 passenger, 115 foot long, 30 foot wide, 120 ton tour boat.

Above, *Defiance* launched from Beach Road, 1983.
Left, new *Defiance*, 1983. Courtesy: Jim Quirk.

Defiance today. Photo by author.

Horicon (Shoreline Cruises)

The present 42 ton *Horicon* owned by Shoreline Cruises is the result of a 12 month planning and building project by company owner Jim Quirk and John and Rick Scarano of the Scarano Brothers Boat Builders located at the Port of Albany. The majority of the "cold mold" wooden hull construction was completed at Albany where she was launched on May 4, 1988 into the Hudson, transported northward through the Champlain Canal and hauled 3 miles overland to Ticonderoga where she was launched onto Lake George. She then traveled southward using her own power to Lake George Village where her third deck was added at the Shoreline Cruises docks. On Sunday June 12, 1988, the *Horicon* was christened by the Rev. George Phillips of Sacred Heart Church in Lake George. Her captains to date have been Jim Flowers, Dick Paris, Bill Huus, John Mason, Jim Young and Bob Nason.

The *Horicon* is made entirely of Yellow Pine, mahogany and teak and is powered by twin turbo Cummins Diesel engines producing 700 hp at a speed of 15 mph. She is 85 feet long, has a 22 foot beam, drafts 4 feet and can accommodate up to 300 passengers for sightseeing and charter cruises.

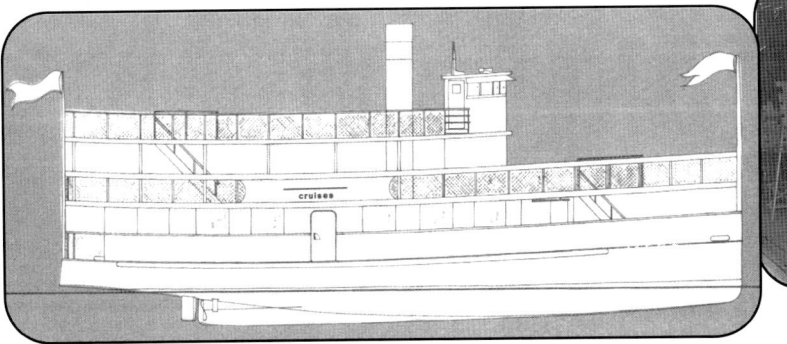

Shoreline's *Horicon* under construction, 1987.
Courtesy: Jim Quirk

Left, *Horicon* into Lake George. Above, *Horicon's* hull under her own power to Lake George Village. Courtesy: Jim Quirk.

Above, *Horicon* passes Bolton. Courtesy: Jim Quirk.
Right, *Horicon's* engines. Photo by author.

Above, *Horicon* construction, 1988. Photo by Author.
Right, *Horicon* today. Courtesy: Jim Quirk.

Ms. Lake George & Spirit of 76

During the winter of 1974-1975, Shoreline Cruise Line in Lake George Village decided it needed to expand its fleet. Owner Jim Quirk commissioned designer, builders Don Perkins and Fred Roeslin of Beacon, NY to build a new boat that would be stable and dependable for speedboat rides. In 1915, the Ms. Lake George began its operation after being launched at the Shoreline Cruise launch ramp. The 25 passenger *Ms.Lake George* is 26 feet long, 9 feet wide at the beam and is powered by twin Merc Cruisers. She is equipped with a PA for narrated tours. In 1976, another identical boat was added named *Spirit of 76*. Both of these boats are still in operation today to ferry passengers out to their parasail rafts.

Photos, courtesy: Jim Quirk.

Minne-Ha-Ha (II)

Throughout the 1950s and 1960s, the *Mohican* and the *Ticonderoga* were the only vessels owned by the Lake George Steamboat Company. The *"Mo"* was making two daily Paradise Bay trips while the *"Ti"* handled the full-length cruises down the lake. It became obvious by 1968 that the public wanted a one-hour trip to accommodate their young families and busy schedules. Steamboat Company owner Wilbur Dow wanted a new vessel to be its own attraction— a showpiece powered by steam.

The initial plan was to build a sidewheeler, but it would have appeared too wide compared to its relatively short length. The sternwheeler which resulted was designed by H.M. Tiedemann Company of New York City. Construction began at our Baldwin Shipyard near Ticonderoga on October 2, 1968 under the supervision of the LGSBC's Marine Superintendent Jim Marvel. The completed hull was launched on December 6th of that year, and it was towed to the Steel Pier in Lake George Village by her sistership, the M/V *Mohican*. She was completed during that winter by our own Lake George Steamboat Company's engineering crew at a cost of $270,000. Initially, the *Minne-Ha-Ha* was 103 feet long and 30 wide at her beam.

Minne-Ha-Ha (II), before she was lengthened. Photo by author.

With a displacement weight of 200 tons, she was capable of speeds up to 7 MPH. Draft was 3 feet, 6 inches.

The Frederick H. Semple Manufacturing Company of St. Louis, Missouri designed and built the steam engine which produces 200 horsepower from 6,000 pounds of steam per hour. The stainless steel boiler was built by the International Boiler Works of East Stroudsburg, Pennsylvania. Two pistons, moving a distance of 4 feet, crank power to the 12 foot diameter paddlewheel at her stern. The engineer operates the paddlewheel by listening to a series of bells rung by the captain; these bells were recycled from a 1910 Hudson River steamer. Her helm is half of the wheel from the old steamboat *Horicon* (II). (The other half is on display inside the *Lac du Saint Sacrement*.)

Minne-Ha-Ha (II) Pilothouse. Photo by author.

Minne-Ha-Ha (II) officers and crew, 1970's. Courtesy: Lee Taber.

Minne-Ha-Ha (II) before and after 34 feet added midship, 1998-1999. Photos, courtesy: Brian Granger.

Wilbur's wife, Ruth, struck the traditional champagne bottle against the jackstaff on July 30, 1969 and the new boat was christened *Minne-Ha-Ha*, meaning "Laughing Waters", the name given to Indian Chief Hiawatha's wife. Two days later, the *"Minne"* began her daily schedule of popular one hour cruises under a series of captains over the past 32 years–Captains Mike Kehoe, Bill Dow, John Miller, Fred Dorr, Tom Thompson, Ron Welton, Steve Boyce, Ed Stanilka, Bill Connor, John McDonald and Dave King. It is interesting to note that much of her crew these days, both captains and deckhands, comes from Ticonderoga.

This boat is so successful that current company owner Bill Dow decided to modify the *Minne-Ha-Ha* during the winter of 1998-99. She was cut into two parts and 34 feet of hull was added to her midsection changing her displacement to 250 tons and bringing her overall length up to 137 feet. Handicap access was improved, and a propeller was added, powered by a caterpillar diesel engine. The propeller was a necessity to assist this much longer vessel in its difficult docking maneuvers. Although the old twin split-stacks have been replaced by a sleek single stack, it is interesting to note that the old stacks have been preserved for everyone to view on the Steel Pier.

Mohican towing extended *Minne-Ha-Ha* to Lake George, 1999. Photo by author.

From our pilothouse viewpoints on the *Mohican* and *Lac du Saint Sacrement*, the *"Minne"* is a beautiful sight to watch when she is steaming at an angle towards her berth at the pier—and when we are up the lake on the *"Mo"* or the *"Saint"*, we always watch the *"Minne's"* steam at the dock to give us an early wind indicator to assist us in our own docking. Perhaps the most enjoyable part of all about the extended *"Minne"* is teasing Captain Steve Boyce about piloting the *"Minne-Ha-Ha-Ha-Ha"*!

Extension on *Minne-Ha-Ha* (II) completed at Steel Pier in Lake George Village, 1999. Photos by author.

Above, Lake George Steamboat Company Officers at rechristening of the extended *Minne-Ha-Ha*, May 1999. Left to right: B.J. Forando, John McDonald, Steve Boyce, Tom Conerty, Ed Stanilka, Lee Taber, Don Cornell, Bill Gates, Darrell Finlayson and Ray Mound. Courtesy: Don Cornell.

Top right, old *Minne-Ha-Ha* stacks on Steel Pier, 2000. Photo by author.

Middle right, *Minne's* paddlewheel rebuilt, 2001. Photo by author.

Right, *Minne-Ha-Ha* today approaching Tea Island, Prospect Mountain in background, 2002. Photo taken from pilothouse of *Lac du Saint Sacrement*. Photo by author.

Henley Regatta

Growing up in Bolton Landing exposed me to many interesting and wonderful people, to incredible regional history and some very unique events. One such event was the American Henley Regatta held in Bolton Bay on June 5, 1971. Back then, summer events never began in Bolton until the end of June when the schools got out. Suddenly, there was an early array of people and activities around town that told us locals that something special was about to happen. My parent's business, Bill Gates Diner, was filled early with promoters, organizers, rowers, timers, spectators and the press.

In 1970, the prior year, Warren County formed a committee to discuss and plan some new activities to promote tourism in the county. Committee President Horst Schroeder and photographer Walter Grishkot heard that the American Rowing Association was considering a location in Arizona to hold the 1971 Henley Cup. This event is so important to the local economy where it is held that a competing Arizona community was actually planning to build a new lake to lure the event to their area. The Warren County committee contacted the ARA and invited them to Lake George to see what we had to offer.

The most important requirement for rowing these racers successfully is calm water. Those of us who have experienced the lake over time know that calm water is a chancy situation that can't be counted upon. When the ARA officials arrived, they were to see our beautiful lake during a promotional tour on the Lake George Steamboat Company's *Mohican*. The lake was so rough in Lake George Village that day that the committee began discussing giving up on us as a site and were about to leave the boat when it suddenly left the pier before they could get off. When the *Mohican* rounded Recluse Island and entered Bolton Bay, the discouraged group from the ARA noticed Huddle Bay, as calm as it could be. If the bay could be calm on a rough day–then it would be suitable for the race. A favorable decision was made immediately.

During the winter, the 2000 meter course was surveyed and laid out on the ice extending from the southern end of Huddle Bay to Rogers Park in Bolton Landing. Holes were cut in the ice by the Glens Falls Seabees for the cement buoy anchors to be dropped through into their exact locations. The course was laid out close to shore where the slight lake currents and wave action would be minimized. Another reason Lake George was selected as a site was that most of the competing rivers never freeze over, making it difficult to lay out an exact course.

The weather on race day was beautiful. With my young son Mike at my side, we watched the event from Rogers Park. Bolton's own Lynn Otto was chosen as the Regatta Queen. Boats ranging in length to 60 feet raced in two, four and eight-man classes beginning at 1:15 PM after qualifying during the morning. Cars packed route 9N while 3,000 to 4,000 spectators lined the Bolton shoreline, estimated by the Chairman of the ARA, William M. Hollenbeck. Police boats kept stray boaters

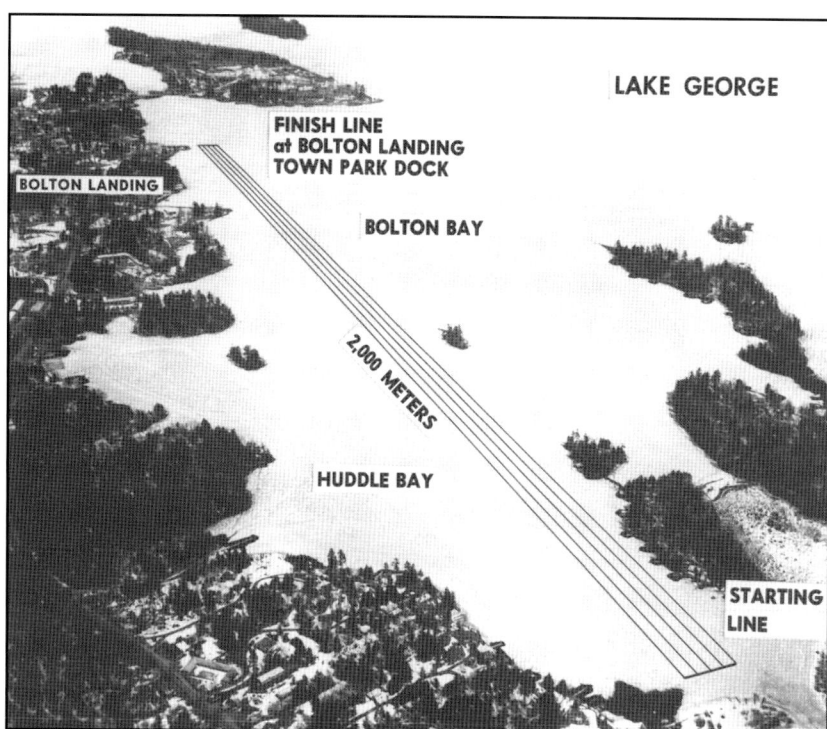

The American Henley Regatta in Bolton Bay, 1971. All photos courtesy: Walter Grishkot.

After the race at the American Henley Regatta in Bolton Landing, 1971. Courtesy: Walter Grishkot.

away from the course and made certain that their wakes were minimized. More than 350 oarsmen attended, far more than the normal draw for those years where 200 to 250 were the norm, in an event that received world-wide attention. At the conclusion of this exciting series of races, the Philadelphia eight man crew upset and beat the Naval Academy crew and won the Henley Cup in the Olympic Elite Eight race by completing the 2000 meter course in 6:43.1 while Navy's time was a close 6:45.1. Cornell finished in a very close third position.

Thanks to the efforts of then Bolton Supervisor Walter Lamb, Chamber of Commerce President Stanley Tonnesen, Warren County Chamber President Robert Hall, Walter Grishkot and Horst Schroeder, to name a few, the event was a huge success and will forever be remembered by the residents of Bolton, boating enthusiasts and historians around the greater Lake George region.

(It is important to note that this was not the first rowing competition here on Lake George. The Rowing Association of American Colleges was formed in 1871 with Cornell, Harvard, Yale, Amherst, Wesleyan, Columbia, Trinity, Williams, Dartmouth, and the Massachusetts Aggies competing. Two of these prestigious early regattas were held here on Lake George, the 1874 races with Columbia winning and in 1875 favoring the Cornell team. The organization collapsed in 1877 when Harvard and Yale resigned. It was later reestablished in 1903 as the American Rowing Association.)

Buccaneer

During the early 1980's, Nick and Caroline Cutro, former owners of the Boardwalk Restaurant in Lake George Village, and Stan and Claire Libert of Saratoga formed a partnership named Medallion Charters, Ltd. Their plan was to operate a pirate ship out of the Village. They purchased a 1961 Liberty Launch off Lake Champlain named the Benedict Arnold which was being used as a fishing boat. She was formerly used as a U.S. Navy Personnel Carrier to ferry naval personnel from their ships to shore. The *Buccaneer*, as she was christened, was 40 feet long, 12 1/2 feet wide at the beam and drafted 4 feet. Her hull was made of glass reinforced plastic and built by Lunn Laminate of Huntington Station, NY.

The Cutro's and Libert's purchased the *Buccaneer* in 1983 and brought her to a barn in West Fort Ann where Stan Libert did a total reconstruction of the boat above the rub rail to resemble a pirate ship.

Buccaneer, 1984. Courtesy: Nick and Caroline Cutro.

Below deck, everything was already up to Coast Guard standards. *Buccaneer* was powered by a single 671 Detriot diesel which produced a speed of 12 knots. There were 2 bulkheads, a 100 gallon fuel tank, and even a lever on the carburetor which read "Battle Speed" to make the boat go faster. She was launched in 1984 at the northern end of Lake George and brought to the Boardwalk Restaurant where the masts and lines were added to her rigging.

Beginning her first season on July 4th, the 15 ton ship could carry up to 50 passengers on each of its seven 1 hour tours beginning at 10:30 a.m., including a 9 p.m. cocktail cruise. With captain and crew all in pirate dress, and the young guests given pirate hats, the *Buccaneer* would sail to Diamond Island and fire her two cannon. There, the crew would climb up the 5 square rigged sails and young Brian Libert would dive into the lake and bring up souvenir gold coins planted there in a treasure chest, while the guests were treated to a glass of "Pirate Punch". On the return trip, the ship had to defend itself from water balloon attacks and cannon fire from other cruise boats.

At 11 a.m. every Sunday, when the boat did not carry passengers, the *Buccaneer* regularly attacked Fort William Henry. After firing both cannon, the fort would return fire. One morning, the fort went all out and fired 22 cannon without waiting for them to cool down. One cannon, therefore, sent a fireball of paper into the rigging of the *Buccaneer* and a sail caught fire. That ended the Sunday attacks altogether.

After 5 seasons here on the lake, the *Buccaneer* was lifted onto a truck at the Lake George Steamboat Company pier in the fall of 1988 and brought by the Cutro's to Green Cove Springs, Florida where she was to be purchased. The deal fell through so the Cutro's son Nicky took the boat through the Inland Waterway to his parent's home at Islanorada in the Keys. She was quite an attraction down there. The bow cabin was removed as was the back of the aft cabin. Many parties were held aboard and she was also used a lot for fishing trips from 1989 to 1993. In 1993, the *Buccaneer* was sold to some local fishermen for $15,000. She is still in use today in Key West fishing for Grouper and Yellow Tail Snappers.

Above, *Buccaneer* on Lake George.
Below, *Buccaneer* in Florida, 1988.
Courtesy: Nick and Caroline Cutro.

DEPARTURES	
10:30 am	- 11:30 am
12:00 noon	- 1:00 pm
1:30 pm	- 2:30 pm
3:00 pm	- 4:00 pm
4:30 pm	- 5:30 pm
7:00 pm	- 8:00 pm
(Sunset Cruise)	
9:00 pm	- 11:00 pm
(Cocktail Cruise)	

Morgan

The Sagamore Hotel in Bolton Landing was completely restored in the early 1980's. Its location on Green Island offers breathtaking views of Lake George, of the Islands of the Narrows to the North, and to the south of the mountains that surround Bolton Bay. With the prospect of large conventions wanting comfortable access onto Lake George itself, the Sagamore decided to build and launch their own cruise boat.

The new boat was built by Bill Morgan of Morgan Marine in Silver Bay. Bill's chief engineer Dave Hoffey oversaw construction in the shore-side warehouse behind Green Island on Sawmill Bay. Naval architect James S. Krogan of Miami, Florida came up with a trawler design that maintained the historic appearance while allowing the interior to be easily utilized for tours and dinner cruises. Construction began in 1985 on the plywood and fiberglass hull which is 72 feet long, 26 feet wide and 1 inch thick. I was extremely interested in the construction and photographed the entire project. One day I asked Bill Morgan, "Who is to be its captain?" He looked at me directly for a moment and said, "You are." I knew right then that I'd do it. Bob Gordon of Whitehall was also hired as captain, and we alternated for days off. I spent the remainder of 1985 and the spring of 1986 getting licensed and trained. Fortunately, growing up in Bolton provided me with a great deal of knowledge about the lake. It was a good starting point; there was still a lot to learn.

Morgan hull launching, July 17, 1985. Courtesy: Evelyn Hersh.

On July 17, 1985, in a very long and complicated procedure, the hull was launched sideways and construction was completed throughout that winter and into 1986, with the boat in the water in front of the warehouse. Bill Morgan's contribution to the project was so significant that the boat was named for him, the *Morgan*. By May of 1986, she was nearly ready. I'll always remember the first time she was underway. The New York State license for the vessel requires stability tests. The generator and single screw diesel engines were started by our engineer Drew Van Der Volgen. Builder Bill Morgan, our other captain Bob Gordon and I were in the pilothouse. Lines were dropped and Bill turned to me and said, "Let's go!" I took it on a one mile

Morgan under construction, summer 1985. Photo by author.

course into Northwest Bay and Bob took her back. There had been much speculation about her handling characteristics, being a single screw vessel. She handled beautifully. The tests were all successful.

On June 6th, 1986 the boat was christened during a festive celebration at her summer pier in front of the hotel. It was a very overcast and hazy day. Bob and I were in the pilothouse. On the bow were Bill Morgan, David Boyd (the hotel's General Manager at the time), and boat owners Norman and Marian Wolgin with their son Ike. Mrs. Wolgin was unable to break the champagne bottle on the wooden rail so instead she poured the champagne onto the bow. (Afterwards, the bottle was forgotten. Late in October that same year, I discovered a paper bag on my front porch. Inside was the bottle and an unsigned note which read, "You will appreciate this and take care of it." If that secret friend should read this—I still have the bottle in its original bag.)

Wheelhouse. Photo by author.

The Morgan's first year was an exciting one. Every place I took her was a thrilling first experience. Boats came from all around the lake to see her and take her photograph. She and I were tested in several severe thunderstorms during June— thunder, lightning and severe winds—she handled them all very well. On July 4th, I had a fireworks cruise with a full boat of passengers. There were hundreds of boats in Bolton Bay gathered around and in front of us. My eleven year old daughter Allison came along that evening. Boats-lights-reflections-fireworks-my

Christening, June 6, 1986. Marian, Norman and Ike Wolgin, David Boyd and Bill Morgan. Photos by author.

daughter with me—and the *Morgan*; it was an evening I'll remember always.

The Sagamore Hotel has always attracted celebrities and many were aboard the *Morgan* that first summer. Among them— Billy Joel and Christie Brinkley, Billy Idol, the Beach Boys, Mary Tyler Moore, Michael York, and Stevie Nicks of Fleetwood Mac. One evening in August I had a corporate charter. A half hour into the cruise, the president of the corporation rushed into my pilothouse. He was surprised that cigars were not available on the boat and he directed me to return at once back to the

Morgan leaving the Sagamore Hotel, 1986.
Photo by author.

Morgan and author at Sagamore Hotel, October 1986.
Courtesy: Ron Alcan.

Sagamore. I radioed ahead and we were met on the dock by a waiter holding a box of cigars on a silver tray. I can still recall the waiter struggling to keep a straight face as he held out the tray. One hour of that two hour cruise was spent chasing cigars.

So many unusual situations came up that summer that nothing surprised me after awhile. One day in the Narrows I received a radio call to stop the boat. A speedboat from the hotel pulled up and a tuxedoed gentleman boarded to dine with his friends. On another occasion a seaplane landed and its passengers came aboard—and off we sailed. One evening an intoxicated woman suddenly appeared at my doorway and fell headlong onto the pilothouse floor. I immediately summoned my crew who took her below and fed her coffee. Fortunately she was uninjured, but my crew teased me for weeks about finding her on my floor in the darkness. During another afternoon charter, the *Morgan*'s single engine began overheating and

Sunset cruise, 1986. Photo by author.

needed to be shut down. The boat had to be towed back to her pier. Someone on the lake photographed the event and the picture found its way across America's newspapers as an AP Laserphoto. The problem was caused by a faulty water pump impeller which I still have in my collection.

My son Mike always enjoyed Fork Island at the northern end of the Narrows. I would often think of him as I passed his favorite dock. One evening, as I was passing Mike's dock, I decided that the *Morgan* was ready to enter Paradise Bay for the first time. As I took her in from the north, engineer Drew climbed onto the pilothouse roof with my camera to record the moment. A very satisfying accomplishment—everyone aboard applauded.

At the end of the season, Captains Tom Conerty and Ed Stanilka, longtime friends, asked me to pilot the *Mohican* for the Lake George Steamboat Company. I've been at the LGSBC ever since then, but to be Captain of the *Morgan* during her first season was, for me, a once-in-a-lifetime experience. I'm often asked which is my favorite boat. I always reply honestly, "Any boat as long as it is on Lake George."

Above, *Morgan* at Sagamore today piloted by Craig Clesceri, Ed Kluck, engineer.
Left, *Morgan* out for maintenance, late 1980's. Photos by author.

Lac du Saint Sacrement

In 1950, the Lake George Steamboat Company launched the *Ticonderoga*. This converted World War II vessel provided daily passenger service on Lake George for four successful decades. By 1978, it became clear to Wilbur Dow, the company's late owner, that the *"Ti"* would become obsolete by the end of the 1980s. She would soon be unable to provide the upscale services which the future passengers would be seeking. He understood there would be a growing demand for private charters, convention facilities, entertainment and cuisine while cruising the majestic waters of Lake George. The decision was then made to construct a luxurious new vessel—in Wilbur's own words, "The finest the Lake had ever seen". The plan was to construct a new vessel which would comply with all of the modern safety regulations, yet still present the appearance of a traditional early steamboat. The first idea considered was to build a side-wheeler, however, its hull would be too narrow, which would have caused a stability problem. Wilbur and his son Bill, current owner and president of the company, liked the classic style of the old Hudson River Dayliner, *Peter Stuyvesant*, which had run from New York City to West Point, but it would have been too heavy and large for the Steamboat Company's dry-dock at Baldwin near Ticonderoga.

Peter Stuyvesant, Hudson River Day Line. Photo, author's collection.

Wilbur Dow was able to obtain the original plans for the *Peter Stuyvesant* from an old gentleman in Brooklyn who had stored them in his attic. Prominent marine architect Robert Simmons was then hired to design a 3/4 replica from these plans. His new design depicted a vessel of 190 foot length with a 40 foot beam which would hold over 1000 passengers. This elegant new ship would be named *Lac du Saint Sacrement*. Jesuit missionary Isaac Jogues, the first European to arrive here, had christened the lake with this name in 1646.

Saint's hull at Baldwin, 1980's. Photo by author.

The keel was laid in August of 1979 at the Baldwin dry-dock under the supervision of former marine superintendent Wayne Anderson. The company was unable to obtain financing for such a huge project at the time, so about $100,000 of the company's annual profits were earmarked towards it for the next eight years until Key Bank was finally willing to lend the money to complete it. Only the *Saint's* bare hull was launched into the early morning haze on September 9th, 1987 with Bill Dow doing all of the risky underwater diving procedures himself. Long-time employee Sophie Nesji struck the bow with the traditional champaign bottle during the small ceremony as Bill Dow solemnly spoke, "Bless the men who built her—the men who will sail her—Bless the boat, and hope that she will always sail in untroubled waters." The *Mohican*, in the experienced hands of Captain Ted Kalisz, then towed the *Saint's* hull safely to the end of the Steel Pier in Lake George Village, where construction continued at a fever pitch for the next 21 months. This successful project was a total team effort by all departments of the company.

The official dedication ceremony took place on a very rainy June 15th, 1989. Wilbur Dow praised the local men who had built his ship. He proudly pointed out that "they didn't come from the shipyards of America. They came from nearby towns

Oval, *Mohican* towing *Saint*, September 9, 1987.
Above, Saint under construction, 1988. Photos by author.

such as Warrensburg, Ticonderoga and Bolton." Bill Dow praised the boat's "finely designed hull", the "rounded cruiser stern" and "high transom" which not only minimizes her wake, but almost totally eliminates it. Bill's daughter Rebecca christened the completed ship by striking the bottle on the capstan (anchor winch) as she said, "I christen thee *Lac du Saint Sacrement*." We all had a good laugh when the champaign sprayed all over Captain Kalisz's trousers. It was a good omen.

Once the Saint was under way, the new galley served up the food and everyone danced to the Dixieland band. News reporters and television crews were everywhere. The mood in the pilothouse was also very festive. Although all of us in the pilothouse were dressed in full officer's uniforms, only Captain Ted was in command on the maiden voyage. While visiting the pilothouse during this historic cruise, Wilbur Dow excitedly summed it all up for everyone by saying, "It was worth the ten years!—"There couldn't be a better!"—"The finest ship we could ever leave on Lake George!"

Since her completion, the *Saint* has been piloted by Ted Kalisz, Tom Conerty, Lee Taber, Ed Stanilka, Darrell Finlayson, Don Cornell, this author Bill Gates, Ray Mound, George LaPointe, Ann Buckell, Rick Connors and Adam Bombard.

Ballroom and Grand Staircase, 1988. Photo by author.

Saint's hull painted, 1988. Photo by author.

Christening Ceremony, June 15, 1989. Photo by author.

Author's boarding pass for christening ceremony.

Saint's pilothouse, 2002. Photo by author.

Saint approaching Steel Pier, 2002. Photo by author.

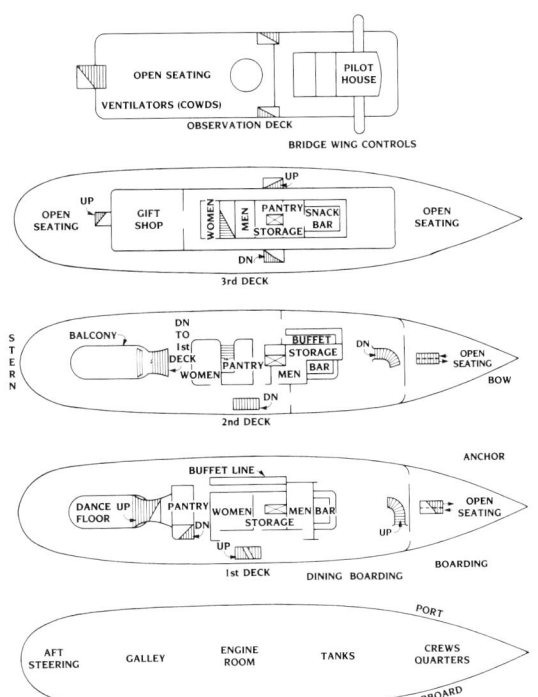

Above, *Saint* on Baldwin drydock, October, 1997. Courtesy: Brian Granger.
Left, *Lac du Saint Sacrement's* floor plans. Courtesy: Bill Dow.

Saint sliding down the ways at Baldwin, 1997. Photo by author.

View of Narrows from pilothouse, 2002. Photo by author.

Above, *Saint* viewed from *Mohican*, 2002. Right, Top deck. Photos by author.

Above, Lake George Steamboat Company fleet, 2002.
Photo by author.

Left, *Lac du Saint Sacrement,* piloted by Tom Conerty, closely passing *Defiance* on her way to winning the Queens Boat Race in 2001. Beginning in 1997, the large boats *Mohican, Horicon, Defiance, Morgan* and *Lac du Saint Sacrement* began racing from BoltonLanding to Lake George Village every May in the annual Queens Boat Race. Many people ride along during these races and enjoy the competition in hopes that their boat will win.
Photo by author.

Ellis Barber Rowboats

Ellis Barber was born in 1872 and died in 1951, spending most of his life in Bolton Landing. He was a skilled craftsman and used his gift to design and build beautiful rowboats. His shop was located just south of the Algonquin. Every Barber boat was planked with cedar, attached by copper rivets to spruce ribs. Barber rented his boats to fishermen and tourists who vacationed here during the summer. It is not known how many of his rowboats were built, but only three of his boats still survive today. In addition, one of his small design-models is on display at the Bolton Historical Museum.

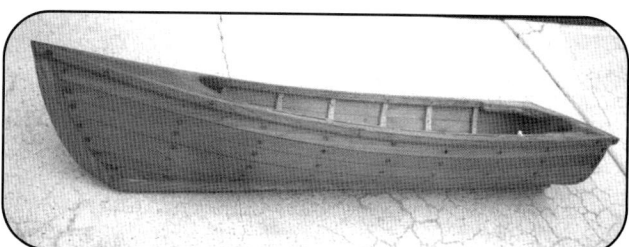

Ellis Barber model rowboat at Bolton Historical Museum.
Photo by author.

One of his rowboats, which was built by Barber in 1912, was owned by the Rose family who lived on Clay Island. Charles "Juddy" Peer of Bolton worked for the Rose family during the 1930's. Their Barber rowboat was in poor condition, so they gave it to Juddy who expressed an interest in repairing it. Juddy returned the rowboat to its original condition and painted it exactly as Ellis Barber had painted most of his boats, green inside and black on the outer hull. Recently, Juddy sold it to his friend Fred Brown, also of Bolton. Last year, 2002, Fred entered his Barber rowboat in the annual Smith-Granger rowboat race which is now open to all makes of vintage rowboats.

"Juddy" Peer's Ellis Barber rowboat, now owned by Fred Brown, 2002.
Photos by author.

Indian Pipes

John Orlando first came to Lake George in 1959 and immediately he fell in love with it. In 1971 he brought his wife Anita and their children here. For 16 consecutive summers they lived on their boat in Red Rock Bay in the Narrows. When the Sagamore Hotel was reopened in the early 1980's, Ray Ciccarelli of Chic's Marina acquired the franchise for the boat rentals at the hotel. John approached Ray about adding a large captained boat to the rental fleet and Ray was willing to try it out.

Anita had been fascinated since 1974 with some delicate little plants she had discovered while hiking in the woods near Paradise Bay. The large new boat John and Anita purchased was to be named for these plants, the *Indian Pipes*. The *Indian Pipes* was built in Taipei, Taiwan under contract to Fred Peters of Albin of America of Cos Cob, Connecticut. The Albin company was originally a Swedish sailboat and deisel manufacturer. Fred, a former officer in the Swedish navy, once worked for them. Later he purchased the company and brought it to America.

Indian Pipes, 2002. Photos by author.

John and Anita ordered the boat in 1985 and had it constructed to their specifications. A special ladder was built so their guests could easily come aboard after swimming in Lake George. The interior can sleep 6 in separate state rooms—there is a full galley, a dining area and a sofa—the aft cabin has a queen sized bed–and there are 2 bathrooms with showers. A Chinese family does all the interior construction in Teak-wood. Importantly, all exterior drains were sealed to insure that nothing harmful could discharge into the lake. *Indian Pipes* is 36 feet long and is powered by a single 135HP Lehman-Ford diesel engine. The completed Albin was then loaded on a ship and sailed to Port Newark, New Jersey. There, it was hoisted into the water and piloted to the Albin headquarter's shipyard at Cos Cob. With the flying bridge removed, it was placed on a trailer and driven to the Harris Bay Yacht Club on Lake George. After launching in May of 1986, she arrived at the Sagamore. *Indian Pipes* is economical–burning only 3 gallons of #2 fuel oil at cruising speeds of around 7 knots. On one occasion, John says it ran for 18 straight hours. She handles beautifully–I can agree with this because I piloted her myself back in 1986. Today, the *Indian Pipes* is a popular and successful commercial boat, and I personally have always found her trawler design to be very visually appealing.

Pamelaine (I)

In 1972, Doctor Mason Saunders, a retired Albany dentist who now resides in Bolton Landing, purchased a 1918 Fay & Bowen which he converted into a fast and successful racing steam launch. She was named *Pamelaine*, a name constructed from a combination of his two daughter's names, Pamela and Elaine. *Pamelaine's* hull was 28 feet long and was purchased from Norm Lamb of Lamb Brother's Marina in Bolton Landing in 1968. Saunders loved racing and won the steamboat races on Lake George three times with a winning speed of 7 mph. Three weeks before the 1974 races, *Pamelaine* overturned near the Narrows in a strong wind storm and all of his equipment sank to the bottom of the lake. After winning many events with this boat, "Doc" eventually sold it in the early 1980's to a buyer in Chicago.

Pamelaine (I) and *Minne-Ha-Ha*. Photo by Walter Grishkot. Courtesy: "Doc" Mason Saunders.

Pamelaine (II)

Doctor Mason Saunders began focusing heavily on his career once again after he sold *Pamelaine* (I). By the mid 1980's, he realized that something was missing in his life. Work was taking its toll and he knew right away that he needed to achieve a happy balance again between work and pleasure. "Doc" often thought fondly of his earlier steam boating days and decided that another steam launch would remedy his situation. After an intensive search, he contracted Walter Beckmann, a popular boat builder from Rhode Island, to build his new hull. The basic green and white fiberglass hull was completed during 1987. He bought a new 670 pound Semple "Vertical Fire Tube" boiler that was exactly the same as his previous one because he was totally familiar with its operation and dependability. By September of 1988, *Pamelaine* (II) was ready for a brief christening ceremony at Hugh Wilson's dock in Bolton Landing. Doc's wife Billie struck the hull with the traditional champagne bottle, only to spray much of it all over her husband's pants. Doc quickly quipped, "Great! Maybe now I can walk on water!" With an overall length of 22 feet, a beam of 7 feet and a draft of only 2 feet, she was ready for her maiden voyage. It takes years to perfect a boat of this kind. Many adjustments had to be made every week–every year. In the beginning, *Pamelaine* (II) was steered by a lever. Later he changed to teleflex with gear boxes with two wheels in a series so steering could be achieved from both the front and rear. The spotlight was originally an old carbide powered lamp, but for dependability it was later converted to a sealed beam. A functional brass enunciator was added as was a carved wooden eagle, and Doc's wife Billie finally agreed to loan him a Brazilian trolley bell which she was using as a doorbell. It is now a pleasant sounding addition to the *Pamelaine*. There are two steam whistles–the small one came from a New York City subway car–the larger one came from the Long Island Railroad.

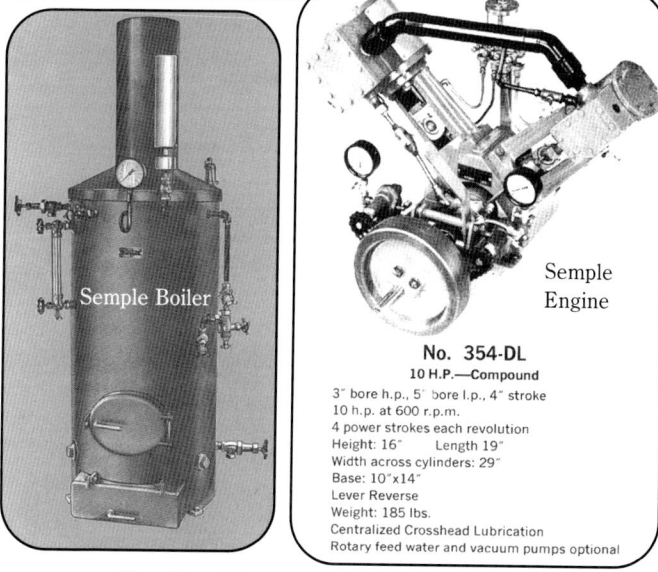

Top, *Pamelaine* (II). Photo by Bea Lewis.
Semple Boiler burns wood or coal, and Semple Steam Engine.
Courtesy: Doctor Mason Saunders.

This Pamelaine is intended for pleasure only–no more racing. "Racing is too hard on the equipment", Doc says. "The boat can travel at 5 to 6 miles per hour after a 30 minute warm up period. She has always burned wood because coal is too dirty." Doc Saunders stores 36 bags of wood under the seats and beneath the deck. Each bag will fuel the engine for 1 1/2 miles giving the boat an approximate 50 mile range.

It is always a pleasant sight to suddenly spot the *Pamelaine* out on Lake George. With her red and black "Turtle Flag" blowing in the breeze and her steam streaming across the horizon, the *Pamelaine* is like a vision from the past. Doc says that is the reason why he is so drawn to steam power. "That is what was originally here on Lake George and I want to help to keep it alive. I want the present generation to experience what our ancestors enjoyed here over a century ago." "Doc" Mason Saunders and his other steam boating friends have certainly achieved their goal. When we spot the *Pamelaine* while piloting the *Mohican* near the Narrows, we always alter my course to give our passengers a pleasant glimpse of her. Doc recently confessed to me that he is thrilled when we blow our whistle to him first. Of course we'll salute her! We salute her in appreciation–and we salute her because we are thrilled to hear her steam whistles singing out the sounds of old Lake George.

Tuscarora

The *Tuscarora* was designed and built between 1975 and 1979 in Saratoga by Tom Rhodes. She is 29 feet 2 inches long, 10 feet wide at her beam, draws only 2 feet 6 inches of water and was patterned after the Puget Sound small steamers of the 1890's. *Tuscarora* was named for the *Tuscarora* at Blue Mountain lake which today rests on shore as a private camp. Her boiler is a Semple 40 Sq. ft. steam tube and her engine is a Semple 2 cyl. model. Tom built her hull of white oak, mahogany, teak and fiberglassed marine plywood. She is equipped with steam heat, electric lighting, a head, a galley, pilothouse controls and engine room bells.

The completed *Tuscarora* was moved to Lake George by Rod Anderson of Burnt Hills and launched at Castaway Marina at Katskill Bay. During her first year of operation, *Tuscarora* burned only the scraps of wood which remained following her construction. For nine years, *Tuscarora* was moored at Hugh Wilson's in Bolton Landing. Her normal cruising route was between Paradise Bay and Basin Bay.

Tuscarora. Courtesy: Tom Rhodes.

In 1991, Tom sold *Tuscarora* to John Patton who continued to operate her on Lake George from Hugh Wilson's dock. Patton eventually stored the boat for three years, and Tom Rhodes bought her back again at a marina on the Mohawk River. In November of 2001, she was sold to Preston Claytor who moved her to Virginia. After a year-long restoration, Claytor launched her on a river near Richmond and rechristened her *Pocahontas*.

Osprey

Osprey was launched in 2000 by her builder Dean Merrill of Queensbury. Named for the *Osprey* at the Adirondack Museum in Blue Mountain Lake, her fiberglass Beckman hull is 21 feet long and has a 5 foot 6 inch beam. The "Tiny Power" steam engine produces 5 hp from a 3 inch bore and a 4 inch stroke. Her 39 square foot boiler burns either wood or coal.

Courtesy: Dean Merrill.

Aggie Belle

Aggie Belle is also owned by Dean Merrill of Queensbury. She is a 19 foot fantail launch with a 5 foot 6 inch beam. Her wood burning boiler is of 21 square feet capacity and her 2 inch stroke compound engine creates around 5 horsepower. *Aggie Belle* was named for Dean's grandmother Agnes Belle Carty who broke the traditional christening champagne bottle during her 1993 launching. Agnes Belle Carty was the first Iowa woman to join the US Navy in WW I.

Courtesy: Dean Merrill.

Isa Victoria

Isa Victoria was owned by Carl Kriegeskottes of Mount Kisko, NY. She is named for a combination of his daughter and wife's names, Isa and Victoria. She and Dean Merrill's Osprey represented Hague during the summer of 2001 when the Lake George Monster was returned to Hague. Her hull is by Jim Thayer and is the same as Dean Merrill's Aggie Belle. Isa Victoria is powered by a Semple boiler. Carl recently sold the boat to a new owner in Florida.

Courtesy: Dean Merrill.

Aurora Borealis

Aurora Borealis was designed and built by Al Dunlop of Echo Bay in 1997. She is 21 1/2 feet long, 6 3/4 feet wide and draws 2 1/2 feet. Her boiler was designed by Al and a friend, and her engine is a 5 hp Semple with 3 inch diameter and 4 inch stroke. She burns a bushel of wood per hour and travels at a speed of 6 mph. Coal can also be burned.

On his first ride, Al steamed all the way from Echo Bay to Camp Andrews Bay. During this evening trip, Al was thrilled to see the Northern Lights, and that is why he named the boat Aurora Borealis.

The Aurora Borealis has made other interesting journeys–a 64 mile tour of the Champlain Canal and a 300 mile trip on the Erie Canal from Rochester to Troy.

Photo by author.

St. Louis

The Elco Electric Launch Company at Morris Heights, New Jersey built electric launches for the 1893 Worlds Fair in Chicago. These beautiful boats plied the fair's numerous canals giving visitors silent rides for the very first time in a boat that did not require hand power, wind power or steam. Eventually, the Elco Company grew into General Dynamics which made submarines and PT Boats.

William K. Bixby owned the "American Car & Foundry" in Saint Louis. (His son Harold later received world wide attention for financing Charles Lindberg's solo flight across the Atlantic in 1927 in the "Spirit of St. Louis" which was named by Lindburg to honor and thank Harold.) William Bixby saw over 30 of these Elco boats at the Chicago Exposition in 1896 and he bought one afterwards to use as his fishing boat. Knowing that

W.K. Bixby's 36 foot Elco launch, St Louis, in 1902.
Courtesy: Charles Houghton, Elco Electric Launch Company, Inc.

railroad flatbed cars were 36 feet long, he purchased a 36 foot Elco for easy delivery on one of his railcars- and he named it the *St. Louis.* He also ordered a smaller Elco for his wife. In 1904 he shipped his boat to his new summer home on Mohican Point in Bolton Landing on Lake George. It was launched on the submarine railway which is still visible along the Beach Road in Lake George Village.

Besides fishing, it was also used for pleasure rides, family gatherings and weddings- and it is still used for these purposes today. Every August 1st for 50 years up until 1968, the *St. Louis* was motored to the Dollar Islands above the Narrows for the family's annual fishing expedition. Bolton's Judge James Ross was her skipper. Family members Doug Houghton, Henry and Ted Caldwell would go up early to set up camp so the fishermen could play Bridge games. When the *St. Louis* turned 100 years old in 1996, there were many family celebrations held in her honor.

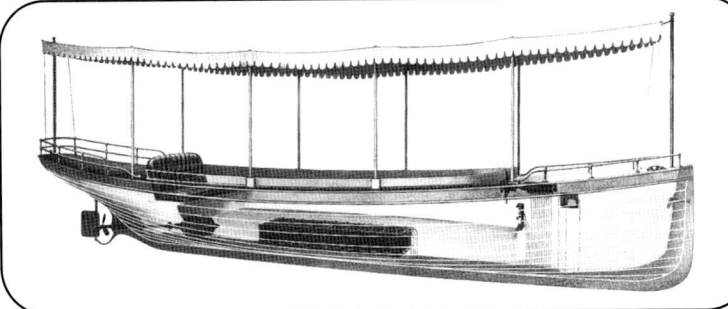

36 foot Elco launch from 1902 Elco catalogue.
Courtesy: Charles Houghton, Elco Electric Launch Company, Inc.

The *St. Louis* is 36 feet long, 6 feet wide across her beam, and is powered by the original Elco 9 1/2 HP electric motor which turns an 18 inch, 3 blade propeller. When new, the boat had 5 forward speeds and 2 reverse—recently the speeds have been modified to 2 forward and 2 reverse, and her batteries need charging every 12 to 14 hours. Every year her eighteen 8 volt batteries have to be installed in the spring, and later removed and stored for winter. Many times I've helped out in this activity and can say that "many hands always make for lighter work" for carrying these 160 pound batteries to the storage bunker.

With a lifelong interest in this Elco, it isn't too surprising that family member Charles Houghton now owns the Elco Boat Company located today in Athens, New York. It is very rare that a boat of this age and caliber still exists, and it is even more remarkable that it has always been owned by the same old Lake George family. Not only does Charles Houghton provide the technical assistance, but his brother Doug Houghton of Bolton's "Adirondack Boat Works" does all of the maintenance on the hull and oak decking. There are only 26 of these boats left in existence and 4 of them can be found on Lake George in Bolton Landing. A 5th was always on Lake George and is now on nearby Lake Champlain.

In an age where too often the sounds and silence of nature are disturbingly interrupted by a loud roaring boat engine, it is an absolute pleasure to glide along in the *St. Louis* and hear only the pleasant sounds of Lake George's water rippling along her hull. How nice it is to have conversations and hear what everyone is saying. Bolton's old Bixby family deserves a lot of credit for appreciating and preserving such a rare and wonderful old electric boat.

Barbara

The 1907 *Barbara* was originally named the *Queen.* This 33 foot electric Elco launch was enjoyed for many years, but went into disrepair and sank. She lay under water for four years across the lake from Bolton. Joe Smith of F.R. Smith and Sons Marina heard about the boat during the mid 1920's and it was given to him for removing it. Joe raised her, restored her and renamed her *Barbara.* Joe loved using the *Barbara* for fishing because she was very quiet and could sneak up on the fish. In 1956, the quiet *Barbara* helped to accompany U.S. Marathon swimmer Stella Taylor for the final 10 miles of her 32 mile swim of Lake George.

Joe Smith and family in *Barbara.*
Courtesy: Marilyn Smith and Greg Smith.

When Smith's Marina burned in May of 1957, Joe was able to rescue the *Barbara* a second time by pushing her to safety out onto the lake. After rebuilding the business, there wasn't much of a need for an electric boat in 1959, so Joe winched her into the second boathouse on the west side of Green Island. She remained there for 20 years. Around 1975, Joe and his son Fred Sr. took her out and cleaned her up. *Barbara* is powered by 12 eight volt batteries and can reach speeds up to 10 mph. Every year thereafter for the next 7 or 8 years, Fred and his wife Marilyn, along with the Vilmars and the Daters, would celebrate

Christmas in July. A Christmas tree was decorated on the bow, Fred and Marilyn would dress as Santa and Mrs. Claus and they would hand out candy canes to children in Log Bay while singing Christmas carols. Today, the *Barbara* can still be seen inside F.R. Smith's.

Fred Sr. and Marilyn Smith in *Barbara*,
July 21, 1979.
Courtesy: Marilyn Smith and Greg Smith.

McGuffy

There were two *McGuffy's* owned by Jim Miller Sr. of Bolton Landing. (This was actually his second named *McGuffy*. His original is now owned by the Wolgin family of Bolton and is named the *Whim*.) *McGuffy* is owned today by Jim's son, John Miller. Years ago, this boat was one of a fleet of rental Elco electrics that belonged to Joe Smith of F.R. Smith and Sons which was used for fishing charters. Eventually she was sold to a family on Saratoga Lake. Jim Miller Sr. purchased her from them and brought her back to Lake George around 1980. She is a 25 foot Elco built in 1905 and is powered by a 5 hp electric motor which can mover her along at 5 knots, thanks to the help of 10 eight volt batteries and an efficient 3 blade prop. *McGuffy's* hull is made of cedar over an oak frame with decking of Mahogany and Oak.

Top, Jim Miller Sr. aboard his *McGuffy*, 1986.
Photo taken by author from the *Morgan*.
Right, John and Lisa Miller aboard *McGuffy*, 2000.
Photo by author.

Whim

The *Whim* was owned by Jim Miller Sr. until he sold her to the Wolgin family of Bolton around 1980. She was originally named the *Whim*, Miller named her *McGuffy*, then the Wolgins renamed her *Whim* again after finding her original name boards hidden below her floorboards. She is a 1907 25 foot Elco electric launch, hull number #499. She is a sistership to the Miller's *McGuffy* with only a slight difference in freeboard height. She is powered by her original 5 hp motor which was rewound in 1990. Her decking is of Oak and Mahogany. The brass rails were made for the *Whim* by the Elco Electric Launch Company which is still in business in Athens, NY. The spotlight on the bow was given to the Wolgin family by my uncle, Bob Gates, in 1983. Uncle Bob got the light from U.S. Senator Kavinaugh's boat which was burned up in a boathouse fire on Green Island.

Ike Wolgin aboard the *Whim*, 2002. Photos by author.

Wenona

Wenona on Lake Champlain, 2002.
Photos courtesy: Kam Hoopes.
Information courtesy: Ray & Barbara Wright.

Wenona is no longer on Lake George, but she once was an important Lake George boat. She was owned by the Rev. Dr. Ernest M. Stires. Stires became a priest in 1892. He served in many parishes in Virginia, Chicago and New York City. His family spent many summers at the Sagamore Hotel before he purchased Brook Hill Farm on lake George, just north of Bolton Landing. His estate became known as Lagoon Manor.

His son, Ernest Van Rensselaer Stires, became a minister after spending most of World War I as an ambulance driver. After the war, he served for 41 years as minister at St. James Episcopal Church in Lake George Village. Stires married Metropolitan Opera soloist Louise Homer's daughter, also named Louise. With two family homes on the lake, the Stires enjoyed boating in their 36 foot Elco electric launch named *Wenona*. The *Wenona* is actually slightly different that the 36 foot *St. Louis*. She has a flat transom, where the *St. Louis* has a fantail. Today, the *Wenona* is docked on Lake Champlain on the Vermont side, just across the Champlain Bridge.

Sal

Sal is a rare and wonderful 1903 Osborne that has been in the same family here at Turtle Bay on Lake George since she was built 100 years ago. She was built at Croton on the Hudson for the Great Uncle of her current family owner, Rich Watkins. In 1903, the completed boat was piloted up the Hudson by Sherwood Day and trailered over to Lake George for launching, and she was brought to his new camp which was built that same 1903 year. Rich told me that his Great Great Grandmother actually rode in her when it was new. Interestingly, *Sal*'s original name was *Sarah*, but everyone called her *Sal*, and the new name stuck. *Sal* is 25 feet long, 6 1/2 feet wide and draws 16 inches. Today she is powered by a 4 cylinder 1941 Grey Marine engine which is her 5th engine over her lifetime. The original engine in 1903 was a Twin Cylinder model with a reversable propeller instead of a reverse gear.

My memories of *Sal* extend all of my life as well, because Rich's late father, Asa Watkins, was a very good family friend. One of the last times I talked with Asa was in 1996 when their 100 year old camp tragically burned at Turtle Bay. Fortunately, *Sal* was saved, as was many of their old photographs which were recovered.

Top right, *Sal*, early 1900's. Photo salvaged from fire.
Oval, *Sal* launching, 1915.
Bottom right, *Sal*, 1996. Courtesy: Rich Watkins.

Lozier Boats

Peer's (No Name)

Lozier's were built by the Lozier Motor Company in Plattsburgh, New York at the turn of the last cenrury. At first, Lozier built engines only. To help their sales, Lozier contracted George Mathews of Port Clinton, Ohio to build boats for their engines. Lozier also built cars. Cyprus was used for the hulls, mahogany for the decking. In these two 1950's photos, "Juddy" Peer and his wife Arlene of Bolton are enjoying their rare Lozier which was never named. It was originally owned by Fleet Corcoran of Bolton. Fleet gave it to my uncle, Bob Gates, who stored it in our woods in Bolton's Huddle. Bob then gave it to Juddy who totally restored it and used it for pleasure and fishing.

Courtesy: Charles "Juddy" Peer.

Newport, 1903 Lozier. Courtesy: John Hilton.

Newport is a 26 foot 1903 Lozier. Her engine was a Lozier 2 cycle, 2 cyl. 10 hp. She was probably named *Newport* to market her to the wealthy who summered at Newport, RI. *Newport* came from one of the early mansions along Millionaire's Row between Bolton Landing and Lake George Village. She eventually ended up at Lamb Brothers Marina in Bolton where she was used for fishing charters. Lamb Bros. replaced the engine with a small Universal with reduction gear. Her current owner, John Hilton of Pilot Knob, noticed that one of her early fishing renters wrote in pencil beneath her deck, near the bow stem, "Jimmy Brown rented this boat in 1936".

Seagull

Seagull is a 1909 Consolidated 30 foot Speedway built by Charles L. Seabury of the NY Gas Engine & Power Co. Consolidated. Today, she is owned by John Hilton. *Seagull* came from Saranac Lake from the William Bucknell estate (Bucknell University). Interestingly, Mrs. Emma Elizabeth Ward Bucknell was a survivor of the *RMS Titanic* disaster. She is documented as being rescued from *Titanic* lifeboat #8 along with Countess of Rothes and "Pepita', the Spanish newlywed. During the early 1920's, the Bucknell's moved to Lake George for the summer while their home on Saranac Lake was being extensively remodeled. They had the *Seagull* shipped here onto Lake George for their use.

Seagull. Courtesy: John Hilton.

Zonta

The *Zonta* is a wonderful boat, rich in history. She was first owned by Katrina Trask of the Three Brother Islands on Lake George, whose husband, Spencer, had been tragically killed in a railroad accident in 1909. Katrina bought the *Zonta* new in 1917. When she died in 1922, an advertisement was placed in the New York Times to help settle her estate by her second husband, George Foster Peabody. The boat was then purchased by Howard White Starr of Hulett's Landing. From 1922 to 1993, generations of the Starr family at Hulett's enjoyed the *Zonta*, and caretaker Harlan Foote gave her the best of care. In 1993, the *Zonta* was donated to the Antique Boat Museum at Clayton, NY. *Zonta* is a 1917 Consolidated Speedway, hull #2551, length 32 feet, beam 6 feet, engine: Chrysler Crown 115 hp.

Courtesy: The Dan and Judy Starr family of Hulett's Landing.

Top left, Original 1922 NY Times advertisement when the Starr family purchased the *Zonta*.
Top right, Stern view of the *Zonta* at Hulett's with the Starr and Brady families aboard.
Above, *Zonta* with Doug Condit and Carolyn Starr aboard, 1984.

Sadie Mae

Sadie Mae is a 1914 Consolidated Speedway owned by the Paul Eckhoff family of Nirvana Farm on Lake George in Bolton Landing. Nirvana Farm originally belonged to John Boulton Simpson who built the first Sagamore Hotel in 1882. He used this small farm to supply some of his summer needs of vegetables and flowers for his mansion on Green Island. This property remained in the Simpson family until 1973, with the last Simpson owner being Helen Simpson, J.B.Simpson's daughter.

Sadie Mae is 26 feet long, has a mahogany deck, a 5 foot 4 inch beam and drafts 2 feet. Paul Eckhoff bought her from F.R. Smiths in 1973 when she was first named the *Lure*. Paul replaced her old 4 cyl. Red Wing engine and gave it to sculptor David Smith who used her crankshaft on a sculpture. Paul then installed a 5 hp Semple steam engine in her for awhile before converting back to gasoline.

Sadie Mae with steam engine.
Courtesy: Paul Eckhoff.

Scuppers

Scuppers is a boat of an unknown make, circa 1900. Owner Paul Eckhoff named her from the popular children's story, "Scuppers the Sailor Dog." Paul saw Gus Bellenger in this boat at Oahu Island before World War II and loved it. He bought it from Gus in 1948 for $50, including three engines. *Scuppers* has Oak and White Pine decking, is 18 feet long, has a beam of 5 feet and drafts 18 inches. Paul's dad bought him the whistle as a gift and his uncle gave him an old oil lamp for the bow. The stern lamp is also a classic oil lamp. Today, she is powered by a Kermath engine.

Paul Eckhoff at Nirvana Farm in *Scuppers*, 2002. Photo by author.

Old Boy

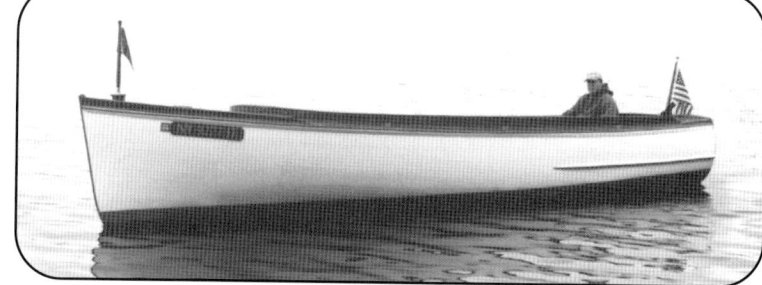

Todays *Old Boy* is actually *Old Boy* (II). *Old Boy* (I) was owned by Fred Streever, famous sportswriter for Field and Stream Magazine and an author of many books on the art of fishing a half century ago. Fred is also credited with inventing the Luna Lure, a fishing lure that glows to attract fish in deep water. Fred's *Old Boy* (I) was a 30 foot Osborne launch. Fred's nephew, Bill Streever of Ballston Spa and Bolton Landing, sold the *Old Boy* (I) after Fred died, and Bill replaced her with the present *Old Boy*. *Old Boy* had been sold by the Antique Boat Museum in Clayton, N.Y. to Bill Morgan of Morgan Marine in a move to cut back on their surplus boats. Bill Streever then bought her as a present for his wife Barbara in 1987. In 1998, Bill Streever sold *Old Boy* to Tony DePace of Bolton Landing. *Old Boy* is a 26 foot Lindsey powered today by a 4 cyl. 30 hp Grey Marine engine.

Top left, Fred Streever's Luna Lure. Courtesy: Henry Caldwell.
Top right, *Old Boy*, late 1980's. Courtsey: Bill & Barbara Streever.
Above, *Old Boy*, 2002. Courtesy: Tony DePace.

Ol' Timer

Ol'Timer is owned by Al Dunlop of Pilot Knob. She was built in Hague by an unknown builder during the early 20th Century for an early youth camp. She is 21 1/2 feet long and is powered by a 5 hp Sears 1923 Motorgo engine made by Lockwood Ash, who based it on using mostly standard parts from a Model T Ford automobile engine. Her hull has Oak ribs and Cedar siding. *Ol' Timer* can travel at speeds up to 6 1/2 mph.

Al Dunlop's *Ol' Timer*, 2002. Photo by author.

Carney's Fay & Bowen (No Name)

This Fay & Bowen has been owned by only two old Lake George families for the past 77 years. Furthermore, it is a "one-of-a-kind", but before I tell its story, I am compelled to tell you first about Fay & Bowen boats.

The Fay & Bowen Boat Company began in Auburn, New York as a bicycle spoke factory. By 1900, it developed into a gasoline engine manufacturing operation. Soon thereafter, Walter L. Fay and Ernest S. Bowen raised $25,000 to expand their company into boat building on Owasco Lake. In 1904 the growing business moved to Seneca Lake near Geneva, New York for easy access to the railroads and the Erie Canal. The business shipped boats all over the world, however its largest dealer was right here on Lake George. My grandmother's cousin, Walter Harris of Harris Bay, owned that Lake George dealership.

Jack Carney's Fay & Bowen Golden Arrow. Courtesy: Henry Heller Smith.

Powered by dependable two-cycle engines, many of these sleek well constructed craft are still seen on the lake today. Round bottom hulls were constructed of either mahogany, white cedar or red cypress and featured passenger compartments located behind the engine beneath a long forward deck. One of their trademarks was the "gooseneck" air vent just ahead of the engine compartment. Ernie Bowen died around 1918 and the company was sold in 1921, but Walter Fay remained in control of the Board of Directors into the 1930s, focusing the primary business on the construction of pleasure launches rather than on boats of speed. The company finally closed its doors in 1937 because Chris-Craft and other competitors cornered the market with its new faster "V" bottom hulls. With so many Fay & Bowen boats sold to Lake George owners, it is not surprising that many are still around.

The 1925 Fay & Bowen Golden Arrow model #800 I am featuring here was custom built in 1924 for the New York City Boat Show. It is unique because it is one foot wider than any other F & B ever built, and because its entire hull is the only one constructed completely of varnished mahogany. It is 30 feet long and was originally powered by a 4 cylinder engine producing 1000 rpms at 45hp. The original propeller had a 22 inch diameter. This valuable launch was purchased at the boat show by the Wallace McCaw family of Bolton Landing for $4500. They used it every summer except during World War II when it was stored on Green Island in the Smith's Boathouse barn. The McCaw's sold it in 1945 to Bruce Carney who owned and operated the Sabbath Day Point Hotel which was torn down in 1957. Boat ownership passed on to his son John K.(Jack) Carney who is the boat's current owner. In 1955, it was repowered with a Chris-Craft "K" 95hp 12 volt engine and the propeller was downsized to 13 inches. At speeds of 25mph, it was sometimes used for skiing. Jack often took 6 or 8 of the hotel guests for nighttime trips to Paradise Bay in the boat. He lived at Sabbath Day Point all of his life until he sold his lakeside home just a few years ago.

Right, Advertisement. Courtesy: Wauneata Waller.
Below, Advertisement. Courtesy: Henry Caldwell.

Fay & Bowen Motors and Boats

Comfort, speed, safety and pleasure is combined in the highest degree in these luxurious and classy boats. Fay & Bowen motors realize highest efficiency and minimum expense of upkeep. Nearly one quarter of all the boats on Lake George of 21 foot and over are Fay & Bowen. Ask their owners.

Gasoline and Supplies

Highest Grade Lubricating Oils
to be obtained on Lake George

All Standard motor boat appliances, greases of all kinds automatic bilge drains, boat cushions, etc.
SUBMARINE RAILWAY
with power hoist will pull your boat out safely and quickly, at a moderate charge.

WALTER P. HARRIS
Lake George, N. Y.
Representive, Fay & Bowen Co.
Geneva, N. Y.

The Carney's used the Golden Arrow for everything. Often it was seen over at Hulett's Landing at the Casino. Jack told me he had his best times in the Fay & Bowen while at the Casino. Often, he and his late wife Florence would take it to the Algonquin Restaurant in Bolton Landing. In 1980, he and Florence had the only mishap the boat ever experienced, and a serious one. While returning from the Algonquin, they were surprised by a violent thunderstorm which suddenly appeared over the northern Tongue Mountain Range. We captains at the Lake George Steamboat Company call these violent sudden storms "Swoopers". The Carney's made it through lightning and turbulent windswept waters to Vicars Island and tied the boat to a dock with help from nearby campers. The wind became so

BULLETIN NUMBER 106-A
FAY & BOWEN ENGINE CO., GENEVA, N.Y., U.S.A.

MODEL L-64 ENGINE
SIX-CYLINDER, FOUR-STROKE-CYCLE ENGINE, T-HEAD TYPE

severe that its force against the boat's hull pulled the dock over, puncturing two bottom planks and sinking the boat. The next day it was rescued by Morgan Marine of Silver Bay and was soon repaired. During the past few years, this old classic has been stored in Rob Henry's boathouse at Hague. Jack told me that at 82 years of age and with a permanent knee injury, he wants to make certain that his boat goes to a new home where it will be appreciated and preserved. In his own melancholy words, "It's time". Jack Carney is currently discussing with Henry Heller Smith, Chairman of Bolton Landing's Antique Boat Museum, a possible "bargain and sale" arrangement which would transfer title to the Museum. Henry Smith proudly describes her as—the "Queen of the Golden Arrows".

F&B Gauge. From author's collection.
Carney's Golden Arrow, 2001. Photo by author.

Bonita (I)

Bonita (I) was owned by Harry Hayden who is sitting on the bow. Elizabeth Hayden is on the dock. The Hayden mansion once stood along the west shore in Lake George Village across the road from todays Lake George High School on Canada Street.

Courtesy: Hugh Allen Wilson

Bonita (II)

Bonita (II) was purchased at the New York City Boat Show in 1924 by Captain Clarence E. Wilson for owner, Miss Jessie S. Robertson, who was a Bolton summer resident. Wilson had also built Berylheath, Robinson's lakeside Bolton home. Interestingly, when Berylheath was sold during the mid 20th century to the William Hoffman family, the *Benita (II)* went along with it. *Benita (II)* then passed on to Hoffman's daughter, Corin. Today, *Benita (II)* is owned by Tony DePace and named *Big Girl*.

Bonita (II), now named *Big Girl* off the Robinson dock, 1920's. Courtesy: Hugh Allen Wilson.

The Old Man

The Old Man is a 1904 Fay & Bowen that was originally owned by Captain Wesley Finkle, the famous steamboat captain and Lake George guide. She is 27 feet long, has a classic torpedo stern, White Oak frames, a Cyprus hull and Mahogany deck. When new, she had a standing wooden top and high brass railings on both her bow and stern. During the 1950's, The Old Man was stored in a garage on Mohican Hill in Bolton Landing. During the mid 1970's, the boat was for sale in a newspaper ad in Old Forge, NY. That is when current owner John Hilton of Pilot Knob bought her.

The Old Man. Courtesy: John Hilton.

Osprey (Hilton)

Osprey originally belonged to the Reverend Bishop Stires, of Lagoon Manor north of Bolton Landing. She is a 25 foot 1907 Fay & Bowen, originally powered by a 2 cycle 2 cylinder 19 hp F&B engine. When Stires died, his son owned the boat and kept her at Shelving Rock. She races in and won many races from the Sagamore Hotel to Dome Island. Baird Maranville owned Osprey next, followed by Ray Nelson, who sold her to John Hilton who had the boat restored in the 1980's.

The Hilton family in the *Osprey*. Courtesy: John Hilton.

Eyrie (II)

Eyrie (II) is a Fay & Bowen with Cedar sides and a Mahogany deck, built around 1912. She is 32 feet long, has a 6 foot beam, drafts 2 feet and is powered by a Chris-Craft K 95 hp engine. She was owned by George O. Knapp of Shelving Rock, first President of Union Carbide Corporation. Knapp's Great Grandson, John Sprole, owned Eyrie (II) during the 1970's and once her to rescue a lone diver who was drowning. The next owners were Roy Anderson and then Geoff Cahill of Tongue Mountain, who then sold her to current owners Sherwood and Betty Finley on Fourteen Mile Island.

Eyrie (II) off Fourteen Mile Island.
Courtesy: Sherwood and Betty Finley.

'Tonka

'Tonka is a shortened version of this 1911 Fay & Bowen's real name, *Minnetonka*, named for Lake Minnetonka, Minnesota. She came from Dunham's Bay and is owned today by John B. "Jack" Newkirk of Turtle Bay. Before him, she was owned by his parents, Burt and Louise Newkirk who purchased 'Tonka in 1932. The 26 foot 'Tonka was used first as a fishing boat and for early camping excursions to Hazel and Sarah Islands. She was originally powered by a naptha 2 cylinder engine, and later a marine conversion of a Model T Ford engine. Her engine today is a grey Marine.

Jack Newkirk in *'Tonka*, 2001. Photo by author.

Blue Angel

Blue Angel, 2002. Photo by author.

In July of 1989, Dick and Yona Freiden of Homer Point purchased their 1916 Special 25 foot Fay & Bowen from Bill Foster of Ruah in Hague. Foster had owned her for 20 years, and even her 2 wicker chairs came from Ruah, once the home of Harry Watrous who built the Lake George Monster. This boat, with hull #469, originally cost $875. *Blue Angel* is 25 feet long and 5 feet at the beam. Her deck is of Mahogany; the rest is Southern White Pine. She is powered by a gravity fed 1940 4 cyl. Chris-Craft engine. If *Blue Angel* looks familiar, she appeared in the popular 1987 "Morning Mist" poster with the *Mohican*, a photo taken the same morning the *Lac du Saint Sacrement's* hull was launched at Baldwin.

Flossie

The Simon's and Bartlett's *Flossie*. Courtesy: Dick and Claire Bartlett.

To know *Flossie*, you must first know of her famous former owner, the late Elsa Kny Steinback of The Point at Shelving Rock. Elsa was an artist, a poet, and is best known for her local history book, "Sweet Peas and a White Bridge". She was a shy woman who loved her dogs. Elsa was born in 1911 and she died in 1996. She spent every summer of her life at Shelving Rock.

Flossie is actually short for *Flosshilde*, one of the Rhine Maidens in the Wagner Opera, Ring of the Niebelungsuk. The boat is a 30 foot 1917 Golden Arrow, hull #621, only one number from the Gabriels' Fay & Bowen on Green Island. She was originally powered by a 6 cyl. 50 hp engine and could travel at 21 mph. Today, she is powered by a Chris-Craft engine which was recently installed by John Miller of Bolton, an expert in rebuilding and maintaining antique engines.

Flossie was purchased new by her grandfather Richard Kny from Walter Harris who owned the Fay & Bowen dealership on Lake George. When Elsa was a young girl, she piloted *Flossie* which was in lake George every summer, except from World War II and on into the 1960s when she was stored in the boathouse. Today, *Flossie* is co-owned by Elsa's nephew Peter Simon of The Point and the Dick Bartlett family of Fourteen Mile Island.

Van Dyck's (No Name)

Peter and Carol Van Dyck's Fay & Bowen, 2002. Photo by author.

Peter and Carol Van Dyck of Clay Island own a 1920 Fay & Bowen that had never been named, and she still is unnamed today. The boat belonged previously to the Hoolihan's. A friend of Peter's mother, Olive Kline Hoolihan was a famous Broadway star who also was featured in early radio programs. She also starred as Miss Palmolive. Olive Kline Hoolihan piloted this boat well up into her 80's. The Van Dyck's got the boat from her at the same time they purchased their Clay Island home in 1971.

Her length is 24 feet, beam is 5 feet 4 inches and she drafts 2 feet. She is now powered by a Chevy 6 cyl. which was installed in 1990.

Minnie Henry

Minne Henry is a 1916 Golden Arrow 30 foot launch owned by the Kiernan-Gabriels family on Green Island. *Minne Henry* is named for their housekeeper of many years ago who helped raise their children. The boat was purchased from John Hilton of Pilot Knob in the early 1970's. It had come from another lake and was once owned by the former Governor of Pennsylvania. Her hull number is #620, one number different from Elsa Steinback's *Flossie*. *Minne Henry* is powered by a dependable Chris-Craft 95 hp K engine.

Zandy Gabriels in *Minnie Henry*, 2002. Photo by author.

Carroll

The *Carroll* was an early Fay & Bowen owned by Peter D. Kiernan. He purchased the boat in 1924 when he purchased the family home on Green Island. The *Carroll* was named for his wife Carroll. They sold her in 1930. The family had three or four old Chris-Crafts through the years as well; each also bore the name *Carroll*.

Peter D. Kiernan in *Carroll*.
Courtesy: Jane Gabriels.

The Black Swan

Peter D. Kiernan of Green Island purchased *The Black Swan* in 1929. She is a Gar-Wood Baby Gar 40, the same as George Reis' *El Lakayo* which is now owned by F.R. Smith's Marina. *Black Swan* is a 28 foot runabout which was originally powered by a 200 hp Scripps. Today, she is still owned by the Kiernan-Gabriels family and is powered by a 1950's Chrysler M14L. Her serial number is #29347. Her hull number is #83 out of only 352 ever made.

Zandy Gabriels in *The Black Swan*, 2002. Photo by author.

6+1

On April 9, 1947, *6+1* was purchased from the Hall's Gar-Wood dealership in Lake George Village on the last shipping day before the Gar-Wood factory closed down. She is a 1947 "706" Deluxe Gar-Wood Runabout. Her original engine is still in use, a Chrysler Crown Six with 115 hp. Of only 84 built, *6+1* is hull #83. *6+1*, owned by the Kiernan/Gabriels family, was named to represent the children: 6 boys and 1 girl. Every Christmas morning, we use the *6+1* for a water skiing event in Bolton Bay featuring skiers Zandy Gabriels and Debbie Gaddy.

Zandy Gabriels in *6+1*, 2002. Photo by author.

Raymond's F&B

In the 1920's, Dr. Raymond of Pilot Knob Road owned a Fay & Bowen which was regularly enjoyed by his family and the Granville Beals family of Assembly Point. Dr. Raymond owned a successful factory in Glens Falls on Logan Avenue named "Dr. Raymond's Pectoral Plasters". He made medical plasters which were placed in an oven and heated, and were then applied to the chest which relieved ailments similar to the method achieved by a hot water bottle. He also made adhesive bandages and tape for the military during World War II.

Above, Philis Beals.
Left, Jim Harris, J.L. Beals & Granville Beals.
Courtesy: John Beals.

Rags

Rags is a 20 foot 1931 Chris-Craft Triple Cockpit Cadet, Model 200, hull # 7278. Originally, she was owned by Coolidge 'Cooly" Thomas in Harris Bay. Cooly painted her sides black instead of using varnish to simplify maintenance. My uncle, Bob Gates, purchased Rags from Thomas after World War II. Bob stripped off the black paint and totally restored the boat to her original condition. In the early 1960's Uncle Bob replaced the original 6 cyl. engine with a 312 Ford Interceptor V-8. The name Rags represents my uncle's initials– Robert Alexander Gates.

I grew up with the Rags and am very fond of her. I attended Camp Chingachgook for two summers in 1953 and 1954–my parents brought me there in the Rags. All of our early family outings on the lake were in the Rags. At the end of the 1960's, most of my generation grew up and were enjoying our own boats, so Rags was stored away, but never forgotten. In 2001, I rolled Rags out of storage where she has rested for 34 years. In the near future, I plan to reinstall Rags' original engine and enjoy her once again.

Clockwise: Rags in Bolton Bay, 1960's. Bob Gates, Lorraine Cushman and Barbara Gates Lawrence in Rags. Rags removed from 34 year storage in 2001. 1931 Chris-Craft illustration. Courtesy: Henry Caldwell.

Owaissa

Owaissa is a 26 foot 1925 Chris-Craft Cadet Runabout. *Owaissa* is an Iroquois term meaning "Blue Bird of Happiness". Originally, she was owned by Judge Railey of Glens Falls, so his daughter Roselyn could take her college friends around the lake. His chauffer would tow Judge Railey around Basin Bay on his aqua-plane every evening. When he wanted to quit for the day, he would entertain his neighbors by gliding to his dock where he would do a back flip into the water.

Roselyn eventually married Donald Braley of Braley Hill. *Owaissa* remained in their family for a total of 62 years before she was purchased by her current owner, Henry Heller Smith of the Lake George Antique Boat Society.

Owaissa at Antique Boat Museum in Bolton Landing, 2000. Photo by author.

Alli

The *Alli* is a 17 foot 1938 Chris-Craft utility that was enjoyed by many. She was purchased new by a family on Clay Island. They used her almost daily to haul their supplies out to their summer cottage. A few years later, Burto Warren wrote to the owners and they sold it to him. Warren next sold her to Ervin Sheridan in the late 1940's. Sheridan named her *Jughead*. During the 1950's, Sheridan sold her to the Hinman family on Trout Lake Road. They named her *Joy Boy*. The Hinman's all grew up with *Joy Boy* and loved her. *Joy Boy* became difficult to start, so they sold her to my Uncle and Aunt, Jim and Zilpha Francis who named her the *Zip*. Uncle Jim was the ranger on Long Island during the 1950's, so my Aunt Zip used the *Zip* to transport supplies to the island. My brother Bud and I made many trips in the *Zip* out to Long Island. When my aunt died in 1972, she left me the *Zip*. I renamed her *Alli*, for my daughter Allison, and my own family enjoyed her for the next 16 years. In 1988, she needed restoration, so I sold her to a man I met at the Saratoga Racetrack. He took her to a lake in Florida, restored her and she is still in use today.

Top, Mike Gates at Fork Island, 1975.
Above, Allison Gates in *Alli*, Bolton Bay, 1985.
Left, *Alli* at Hersh's dock, Bolton, 1975. Photos by author.

Black Arrow

This boat has had at least owners. *Black Arrow's* first owner was Dr. Curtenius Gillette of Bluff Head. Dr. Gillette purchased this 1930 Sea Lyon Model 94 from F.R. Smith & Sons in Bolton and named her *Rabs*. He ran her almost daily to Huletts, Silver Bay and the Uncas Inn. In 1940, the *Rabs* struck a canoe, injuring the two passengers aboard. The *Rabs* was then placed into storage. In 1945, *Rabs* was sold to Walton Wallace and renamed *Marty*. A third owner then sold her again to Walter Grishkot of Glens Falls who named her *Black Arrow*. Grishkot kept *Black Arrow* in his boathouse near the Tongue Mountain lookout. In 1966, he sold her to the Dock and Dine Restaurant at Hague, who then sold her to a dentist in Maine, and they, in turn, sold her to James S. Rockefeller Jr. of Maine. In 1989, owner number eight became Dick Brown of California; he totally restored *Black Arrow*.

Black Arrow. Courtesy: Walter Grishkot.

Snoah's Ark

This 1940 Chris-Craft cabin cruiser is owned by Don and Dottie Vilmar who live south of Log Bay on the former Huntington property. In 1939, Dottie's uncle, Homer H. Snow, ordered it at the New York City Boat Show. He was then caught in a 4 hour snow storm and decided to name her *Snoah's Ark*. The boat was shipped directly to Lake George from Algonac, MI on a D&H Railroad flatcar and launched at Lake George Village where it was then picked up and piloted to Bolton by a young 12 year old Fred Smith Sr. *Snoah's Ark* is 24 feet long, 6 1/2 feet wide and drafts 2 1/2 feet. Originally powered by a 4 cyl. Grey Marine 60 hp, she was repowered in 1982 by a Chevy V-6 4.3 liter. The *Ark* is, and always was, white and green painted mahogany. In 1981, an Encon boat struck her in the darkness, and only then was it discovered that her hull was mahogany. Fortunately, her damage was slight. *Snoah's Ark* makes a trip to Bolton and back almost daily every summer and thus has made several lifesaving rescues.

Snoah's Ark, 2002. Photo by author.

Silver Spray

During the summer of 1899, Dr. Luther D. Wishard was confined to a hospital in Chicago. He then heard that his friend Silas H. Paine had just purchased a hotel on Silver Bay, Lake George from Judge John W. Wilson. Wishard visited the hotel and conceived the idea of converting it into a summer meeting place. With the help of Harlan P. Beach, the men planned the first conference in 1901, The Forward Movement Council in Bible Study and Foreign Missions with over two hundred in attendance.

In 1902, Silas Paine sold the hotel and property to the Silver Bay Association, and in 1904, it incorporated.

Silver Spray at Silver Bay Association, 2002. Photo by author.

Throughout the past 200 years, the Silver Bay Association has relied on a large number of boats for transporting guests around Lake George. Their first large vessels were the *Iroquois* and the *Oneita* which stopped running in the late 1920's. Throughout the 1930's the large commercial steamboats were used for transporting guests, while a large fleet of small rowboats and canoes were always available.

Above, Boat Building at Silver Bay Association. Courtesy: Esko Virta
Left, Boathouse sign to "Skipper Mac", 2002. Photo by author.

In the early 1950's, the Association began acquiring a series of power boats, all named the *Silver Spray*, with lengths of 28 feet, 24 feet and 26 feet respectively. Until recently, *Silver Spray* (I) rested in the children's playground. Her beloved skipper was Norman "Mac" Meglathery of Snug Harbor. Skipper Mac piloted all three of the *Silver Sprays* until he died in 1986. Mac became local legend by climbing 2,665 ft. Black Mountain 250 times.

One of her current eight skippers is Don Dieterrick who came to Silver Bay in the early 1960's and has piloted *Silver Spray* (III) from 1993 to the present. She is a 26 foot wooden 1970 Lyman lapstrake, powered by a Crusader engine. Today, *Silver Spray* takes daily tours to the Mother Bunch, Paradise Bay, the Narrows, Gull Bay, Roger's Rock, Black Mountain and through the Needle's Eye.

Skunk

In 1956, Joe Scully of Lake George purchased a new Chris-Craft Continental from Nemith's car and Chris-Craft dealership in Troy. Almost immediately, Joe had Bill Lockhart rebuild the bottom into a faster, smoother hydroplane style, and Joe also replaced the stock 6 cyl. engine with a Supercharged V-8 Chrysler Hemi. His friends at Halls, where the boat is docked, told him he should name this very fast new boat *Skunk* because, "Nobody messes with a skunk"–and that is how the boat was named. *Skunk* is 23 feet long, has a 8 foot 6 inch beam and drafts 2 1/2 feet. Ever since this boat was new in 1956, Joe has made a full length tour of Lake George and back almost every summer day, beginning early in the morning. Joe knows the lake well; throughout the 1960's, he was a member of the lake's

Skunk, 1956 Chris-Craft Continental. Courtesy: Joe Scully.

Sheriff's Patrol when he wasn't at work at his career job as an official for the U.S. Federal Court. Joe recently told me of a time when he was caught in a severe hail storm in the Narrows in the late 1960's. The stones were so large and plentiful, they dented the *Skunk's* varnish and filled the back seat with ice.

Loon

The *Loon* is a 28 foot 1928 Gar-Wood owned by F.R. Smith's that was a twin to their *El Lakayo*. Her green paint and tan deck make her easy to identify out on the lake. When Smith's business burned in May of 1957, the Loon was badly damaged, but repairable. Rod Lagoy repaied what was left of the woodwork and my uncle Bob Gates did the mechanical work to convert the *Loon* to Smith's work boat, a job she still handles today.

The *Loon* at F.R. Smith & Sons, late fall 2002. Photos by author.

Canoe Island Lodge Boats

Canoe Island Lodge's 28 foot Interclubs, 1960's. Courtesy: Tom and Carla Burlhoe.

Immediately following World War II, Bill and Jane Busch began construction on a new Lake George resort named Canoe Island Lodge. In the early 1950's, the Busch's purchased two 28 foot wooden Interclub racing sailboats from Long Island Sound for entertaining their guests. These boats were used faithfully every summer until 1989. Because they were of wood construction, they were becoming difficult to maintain, and because they had a low freeboard, they could easily take on water. The time had arrived to replace them. Bill Busch commissioned Scarano Boat Builders in Albany to construct three new sailboats that were comfortable, safe and simple to operate. The two lead keels from the Interclubs were reused, and they were then destroyed. The *Jane*, *Nighthawk* and *Word of Life* have high freeboards, bench seats and cabins for storing equipment, and high 46 foot masts which require frequent reefing. Each Canoe Island 30 is made of laminated yellow pine, yellow and red cedar, and is painted black with white trim lines. Each is actually 31 feet long, 8 foot 4 inches at the beam and drafts 4 feet 6 inches.

In 1972, the Busch's purchased their inboard Monteray named *Ark*, white with a red stripe, and in 1986, the red 8.2 liter diesel powered *Sisu* was acquired for transporting guests to Canoe Island, the Narrows or to Paradise Bay.

Sisu, 2002. Photo by author.

Canoe Island Lodge 30's, 2002. Photo by author.

Bateaux Below's Tuff Boat

The underwater explorers of Bateaux Below, Inc. use an R.W. Series (Rough Water) Tuff Boat that was built in the State of Washington and shipped overland to Lake George. It is a 22 foot hardtop model with a 1/4 inch welded aluminum hull. The Tuff Boat was designed with a dual purpose in mind, for diving and survey use. She is powered by a 140 hp Tohatsu engine. Bateaux Below, Inc. formed its charter on January 22, 1992 and exists to preserve submerged maritime-related resources such as historic shipwrecks and piers–and it engages in archaeoligical projects designed to discover and collect data on historical shipwrecks to nominate these discoveries to the National Register of Historic Places. Bateaux Below, Inc. is a totally volunteer group. No member receives a salary. Working with the State of New York, Bateaux Below, Inc, under the direction of Joe Zarzynski, has helped to create New York State's first shipwreck preserves.

Bateaux Below, Inc's Tuff Boat in Lake George Village, 2002. Director, Joe Zarzynski & Bob Benway. Photo by author.

Darrin Fresh Water Institute Boats

The Darrin Fresh Water Institute formed its charter in 1967. It has been housed since the 1980's on the grounds of "The Mooring's , an estate that was built between 1894 and 1896 in Bolton Landing by the retired commandant of the Brooklyn Ship Yard, USN Admiral John W. Moore. Since 1970, David M. Darrin has established a series of endowments to fund the Institute with RPI College maintaining all of the facilities. The Institute provides opportunities for Rensselaer faculty, students and visiting scientists to study Lake George's ecosystems, and to research important environmental problems.

To access their research locations on the lake, they purchased an aluminum 22 foot Henley research vessel in 1985 which has served them well. She has been used to install benthic barriers against the Eurasian Water Milfoil plant and for hauling tons of the invasive plant from the waters of Lake George. She is powered by a new Volvo Penta engine.

Above, 22 foot Henley.
Below, Aussie Cat arrives, 2002.
Courtesy: David Diehl.

A second boat, a 19 foot Mako, was purchased in 1994. Its traditional "V Hull" make sit a faster boat than the Henley. The Institute uses this Mako to shuttle gear and supplies to research sites on the lake. She is powered by a new Honda four-stroke engine which improves fuel efficiency and reduces oil and exhaust emissions.

A third boat, a 23 foot Aussie Cat, arrived at the Institute in September of 2002. She is to be used as an additional dive platform and can access shallow areas safely due to her low draft of only 17 inches. In addition, her tunnel hull makes her very stable in rough water conditions. Her four-stroke engines are each 115 hp Yamaha's. All three of these boats are equipped with GPS navigation systems for boating safety and for exactly marking research sites .

Lake George Club

The Lake George Yacht Club was organized by a group of summer "cottagers" in 1888. Their first summer home in Basin Bay burned, and for several years, they were without a home. On September 5th, 1908, the group reorganized to form the Lake George Club. During the winter, architect Charles S. Peabody designed the current clubhouse which opened to its members on August 14, 1909. This new club was built to be a social center for both cottagers and summer visitors. Spencer Trask was elected as the club's first president, and he served in this position until December 31st of that same 1909 year when he was tragically killed in a train accident at Croton on the Hudson.

Boating has always been one of the many focuses for entertainment at the club. At first, the boats were all the new motor boats that became of interest after the gasoline engines replaced steam. The boating regattas were very popular events and prizes were always awarded. Sailing first became the new focus as late as 1936 when the idea was introduced by Harold "Pappy" Pitcairn and Dr. E.F.W. Alexanderson. Pitcairn had seven children, five of them boys, and wanted to keep them busy and out of mischief. At first, the fleet consisted of two Stars, two Cape Cods and two Sound Interclubs. During World War II, there wasn't any sail racing, and the 9 hole golf course closed when the Marion House Hotel next door was demolished. By the early 1960's, Interclubs were done racing and the 24 foot Rainbows appeared, introduced by Merle Smith. Today, the Rainbows are not racing either, but a few are still around. Some were donated to Camp Chingachgook. The 19 foot Cape Cod's were still around up to the 1980's, and there were around 15 Stars around then, also, at their peak. Next came the J-24's and the J-22's. There have been as many as a dozen of these each entered in club races which are held every Saturday, and on Wednesday evenings, races are open to any style of boat with the handicap rule equalizing the competition.

Above, Interclubs, 1957.
Photo by Art Knight.

Above left, racing with spinnakers, 1984.
Above right, model of 24 foot Rainbow at L.G. Club.
Left, sailboats moored at Club, 2002.
Below, Lake George Clubhouse, Fall 2000.
Photos by author.

Northern Lake George Yacht Club

The Northern Lake George Yacht Club grew from northern members of the Lake George Yacht Club which first formed in 1888. In 1926, sailing competitions were held at the lake's northern end among four Red Wings. During 1931, sailing races began at Glenburnie, and the Rogers Rock Yacht Club organized in 1932 to race Akroid 14 foot dinghies and later, Comets. By 1940, it became apparent that it was in the best interest of all northern sailors to unite into one organization. On March 16, 1941, Commodore John Boulton Simpson's daughter Helen Simpson formally transferred the Lake George Club's burgee to this northern group because the last club Commodore had been John R. Simpson. The burgee's colors consist of a blue field with a central white stripe that contains a red star in its center. To avoid confusion with the Lake George Club, the word "Northern" was added. For the following seven years, races were conducted from the Monsignor Keegan property on Friend's Point. They built their own clubhouse in 1948 with funds donated by members. Through the years, they raced Stars, Turnabouts, Thistles, Flying Juniors, Lazers, and today, a fleet of International Optimists.

The Northern Lake George Yacht Club, 2002.
Courtesy: Marianna Klein.
Photos by author.

Camp Chingachgook

In 1913, a boys camp was established in Basin Bay by the Schenectady WMCA. The camp moved to its present location at Pilot Knob during the following year, 1914, under the direction of Clarence "Pops" Drake, the camp's first director. Camp Chingachgook is one of the oldest youth camps in the United States. The camp's first canoe was named *The Chingachgook*. To honor that first canoe, the camp became known as Camp Chingachgook. The camp also had a large gasoline powered launch named the *Nordic* that took groups on tours of the lake. In the beginning, campers arrived by steamboat at the Pilot Knob Store pier. From here, they would walk to the camp. In 1918, the Boy Scouts began camping here during August and the WMCA group used the facility during July. The scouts began calling their session Camp Rotary in 1922. In 1943, the Boy Scouts opened their own camp in Saratoga. Since 1943, Chingachgook has been totally a WMCA facility.

My brother Bud and attended Camp Chingachgook during the early 1950's. I clearly recall the old 24 foot 1942 Old Town War Canoes which were enjoyed by campers until they were replaced in 1999. These canoes held 8 to 10 kids and taught them the importance of teamwork. Today, one of these

The *Nordic*.
Courtesy: George Painter.

"Old Town 'WAR' Canoe"

Boys' and girls' summer camps and canoe clubs use this canoe for team paddling and group cruising. No water craft is better for team training. It is a pretty sight to see a War canoe crew driving with rhythmic strokes at top speed. Equipped with floor rack, keel, outside stems, 30 inch decks. No. 6 canvas. Stock color Dark Green. Other colors (page 39) for shipment 20 days. Some boys' and girls' camps build a large part of their aquatic program on the team work which is made possible by a fleet of War canoes.

Length	Width	Depth	App. Weight	App. Weight Packed	App. Weight Crated	App. Cubic Meas.	Capacity	Open Spruce Gunwales, C.S. Grade	Code Word
25 ft.	44 in.	14½ in.	180 lbs.	280 lbs.	500 lbs.	256 cu. ft.	6 to 11 Paddlers	$308.00	Remmac

War Canoe Ad, 1940's. Courtesy: Henry Caldwell.

is permanently displayed on the Dining Hall ceiling so everyone can view an important part of Chingachgook's boating history. The 4 new 300 pound, Canadian built, 10 man, 25 foot War Canoes have names which represent the camp's four core values, *Honesty, Respect, Responsibility,* and

Old War Canoe, 1965. Courtesy: George Painter.

New War Canoe today. Courtesy: George Painter.

Old War Canoe in cafeteria, 2002. Photo by author.

Caring. These canoes were dedicated to John and Joanne Mahoney who worked at the camp for nearly 50 years.

The sailboat fleet of today is also impressive, all the way up from Sunfish to 24 foot Rainbows. Recently, the camp has acquired 5 disability boats for their "Camp Y-Knot Sailing Club" program, founded in 1996 by Dick Whalen. George Painter, the camp's current director, told me there are only 80 of these special boats in the world.

Today, Camp Chingachgook consists of a 200 acre plot, 1400 feet of shoreline, 90 buildings, and works with approximately 13,000 youngsters annually. Their total boating fleet consists of 17 aluminum Grumman canoes, 14 Sunfish, 6 Capri's, 4 War Canoes, 9 Rainbows, 5 disability sailboats and several power boats.

Police & Fire Boats

Darrell Finlayson in Warren Co. Sheriff Boat, 24 ft. Chris-Craft, 1960's.
Courtesy: Darrell Finlayson.

R. Frulla in L. G. Park Commission's Whaler, 1960's.
Courtesy: Darrell Finlayson.

Tom Muscatello of the Lake George Marine Patrol, 2002.
Photo by author.

Lake George Marine Patrol, 2002.
Photo by author.

NYS Conservation Police, 2002. Photo by author.

Lake George Fire Dept., 2002. Photo by author.

Bolton Fire Dept., 2002. Photo by author.

North Queensbury Fire Dept., 2002. Photo by author.

Jack Howe & Bruce Lundgren of Warren County Sheriff Patrol, 2001.
Photo by author.

Jack Howe & Bruce Lundgren in new Sheriff Boat, 2002.
Photo by author.

The first New York State Police boat on Lake George was a 17 foot Boston Whaler. She was replaced by this 21 foot 1986 Chris-Craft named *Stoddard's View*. *Stoddard's View,* the only New York State Police boat on Lake George, was named in an essay contest held at Lake George High School. She is powered by a Scorpion 211 engine, and is equipped with a fire pump and a bilge pump for assisting a sinking vessel.

Rich Kober & David Pelchar in NY State Police Boat, *Stoddard's View*, 2002. Photo by author.

Kayaks

"Canoeing on Lake George, the Rendezvous of the Fleet", 1886. Courtesy: Henry Caldwell.

Archaeologists have found evidence proving kayaks to have existed 4000 years ago. The first kayaks were made by the Inuits of Greenland, and by the Alaskan Aleuts. The word "kayak" means "hunter's boat." They were made of seal skins and driftwood which was collected from the beaches. Hair was removed from the skins and rubbed with oil for waterproofing. Sinew was used to lash the frame and sew the skins. When skins were sewn, the stitches did not penetrate completely through the skin which prevented leaking. Some early groups used the two bladed paddle exclusively while others used only the single bladed paddle. Hunting for caribou was done mostly on the inland waters. Sea mammals and fish were hunted at sea.

As far as we know, kayaks first appeared on Lake George during the late 1800's. The American Canoeing Association held Rob Roy Kayak Races

Kayak and Canoes on Lake George, 1898. Courtesy: Mike DeLarm.

 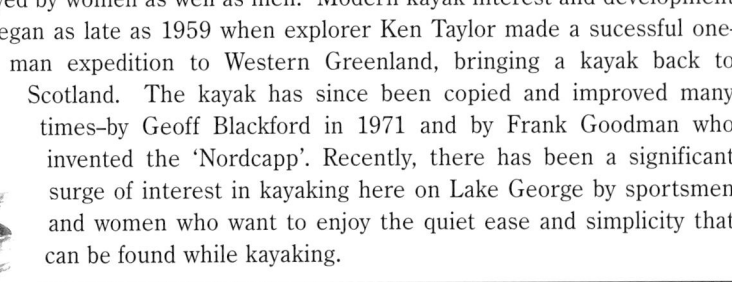

beginning in 1880, and many early lithographs of Lake George show kayaks being enjoyed by women as well as men. Modern kayak interest and development began as late as 1959 when explorer Ken Taylor made a sucessful one-man expedition to Western Greenland, bringing a kayak back to Scotland. The kayak has since been copied and improved many times–by Geoff Blackford in 1971 and by Frank Goodman who invented the 'Nordcapp'. Recently, there has been a significant surge of interest in kayaking here on Lake George by sportsmen and women who want to enjoy the quiet ease and simplicity that can be found while kayaking.

Above, The Rob-Roy Race, Frank Leslie's Illustrated Newspaper, Sept. 3, 1881. Courtesy: Henry Caldwell. Three Kayaks today. Photos by author.

Wrecks & Fires

Throughout Lake George boating history, there have been many serious accidents, sinkings and fires. The following collection of photos were collected over decades by Frank Leonbruno, formerly in charge of DEC operations here on Lake George, and later by Leroy Ryder, who is currently in charge, along with a few others by Darrell Finlayson and Lee Taber.

Hall's Lyman

This 1958 Lyman is owned today by Hall's Boat Corp. in Lake George Village. She is 23 feet long and powered by her original Chrysler Crown 6 cylinder engine. When new, she was purchased from Bob Stewart's dealership and sold to Evelyn Miller at Pilot knob. many years later in the mid 1980's, the Miller's sold it to Hall's. Hall's put on a new bottom and has used the blue and varnished boat as a work-boat. On March 9, 2002, Hall's had a major fire which destroyed several buildings and nine boats. The Lyman was badly burned, but is restorable and will be restored in the near future and put back into use.

Hall's Lyman. Photo by author.

Boats, Scenes & Regatta's

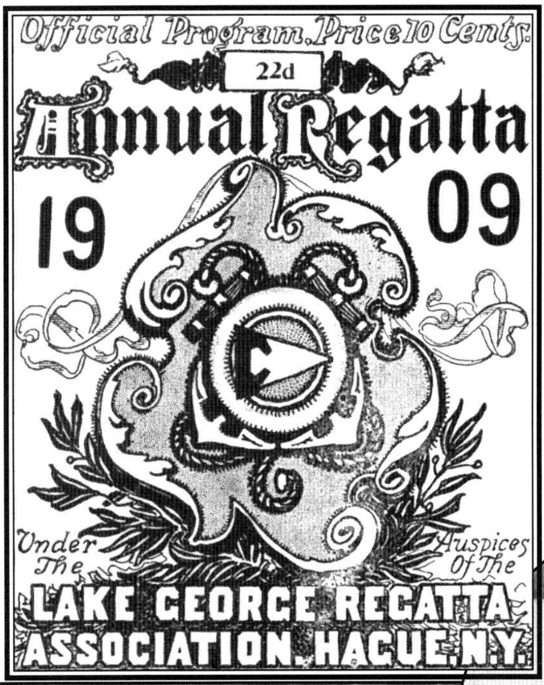

Courtesy: Henry Caldwell.

Courtesy: Bill Richards.

Courtesy: Henry Caldwell & Black Bass Antiques.

Courtesy: John & Betty Barth.

Courtesy: Peggy Edwards, Lake George Village Historian.

Old Buoys from Echo Bay. Photo by author.

Mohawk. Author's collection.

Courtesy: Jane Crammond & The Silver Bay Association.

At Bolton Landing.
Courtesy: Maggie McClure & Lake George Historical Association.

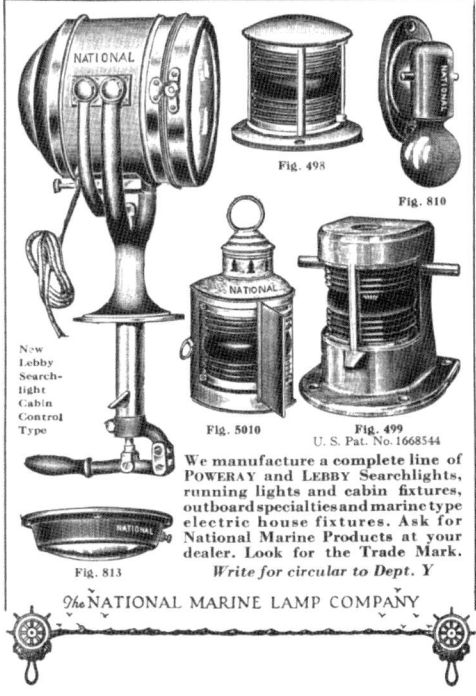

Crusader, Scioto & *Sayonara* at Bolton House.
Courtesy: Bob Benway.

Courtesy: Tom Passaro.

Author's collection.

Trout, from Lorraine Cushman album. Author's collection.

Courtesy: Mike DeLarm.

At Caldwell, 1908. Fred C. Thatcher photo. Courtesy: Peggy Edwards, Lake George Village Historian.

Bob Gates at Sagamore Hotel.
Author's collection.

Postcard. Author's collection.

Courtesy: Ethel Andrus, Hague Historian.

Peter D. Kiernan.
Courtesy: Jane Gabriels.

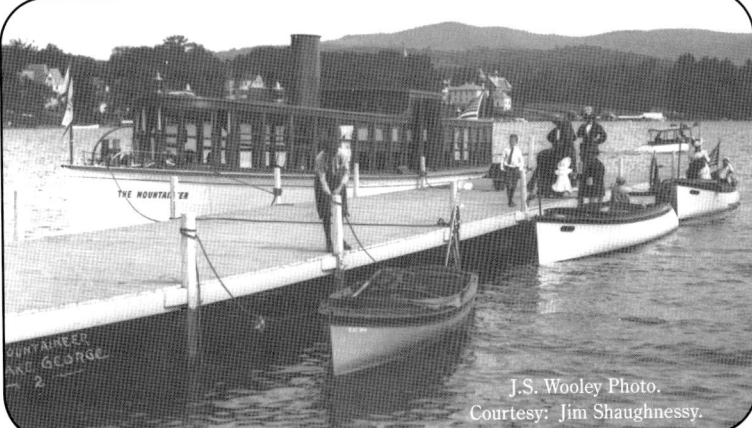
J.S. Wooley Photo.
Courtesy: Jim Shaughnessy.

BE WISE!
Buy the Best at Lowest Price

GILMORE MOTORS

For Kerosene or Gasoline.
Light in weight.
Power and Economy combined. Made in 2-cycle 1 to 4 cylinder, 1½ to 8 H. P. 4-cycle 5 to 50 H. P., 1 to 8 cylinder.

Send for Catalog.

Agents Wanted

Manufactured by

PARK MOTOR WORKS
TRENTON, MICHIGAN

Photo by J.S. Wooley.
Author's collection.

Mohican Point. S.R. Stoddard photo. Private collection.

LAUNCH RACE.
AROUND BUOYS 5 AND 6 TO FINISH—THREE MILES.
TWO PRIZES—FIRST AND SECOND.
Handicap rules as adopted by the Gas Engine and Power Co.
"Camper,"....H. W. Watrous, Hague..........Red
"Middy,".....J. Buchanan Henry, Hague... White
"Saunterer,"..Mrs. E. Mann Vynne, Hague....Blue
"Nahma,"....C. Gillette, Bluff Head....Red, White
"Oneita,"...H. S. Paine, Silver Bay...Orange, Black
"Sophie,"....J. D. Kennedy, Bolton... Blue, White

Courtesy: Mike DeLarm.

Courtesy: Bolton Historical Museum.

Camp Adirondack.
Courtesy: Mike DeLarm.

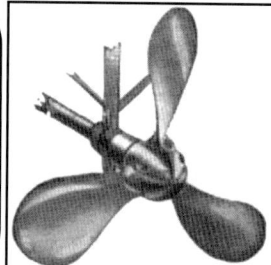

If you want to get real pleasure out of your boat this year
Send for our 1914 Reversing Propeller Catalog.
Buy our outfit and use your gear for an anchor.
Wilmarth & Morman Co.
1173 Monroe Ave. N. W.
GRAND RAPIDS,   MICH.

Ticonderoga (Lake Champlain)

This *Ticonderoga* sailed on Lake Champlain from 1906 to 1953. She is one of only three remaining early steam powered passenger sidewheelers still in existence in the entire United States. Previously built and owned by the Lake Champlain and Lake George Steamboat Company, she is nearly identical to Lake George's own early steamboats *Sagamore* and *Horicon* (II). The *Ticonderoga's* steel hull was built by the Marvel Shipbuilding Company in Newburgh, NY, the same company who built the hull of our current *Mohican* (II). The *Ticonderoga* is 220 feet long, has a 57.5 foot beam and drafts 7 feet. In 1953, she was hauled overland for inclusion in the Shelburne Museum at Shelburne, VT. I highly recommend you explore this magnificent time capsule of early meritime history to help you better understand the great steamboat era that was once here on Lake George from the late 1800's to the 1930's.

Ticonderoga at Shelburne Museum, 2001.
Photo by author.

CONCLUSION: I've spent most of my life, collecting and organizing information and photographs relating to the boating history of Lake George. Many, many boats were never photographed or documented, and our history is so rich and ongoing that it can never be totally complete between the covers of a book, however, I feel content that I have produced a book that is both informative and important regarding our Lake George boating history. I sincerely hope you enjoy reading it as much as I've enjoyed assembling and writing it.

Bibliography

Abbass, D.K. & Zarzynski, Joseph W. *The Radeau Land Tortoise-North America's Oldest Intact Warship.* by M-Z Information, 1993.
Adney, E.T. & Chappelle, H.I. *The Bark Canoes & Skin Canoes of North America.* Washington, DC: Smithsonian, 1983.
Bellico, Dr. Russell. *Sails & Steam in the Mountains.* Fleischmann's, NY: Purple Mountain Press, Revised Edition, 2001.
Bond, Hallie E. *Boats & Boating in the Adirondacks.* Syracuse Univ. Press, The Adirondack Museum, 1998.
Brown, William H. *History of Warren County.* Glens Falls, NY: Glens Falls Post Company, 1963.
Buckell, Betty Ahearn. *Lake George Boats,* Lake George, NY: Buckle Press, 1990.
Buckell, Betty Ahearn. *No Dull Days at Hulett's.* Lake George, NY: Buckle Press, 1984.
D&H Railroad. *The Steamboats of Lake George.* Lake George, NY: The Lake George Steamboat Co. 1817 to 1932.
Dow, William P. *Mountain Steamboats,* Lake George, NY: Lake George Steamboat Company, 2000.
Ervien, Robert. *History of Assembly Point on Lake George,* NY: Self Published. 1956.
Flexner, James Thomas. *Steamboats Come True, American Inventors in Action.* Fordham University Press, NY; 1992.
Gates, William Preston. *Turn-of-the-Century Scrapbook of Jonathan Streeter Gates.* 1 Glenwood Ave., Queensbury, N.Y. 12804: W.P. Gates Publishing, 1999. (518) 798-3609
Halm, Gale J. & Sharp, Mary H. *Lake George.* Charleston, SC: Arcadia Press, 2000.
Heard, A.H. *A Summer Paradise,* Published by the D & H Passenger Dept., 1913.
Holden, A.W. *History of the Town of Queensbury.* Albany, NY, Glens Falls, NY, 1874.
Hulbert, A.B. & Schwarze. *History of the North American Indians.* Ohio State Archives & Historical Society: Heer Printing, 1910.
Knight, A.S. *Adirondack Guide. Lake George, NY:* Adirondack Resorts, Inc., 1945 & 1961.
Leonbruno, Frank. *Lake George Reflections.* Fleischmanns, NY: Purple Mountain Press, 1998.
Manley, Atwood. *Rushton & His Times in American Canoeing.* Syracuse Univ. Press, Adirondack Museum, 1968.
Marvin, Henry. *History of Lake George.* (Courtesy; Black Bass Antiques). Sibells & Maigne, 1853.
Morgan, Lewis H. *League of the Ho-De-No-Sau-Nee or Iroquois.* Vol.II, Dodd, Mead & Co, 1901.
Newspapers: Chronicle, *Lake George Mirror,* Post Star, Adirondack Journal, 1880 to 2003.
O'Brien, Kathryn. *The Great & the Gracious.* Sylvan Beach, NY: North Country Books, 1978.
Offensend, Dorothy Backus. *The Sexton Boatbuilders of Hague.* Granville, NY: Self Published, 1982.
Shaughnessy, Jim. *Delaware & Hudson.* Berkeley, CA: Howell-North Books, 1967.
Steinback, Elsa Kny. *Sweet Peas & a White Bridge.* Burlington, VT: George Little Press, 1974.
Stiles, Fred Tracy. *From Then Till Now.* Fort Edward, NY: Washington County Historical Society, 1978.
Stoddard, Seneca Ray. *Lake George Guidebooks.* Glens Falls, NY: Self Published, 1873 to 1910.
Strum, Richard M. *Ticonderoga.* Shelburne, VT: Sheburne Museum, 1998.
Thorne, Frederick C. *The Pilot Knob Story.* Pilot Knob, NY: Self Published, 1977.
Van De Water. Frederic F. *Lake George & Lake Champlain.* Bobs-Merrill Co. 1946.
Whelden, Ernest J. *History of Pilot Knob.* Vols. 1 to 4: Pilot Knob Association, 1994 to 2000.

Roger's Slide Lithograph.
Courtesy: Jim & Kayce Dimond & Ephemerist Antiques.

Index

'Tonka 172
6 + 1 174
19+ 75
Adelaide 189
Aggie Belle 162
Algonquin, de Champlain, Ethan Allen 144-145
Alli 176
American Canoeing Association 21-22
Amphicar 140
Ankle Deep 87-90
Ankle Deep Too 90
Apperson Canoe 81-82
Arcadie 29
Aurora Borealis 163
Baby Bootlegger 112-113
Baby Reliance V 92
Baby Speed Demon II 91
Banshee 20
Barbara 164-165
Barge Boats 126
Barge Races 96
Bateaux 2
Bateaux Below's Tuff Boat 180
Betty V 116
Black Arrow 177
Black Swan, The 174
Bluebird 30
Blythe 43
Boats, Scenes, & Regatta's 188-195
Bonita (I) 171
Bonita (II) 171
Buccaneer 152-153
Cabin Cruisers, Early 119
Cachalot 119
Cadet 42
Californian 110-111
Camera 50-51
Camp Chingachgook 182-183
Canoe Island Lodge Boats 179
Caprice 46
Carney's F&B 170-171
Caroline 189
Carroll 174
Cecelia 31
Cozy 30
Crusader 60
Cyric 48
D. W. Sherman 27
Darrin Fresh Water Institute Boats 180

Defiance 145-146
Delphine IV 113-114
El Lacayo 104-105
El Lagartito 103-104
El Lagarto (G-18) 106-109
Elizabeth 67
Ella 33
Ellide 46-47
Ellis Barber Rowboats 159
Elm Bark Canoe 1
Ethyl-Ruth IV 114
Evinrude Ad 189
Eyrie (II) 172
Falcon V 102-103
Fanita 37-40
Fanita Jr. 41
Float Plane 126
Flossie 173
Flying Boats 99-100, 193, 194
Folly 41
Forward 75
Ganouskie 10-11
Geneva 49-50
Gilmore Motors 192
Grace 77
Grace (Another) 77
Gypsy (Sexton) 33
Gypsy (Simpson) 43
H. Colvin 14
Hall's Lyman 188
Happy Times 110
Harpoon 93
Harris Houseboat 72-73
Hawkeye 94
Helen (I) 52-53
Helen (II) 53
Henley Regatta 150-152
Horicon (I) 17-19
Horicon (II) 83-86
Horicon (Shoreline Cruises) 146-147
Horse Racing on Ice 139
Hotsy Totsy 11-112
Ice Boating, by Engine 137-139
Iceboating, by Sail 134-136
Idler 34
Imp 115
Indian Pipes 160
Iroquois 62-63
Isa Victoria 163
Island Queen 45
Isolde 59
James Caldwell 4-5
John Jay 7-8
Jolly Roger 98
Josie C 24
Julia 13

Katrina 30
Kayaks 185–186
Kiowa 76
Kismet 54
Lac du Saint Sacrement 156–159
Lady Of The Lake 118
Lake George Club 181
Leisure 189
Lillie M. Price 12–13
Locust 36
Loon 178
Lozier Boats 167
Mamie 51–52
Marion 55
Mary Anderson 58
McGuffy 165
Meteor 14
Minne Ha-Ha (II) 148–150
Minne-Ha-Ha (I) 8–10
Minnie Henry 174
Miss America IX 115
Miss Lake George Boats 122–123
Mohawk 35
Mohawk (steamboat) 190
Mohican (I) 56–58
Mohican (II) 78–81
Morgan 153–155
Mountaineer (I) 5–6
Mountaineer (II) 82–83
Ms. Lake George & Spirit of 76 147–148
Mystic 13
Naomi 68
Nellita 96
Newport 167
Northern Lake George Club 182
Ol' Timer 169
Old Boy 169
Old Man 172
Old Town, 1932 Info. 194
Oneita 61–62
Osprey (Hilton) 172
Osprey (Merrill) 162
Outboard Racing 132–133
Owaissa 176
Owl 11
P.D.Q. V 93
Pamelaine (I) 160
Pamelaine (II) 161
Pampero 15–16, 190
Passaic 35
Pastime 54
Patricia 140–142
Peer's (No Name) 167
Peter Pan 93
Petti-auga 4
Pippa II 101–102
Pocahontas 27–29

Police & Fire Boats 183–185
Pukwudji 189
Racers, More 117
Rachael 37
Radeau 3
Rags 175
Rainbow IV 100–101
Ranger 123–126
Raymond's F&B 175
Resolute 97
River Queen 44
Roamer 120–122
Rushton, J. Henry 20
Sadie Mae 168
Sagamore 68–71
Sal 166
Saunterer 34
Sayonara 65–67
Scioto 73–74
Scotty II 105
Scuppers 169
Seagull 167
Show Me III 86
Silver Spray 177–178
Simplex XV 94
Skate Sailing 136–137
Skunk 178
Smith-Granger Rowboats 23
Snapshot 33
Snoah's Ark 177
St. Louis 163–164
State Barges 127
Submarines 143–144
Tech Jr. 92
Theta 59–60
Ticonderoga (I) 24–26
Ticonderoga (II) 128–131
Ticonderoga (Lake Champlain) 195
Trout 191
Tuscarora 162
Uncas 31–32
Van Dyck's (No Name) 173
Vanadis 64
Vassar 42
Wanda 61
Wapanak 49
Watrous & Lake George Monster 74–75
Wenona 166
Whim 165
Whip-Po-Will 95
Whip-Po-Will Jr. 95
William Caldwell 6
Wilverne 118
Wininnish 76
Winogene 97
Wrecks & Fires 186–187
Zonta 168